A HISTORY OF THE ORIGINAL PEOPLES
OF NORTHERN CANADA

A HISTORY OF
THE ORIGINAL PEOPLES
OF NORTHERN
CANADA

Keith J. Crowe

Arctic Institute of North America
McGill – Queen's University Press
Montreal and London - 1974

© Arctic Institute of North America 1974
International Standard Book Number 0 7735 0220 3
Library of Congress Catalog Card Number 73-93833
Legal Deposit 1st Quarter 1974
Bibliothèque nationale du Québec
Typeset by McGill Students' Society Typesetting
Printed in Canada by the Hunter Rose Company

FOREWORD

It is with pride, hope, and gratefulness that Man in the North presents this publication on the history of the original people of Northern Canada.

PRIDE, because this was requested from us by the participants in the MIN conference in Inuvik, November, 1970. MIN would not have undertaken that difficult task if it had not been then identified as a most important priority need by the northerners themselves.

HOPE, because we feel this can contribute significantly to a better appreciation of the life and the role of the first inhabitants of Canada. This should enhance both the self-esteem of the native people themselves and a true sense of respect toward them on the part of the Canadian society as a whole.

GRATEFULNESS, because this achievement has been made possible through a series of contributions for which we want to express our gratitude. Like the other tasks undertaken by MIN, the History of the Original People of the North was assigned to a task force, whose members could help through field or office research, or in view of their proven competence in northern history and their active devotion to the human dimensions of the northern reality.

Among them, I especially want to thank the co-ordinator of the task force, Keith Crowe, who is also the author of the book. When he heard of the wish expressed by the Inuvik MIN Conference, he told us that he had already done some research into the history of the original people of the Canadian north, and would like nothing better than to resume it on a continuing basis within the MIN program. Eventually, thanks to his immediate superior A. J. Kerr, his services were to be graciously seconded to us for over a year by his employer, the Department of Indian and Northern Affairs. The personal experience of Keith Crowe in various areas of the Canadian north, his familiarity with the situation of the Eskimos and the Indians, his exceptionally good rapport with them, and his keen sense of observation are all reflected in this book.

I want also to address special thanks to the members of the reviewing committee: Father Guy-Mary Rousselière and Professors Richard Diubaldo and Robert McGhee.

ERIC GOURDEAU
Director
Man in the North

PREFACE

For four centuries foreign peoples have encroached upon the ancient territories of Indians and Inuit. The uneven balance of power is reflected in written histories that ignore or undervalue the pre-European period, the native side of trade and exploration, and the part played by individual native men and women.

This history has been written as a classroom text for northern native students of early teenage, but it may serve a wider audience. It leaves much to be desired — reflecting the inexperience of the author and some rather bizarre working conditions. It is, however, a beginning, and its very imperfections may arouse other (perhaps native) authors to write with the same target and better aim.

It is never possible to thank by name all those who collaborate in the making of a history book. The following people have played major and indispensable roles:

A. J. "Moose" Kerr, head of the Northern Science Research Group, Department of Indian and Northern Affairs, approved and nurtured the project.

Pat McCormack supplied the results of several months of research among Athapascan peoples and much theoretical guidance. George Diveky contributed his linguistic skill, scholarship, and experience of life in northern Quebec. Evelyn Clarke provided valuable summaries of historic documents.

Jacobie Ikeperiar, John Pudnak, Roy Daniels, John T'Seleie, and Edwin Scurvey were regional researchers from Baffin Island to the Yukon.

Graham Rowley, Alex Stevenson, and Dudley Copland volunteered their profound experience of the north and of history writing.

Scholars of Athapaskan cultures were most generous with encouragement and data. They include Professors June Helm, Richard Slobodin, and Catharine McClellan, and Annette McFadyen Clarke, Beryl Gillespie, and Margaret Morris.

Paul Robinson, head of Curriculum Services for the Department of Education of the Government of the Northwest Territories, was a constant source of strength. Dr. Jacquie Weitz, education officer for the National Indian Brotherhood, provided one of the most thorough critiques of the draft.

Chief Elijah Smith and his staff of the Yukon Native Brotherhood made me welcome despite the pressure of more urgent matters. Don MacNeill, Superintendent of Continuing and Special Education, Baffin Island, also gave support in many ways.

The resources of the Hudson's Bay Company were not used as widely as they should have been, but they were made available. Malvina Bolus, Helen Burgess, and Shirlee Smith of the Winnipeg office contributed their wide knowledge of northern history with kindness and patience.

CONTENTS

FIGURES

MAPS

Palaeo-Indians of 12,000 years ago hunting mammoth.

Palaeo-Indians hunting the giant bison.

INTRODUCTION:
ACROSS THE CONTINENTS

Man comes to the Americas

This book is about the native peoples of Canada, but their story begins, like that of all peoples on earth, so long ago that we cannot picture the passage of time.

Over two million years ago some very early kinds of human being had learned how to walk upright and how to use stones, sticks, and bones as tools. From their homeland in Africa they spread north into Europe and Asia, becoming more clever and more numerous as centuries passed.

As these first humans changed, so did the climate of the world. It became colder, and great sheets of ice formed over much of Europe, Asia, and North America. Several times the ice grew, partially melted, and then formed again before it finally disappeared from everywhere but the high mountains. The coming and going of the ice, called the Ice Age, lasted several million years.

Close to the ice lived herds of hardy animals such as the caribou, musk-ox, camel, bison, and woolly mammoth. Human hunters learned how to use animal skins and fire for warmth; gradually they moved north, and some of the Asian wanderers found a great region where the land was free of ice, north of what is now China. Perhaps 40,000 years ago the first people came to the place where Asia and North America meet.

During most of the Ice Age the two continents were joined by land, and animals moved freely between the Old World and the New. Toward the end of the Ice Age the sea flooded the land, separating the two continents. Once or twice the land became dry again, but at last the sea remained. The widest part of this lost

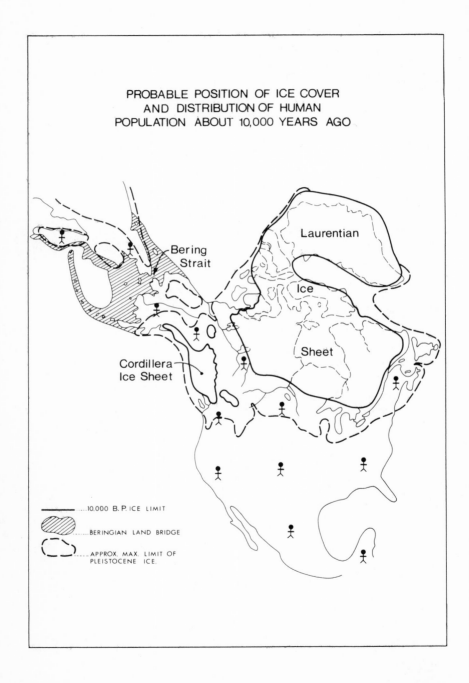

PROBABLE POSITION OF ICE COVER
AND DISTRIBUTION OF HUMAN
POPULATION ABOUT 10,000 YEARS AGO

land, which is called Beringia by scholars of our time, is now covered by the Bering Sea, and the narrowest part by Bering Strait.

The Beringian plain was above water for several thousand years at a time. Even when the crossing was flooded it may have been possible — as it is now — to cross Bering Strait in skin-covered boats, or over the ice during cold winters. By land, by water, or on the ice people certainly moved between Asia and North America. They probably journeyed in small groups, a few families at a time, hunting, fishing, and gathering as they went. Some may have settled in pleasant places, leaving it to their grandchildren to explore a little farther.

Valley by valley wherever there was no ice, or island by island along the west coast, people moved during thousands of years into their new continent. The slow flow of people went beyond the ice sheets and on to South America. By at least 10,000 years ago there were people all the way to Tierra Del Fuego at the southern tip of the continent.

As time passed each kind of region — desert, jungle, woodland, and mountain — became the home of people who worked out a way of life that fitted their country. All of these people were the ancestors of modern Indian peoples, and before any Europeans crossed the Atlantic, great cities of stone were built by the Indians of Central and South America.

Our concern, however, is for the people of northern Canada. As the huge ice sheets melted from the north, plants and animals occupied the land. Indian hunters moved into the northern forest to become the people of the snowshoe. When at last the arctic coasts became free of land-ice, the first Eskimos moved eastward from Bering Strait into what is now Canada and Greenland.

Atoms and arrowheads

"This is quite a story," you may say, "but how can anyone know so much about the people of so long ago?" The answer is that our knowledge of prehistoric times comes from many sides. It has to be fitted together with careful thought and a little guesswork. Each year new discoveries help to fill in the spaces of the puzzle.

Geologists and scientists of other kinds know the ages of rocks, how they were formed by volcanoes or as mud on ancient sea-beds, and which rocks came first. In the rocks may be found fossil shells, insects, and animal bones which show what kinds of creatures lived long ago, how big they were, and when and where they lived. By the study of the teeth, feet, and skeletons of fossil animals, it is possible to tell whether they lived in swamps or dry country, in cold or warm climate.

The glacial ice sheets left many traces of their existence. As they advanced they pushed boulders across the bedrock beneath, leaving huge scratches and grooves which show the direction of movement. Lines of boulders and gravel mark the farthest edge of the ice, and when the huge sheets melted, sand, clay, and gravel were washed onto the land in mounds that are easily seen. Since the enormous weight of the ice has gone, the surface of the earth has risen, and in places ancient beach-lines can be seen one above the other like steps, high above the present sea.

Botanists can read the past by examining the rings of growth in trees — each ring represents a year of the tree's life, and the width of each ring helps to explain variations in climate as the tree grew. Samples of plant pollen from the ground or from the mud of lake-bottoms can be tested to show their age. The plants themselves are a clue to the climates in which they grew.

One of the most important discoveries in the study of prehistoric times has been the invention of *radiocarbon dating*. All living things absorb rays from outer space, and radioactive carbon is formed as a result in the bodies of humans, animals, and plants. After death the radiocarbon disappears at a constant rate. By measuring how much remains in a very old bone or in a fossil plant, scientists can determine its age.

Archaeologists study the bones, the tools and weapons, the houses, and other remains of prehistoric people, and try to put together a picture of the life of long ago. Some archaeologists have lived with the last hunting peoples of Africa, Australia, and the Arctic in order to learn how hunters of ancient time may have lived and thought. Some of these scientists have become expert at making stone tools just as men did many centuries ago.

What did they look like, how did they live?

Once we know about the land, the plants, the animals, and the climate of long ago, and once we know something of the houses people built, their tools, and their hunting methods, we can try to form a better picture of the past. Anthropologists study the habits, legends, and appearance of people alive today and are able to link their knowledge to that of the archaeologists in building up the picture of the past.

Physical anthropologists, for instance, compare types of hair, skin colour, the shape and size of bones and teeth — even the chemistry of the blood. By such methods we know that the Indian and Eskimo people of the Americas are of Asiatic origin like Chinese, Japanese, and many other peoples.

All over the world groups of people have their own languages, foods, games, clothing, and other parts of life. Each way of living is called a "culture", and there are many similarities between the cultures of northern peoples in Asia and North America. There are similar legends, for instance, about the raven and about the woman who married a dog. Many northern tribes on both sides of Bering Strait use similar drums in their music. The kayak, the bark-covered canoe, snow-goggles, and portable cradles for babies are other evidence of links between the northern cultures.

The study of languages is important in making up a picture of the movement of prehistoric people. Linguists estimate that a few thousand years ago the language of the Inuit, commonly known as Eskimos, separated from the language of the Aleutian people. The languages of the Navaho and Apache people of the southern United States are closely related to those of Canada's Athapaskan Indians, and this indicates movements of the tribes long ago.

These are some of the ways in which we can look back into prehistory, and can try to bring the ancient past to life. Now is the time to consider the peoples who first came to live in northern Canada.

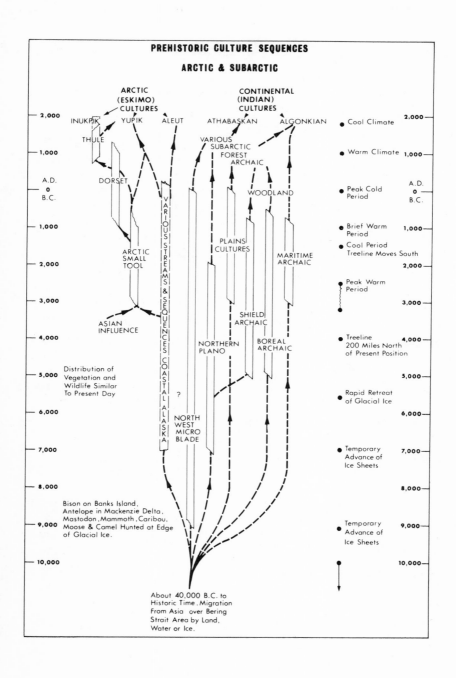

PREHISTORIC CULTURE SEQUENCES

ARCTIC & SUBARCTIC

ARCTIC (ESKIMO) CULTURES

CONTINENTAL (INDIAN) CULTURES

INUKPIK   YUPIK   ALEUT   ATHABASKAN   ALGONKIAN

THULE

DORSET

VARIOUS STREAMS & SEQUENCES COASTAL ALASKA

ARCTIC SMALL TOOL

ASIAN INFLUENCE

VARIOUS SUBARCTIC FOREST ARCHAIC

WOODLAND

PLAINS CULTURES

MARITIME ARCHAIC

SHIELD ARCHAIC

NORTHERN PLANO

BOREAL ARCHAIC

?

NORTH WEST MICRO BLADE

2,000
1,000
A.D. 0 B.C.
1,000
2,000
3,000
4,000
5,000
6,000
7,000
8,000
9,000
10,000

Distribution of Vegetation and Wildlife Similar To Present Day

Bison on Banks Island, Antelope in Mackenzie Delta, Mastodon, Mammoth, Caribou, Moose & Camel Hunted at Edge of Glacial Ice.

About 40,000 B.C. to Historic Time, Migration From Asia over Bering Strait Area by Land, Water or Ice.

● Cool Climate

● Warm Climate

● Peak Cold Period

● Brief Warm Period

● Cool Period Treeline Moves South

● Peak Warm Period

● Treeline 200 Miles North of Present Position

● Rapid Retreat of Glacial Ice

● Temporary Advance of Ice Sheets

● Temporary Advance of Ice Sheets

2,000
1,000
A.D. 0 B.C.
1,000
2,000
3,000
4,000
5,000
6,000
7,000
8,000
9,000
10,000

1 THE FIRST
NORTHERN PEOPLES

Although the great ice-sheets of the Ice Age covered the Rocky Mountains and Hudson Bay, many of the kinds of wild creature we know today lived beyond the ice in the Yukon and southern Canada. There were caribou, beaver, musk-ox, and bear. Human hunters shared the plains and forests, and in those days there were other animals which thrived on the conditions close to the ice — camels, horses, long-horned bison, mammoths, and mastodons of the elephant family.

As the climate changed and the ice melted northward, the wild-life also changed. Some of the Ice Age animals slowly became the species we know today; others died out on this continent. Perhaps the last camels and elephants were hunted down in their dwindling pastures by bands of men. During the thousands of years as the glaciers slowly retreated and disappeared, the first arctic people migrated in search of new and better hunting grounds. They worked out ways of living: cultures that suited the country, the climate, and the animals of their time and place.

The hunters of the Ice Age travelled light and made little mark on the land. Forest and moss have covered their camps and houses, and all that remains are scattered stone tools or a very

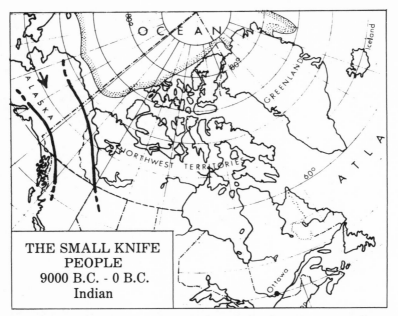

THE SMALL KNIFE
PEOPLE
9000 B.C. - 0 B.C.
Indian

few tools of bone, and the charred earth of ancient campfires.

We do not know whether Indians and Eskimos were once the same people. We do not know whether the people of the northern forests and barrens 10,000 years ago were the ancestors of the present Indians, though it is likely.. All that the stone tools and fires tell us is that the prehistoric peoples worked out several main cultures. The Eskimo cultures came latest, and in the cold, treeless ground of the arctic coast much more of these cultures remains, or has been found, than of the Indian cultures.

The various cultures, the different ways of making spearheads, and the choice of seacoast, plains, or forest changed from age to age. It is likely that changes in climate caused people to migrate, but we do not know just how the groups traded, fought, and generally affected each other.

Archaeologists have traced several main ways of life among the prehistoric northern peoples. Each one is made up of several cultures and lasted thousands of years. If we simplify the names that have been given to their traditions and keep in mind how little is known, this is their story.

1. People of the Small Knife

In the valleys and on the plateaus of Alaska and the Yukon, people of many cultures succeeded each other through the ages. Their camp sites were at fishing places by lakes and rivers or in mountain passes where caribou and other moving herds could be ambushed. Other camps were made on high lookout points.

As the ice melted away from the mountain country of the northwest, people occupied more and more territory, going south into British Columbia and east to the Mackenzie Valley. Probably their way of life was similar to that of the northwestern Indians a hundred years ago. Fishing and caribou hunting would be important, among many other activities. There were probably snowshoes and canoes, but we can only guess.

One thing that the northwestern prehistoric cultures had in common for almost 10,000 years, besides a similar way of life, was a preference for small cutting tools made of flint or other hard stone. From this custom the tradition is named. At Fisherman Lake near Fort Liard in the Northwest Territories, the same fishing place was occupied by various Small Knife cultures for about 9,000 years, and eventually by the present Indian people.

2. The Long Spear People

Some 7,000 years ago, it appears that bison-hunting people of the western plains began to move north into the lands vacated by the ice. They moved around and north of Great Slave Lake, hunting bison in the meadows and parkland there. They learned to follow the caribou during the summer migration onto the barrens, and to retreat back with the herd into the forest each winter.

These hunters made beautifully chipped, long spearpoints of flints as well as other tools for cutting, scraping, and drilling. Their tents or houses were placed at river crossings where they could spear swimming caribou, at fishing sites, or on the *eskers*, the boulder hills pushed up by the vanished glaciers. Probably their way of life was very much like that of the Slavey and other tribes who came after them, before Europeans arrived.

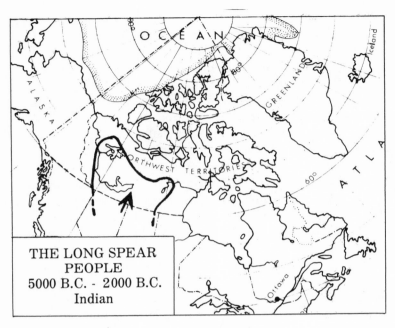

THE LONG SPEAR
PEOPLE
5000 B.C. - 2000 B.C.
Indian

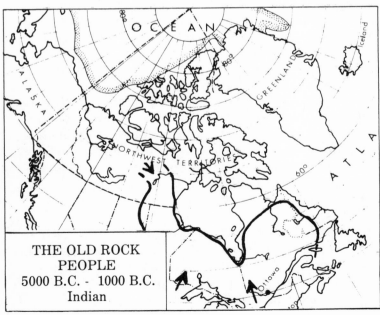

THE OLD ROCK
PEOPLE
5000 B.C. - 1000 B.C.
Indian

3. The People of the Old Rock

Much of the rock underlying the lands around Hudson Bay is very old rock called the Canadian Shield. When the glacial ice melted, the northern Boreal Forest came into being. The great land of rocky ridges, forest, swamp, and a million waterways was occupied little by little by hunters of various cultures.

The people moved north into the new land from Lake Winnipeg, the Great Lakes, and the St. Lawrence River. Some among them made beads of stone, some used the weighted throwing-stick to give their spears greater force. About 6,000 years ago people were living near Lake Mistassini in Quebec.

At roughly the same time, other hunters arrived in Keewatin, where the forest grew farther north than it does now. These people camped at the forest edge and probably followed the caribou in summertime onto the open tundra. Two of their winter houses have been found — shallow oval pits with entrance passages, probably roofed with skins which were held down by stones. In the centre of the floor burned the family fire. By its light maybe, on stormy dark winter days, the hunters worked on their spearheads. Perhaps because of the brittle rock of the Shield, their spearheads were bigger and more crudely made than those of the Long Spear People.

The Keewatin People of the Old Rock may have come originally from the Long Spear country to the west. Whatever their origin, the climate grew colder about 3,000 years ago, pushing trees, caribou, and people southward. As time went by, one main way of life emerged among the People of the Old Rock country.

At Southern Indian Lake in Manitoba people — probably ancestors of the Crees — made pottery a thousand years ago. Here too, and in other places of the region, Algonkian spirits were painted on rock long before the arrival of Europeans.

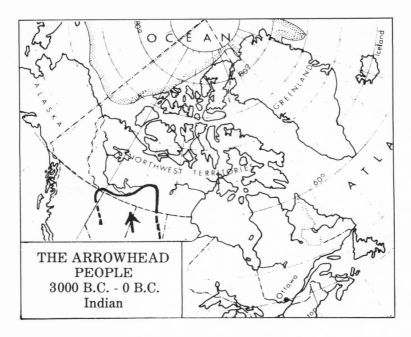

THE ARROWHEAD
PEOPLE
3000 B.C. - 0 B.C.
Indian

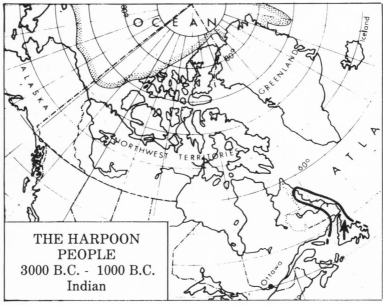

THE HARPOON
PEOPLE
3000 B.C. - 1000 B.C.
Indian

4. The People of the Arrowhead

A second group of plains bison hunters, small in number, appear to have moved north of Lake Athabasca about 3,000 years ago. There, like the Long Spear People before them, they hunted bison and caribou and fished the waters. They made arrowheads of flint, notched at the sides for lashing to a wooden shaft, and from this their name is taken.

5. The Harpoon People

About the same time that the Arrowhead People moved north from the plains, a similar movement seems to have taken place on the Atlantic coast. Seagoing Indians moved up to Labrador. They hunted whales and seals, using harpoons and almost certainly boats of skin or wood. After some 2,000 years, perhaps because of a colder climate, the Harpoon People left the Labrador coast, or at least abandoned sea hunting for land hunting.

6. The Denbigh People

Some modern Inuit of Canada prefer to use their own name for themselves, but the word Eskimo has been used for several hundred years, and we will use it here to describe a related series of cultures of the arctic coast.

About 5,000 years ago a certain style of life developed on the east shore of Bering Strait in what is now Alaska. The people of the first Eskimo cultures used tiny blades of flint to cut bone and ivory for their harpoons and other tools. They set the blades in handles of antler for cutting meat and skins. Some of the most important examples of this "arctic small-tool tradition" come from Cape Denbigh, Alaska, and we will use that name to describe the first Eskimos to occupy arctic Canada.

During the time of the Denbigh Eskimo culture in Alaska the arctic climate grew warmer. Perhaps because of better conditions for hunting and travel, the Denbigh people began to spread eastward, following the coastline. According to the dates of their many villages, they moved very quickly, and within a century or two occupied the arctic coast from Alaska to Greenland; 4,500 years ago they lived in northern Ellesmere Island.

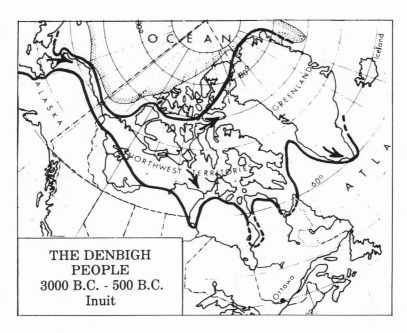

THE DENBIGH
PEOPLE
3000 B.C. - 500 B.C.
Inuit

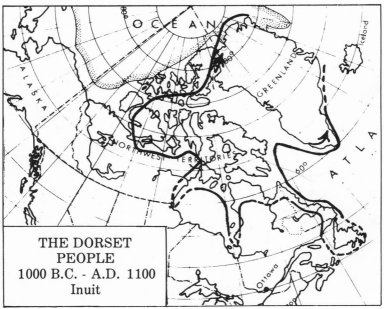

THE DORSET
PEOPLE
1000 B.C. - A.D. 1100
Inuit

Although there are no remains of their boats, it is very likely that they used skin-covered boats, and there is some evidence that they had dogs. They used bows and arrows, and the design of their harpoon heads is vaguely similar to modern forms. With needles of fox bone or bird bone, the Denbigh women sewed the special clothing so essential to arctic living. Their oval houses were partly sunk into the ground and probably roofed with skins. Stone lamps, burning animal fat, were used in some regions, and where possible open fireplaces were used to burn driftwood, brush, or fat-smeared bones.

Like most arctic hunters, the Denbigh people lived in small nomadic groups, spaced over the land to make the best use of wildlife. Their way of hunting, and the animals eaten most, varied from region to region. In northern Greenland, for example, muskox were plentiful and provided much of the food for the Denbigh settlers there.

During the Denbigh occupation of Canada and Greenland there were changes in the arctic climate, and perhaps owing to an increase in cold, the people moved south, abandoning the most northerly places. They moved along the coasts of western Greenland, northern Labrador, Ungava, and Hudson Bay. Some of them moved inland on the barren lands as far as Great Slave Lake, though this may have been just a seasonal visit. It is possible that they met Long Spear or Old Rock Indians near the treeline.

Warmer conditions returned about 1000 B. C., and perhaps wild creatures moved northward again as the snow and ice decreased. The Denbigh culture changed at this time. New styles of houses, lamps, and weapons developed, and a new culture grew out of the old one somewhere in the central Arctic.

7. The Dorset People

The first signs of this second Eskimo culture were found at Cape Dorset on Baffin Island, and the name "Dorset Culture" was given. It probably began in the Foxe Basin region as an outgrowth of the Denbigh culture and like the Denbigh way of life it spread rapidly across the Arctic.

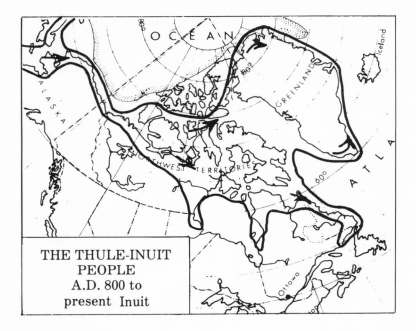

THE THULE-INUIT
PEOPLE
A.D. 800 to
present Inuit

   Dorset immigrants, during an early period of mild climate, re-
settled most of the former Denbigh territory. No evidence has
been found of Dorset settlement in the Mackenzie Delta, and the
southwest coast of Hudson Bay was only occupied briefly. Perhaps
a combination of poor hunting and Indian settlement blocked the
Dorset people there. They moved down the Labrador coast and
around the coast of Newfoundland by A.D. 500. There they may
have met the Beothuk Indians and the first European explorers,
the Vikings.
   Perhaps the climate during most of the 2,000 years of Dorset
culture was at least as cold as at present, for they seem to have
adapted to life among snow and ice. They made snowknives of
bone, and may have invented the snowhouse. For walking on
smooth ice they wore "creepers" or crampons of ivory tied under-
foot. There is no evidence that they had dogs, but they built
sleighs shod with bone and ivory. Their houses were partly sunk
into the ground, with turf walls and skin roofs. They were heated
by open fires and oil-burning lamps of stone.

Between about A.D. 800 and 1300 another warming of the arctic climate occurred, and with it came a new spread of immigration from the western Arctic. The newcomers were well equipped and organized, and aggressive in their search for living-space. After several centuries of mingling with or retreat from the newcomers, the Dorset people disappeared. Modern Inuit know of the Dorset people through stories passed down by their ancestors, who met and absorbed or eliminated the older culture. In the stories the Dorset people are called Toonit, and while some of the tales have become fanciful over the years, many of the facts agree with the evidence of archaeology.

8. The Thule Inuit

In Alaska the original Denbigh culture disappeared about 2,000 years ago, and a series of new cultures followed around Bering Strait. In some of the cultures people concentrated on hunting the huge whales which we now call by various names such as Greenland, Right, or Bowhead.

One of these whale-hunting cultures developed by about A.D. 900. Known as the Thule culture, its people were the direct ancestors of modern Canadian and other Inuit. The original home of the Thule people was on the northern coast of Alaska, and perhaps as far east as the Mackenzie Delta. During a period when the climate became warmer, they spread eastward as the Denbigh people had done long before them. They had dogs to haul sleds or to carry packs, had umiaks and kayaks, and in general were better equipped than the Denbigh or Dorset people had been.

The stories of the Inuit tell how the Thule people invaded and took over the hunting grounds of the Dorset people. The Thule houses are still plain to see all over the arctic, paved with flat stones and walled with turf over boulders or whale skulls. Only the skin roofs are gone, and the whale-jaw rafters which have been used for sled runners. At least one carving on ivory shows the skin tents, bows and arrows, caribou hunting, and fighting of the Thule period.

The Thule reached northern Greenland, and in fact the whole Arctic with the exception of the extreme northwestern islands. Where whales were available they continued to hunt them but all other wildlife — caribou, musk-ox, walrus, seal, white whale and narwhal, rabbit, fish, and birds — was also used. Some groups wandered inland on the Keewatin barren grounds to become the present day Caribou Eskimos.

From about A.D. 1650 to 1850 there was a spell of very cold climate, often called "The Little Ice Age". Perhaps an increase in ice on the sea kept the whales away or made boating difficult. Whatever the reasons, in many parts of the Arctic the Thule whaling villages changed. Smaller groups of people began to rely more on caribou and seal and made their seasonal camps in tents or snowhouses. In some regions, such as the Mackenzie Delta, Labrador, and eastern Greenland, the large villages and the elaborate Thule culture continued up to the time of the first European visitors. There was no certain time when the Thule way of life became the Inuit way, only a gradual change, greater in some places than others. Most people agree that by about A.D. 1700 the true Thule culture had become that of the modern Eskimo, the Inuit.

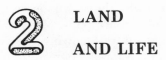 # LAND
AND LIFE

The unmarked land

The Canadian north has two main landscapes. One is the forested country, where grows the *taiga* vegetation of the Subarctic. At its southern fringe there are big spruce trees, fir, tamarack, alder, birch, poplar, and willow. To the north, or high in the mountains, the forest changes; the firs, birches, and poplar thin out and disappear, then the tamarack. Farthest north only the hardy black spruce and willow remain, hugging the shelter of river valleys and hills. Finally poor soil, ground frost, and winter winds defeat the trees, and the open *tundra* stretches north.

The area where trees give way to open tundra or barrens is called the *treeline*. Beyond it to the north, only low plants grow — dwarf willow, berry bushes, arctic grasses, and mosses. Rocks and boulders show up everywhere, and the wind has laid bare whole hilltops, exposing rock and gravel.

Both the northern forest and the barrens have probably changed very little during the past 500 years. If you were able to fly over the north as it was in those days, before any Europeans came, you would see a land without cities, roads, mines, airstrips, or other large evidence of people. In summertime you might see the flash of canoe or kayak paddles on water, or the wakes of moving boats. The colour of meat and fish on drying racks, a file of people and dogs moving over the tundra, or the smoke of fires might catch your eye. In winter the tracks of snowshoes or sleds and the stained snow of villages might be visible, but the snow-banked lodges and domed snowhouses would be hard to see.

There would be stone fishing weirs and caribou ambushes of stones or brush, but the works of people would be very few and far between in the vast land. Wildlife would show itself far more — immense flocks of summer birds, the walrus jostling in water or hauled out like brown sausages on ice-pans, bison and caribou in great herds with their breath in winter following like a cloud. Beaver dams would span waters in the forest country, and everywhere in the north ancient game trails would groove the turf.

The people

Some Eskimo people lived — as they do still — by the forest edge of the Mackenzie and Labrador. Some Indian people lived (and live) by the sea where they hunted seals and whales. Others hunted on the barrens beyond the last tree. In general however, the Eskimos were people of the barrens and the coasts, while the northern Indian people were of the inland forest.

There were possibly 50,000 people in the north 500 years ago — we cannot know exactly. They can be divided into three main groups: First were those who spoke variations of a common Eskimo language, looked alike in appearance, and followed a certain way of life, that of the kayak and snowhouse. Second were those who spoke Athapaskan in its many forms and lived the life of snowshoe and canoe in the inland northwest. Third were the Algonkian-speaking peoples, whose way of life, shaped by similar conditions, was very much like that of the Athapaskan Indians.

Each of the three groups is part of a much larger language and culture area reaching well beyond Canada. The Eskimo language is spoken from eastern Siberia to eastern Greenland. Athapaskan is spoken in Alaska and the southwestern United States. Algonkian languages are spoken across the northern United States.

Long ago, however, the northern people did not think of themselves as part of a great language group, or even as a tribe. They lived most of the time in little bands of a few families. Once or twice a year they might gather to hunt caribou or white whale and to trade, dance, and feast. At such meetings there might be a few hundred, perhaps a thousand people. Almost all, in fact, who spoke a common dialect and had the same customs.

Those who shared a common territory, the same dialect and customs, called themselves *People* and still do among their own kind. The names used now such as Indian, Eskimo, Athapaskan, Algonkian, Copper, Dogrib, and Cree are all "foreign" names, that is, given to the people by "outsiders", native or European.

In the Eskimo language the word for people is Inuit. Among the Athapaskan-speaking Indians it is Déné, Dona, Djinje, or a similar word. The Algonkian versions include Eno, Eyo, and Ewo. Some Eskimo people nowadays wish to use only their own word, and it seems the right thing to do for the rest of this book. It is more difficult however to do the same thing for the two groups of northern Indians. For the rest of our story we will speak of the *Inuit*, the *Déné* (pronounced Denay), and the *Algonkians*.

Within the whole Inuit, Déné, or Algonkian groups certain smaller bands of people would be called by their neighbours "People of the Mountains", "People of the Pointed Coats", or similar names. Those whose language and customs were different and with whom there were fights would be called by rude names such as "Bad People", "Stinkers", or "Louse-eggs".

Although we will look at the life of the northern hunting peoples as it probably was before Europeans came, we should keep in mind that these people still live mostly in their ancient territories. Their languages have changed a little but are widely used, and many old customs exist side by side with modern ways. The past and the present of the northern cultures are not distinct and separate like black and white, but are joined together by history, written and remembered.

Deep northern roots

Perhaps the most important thing we can learn about the Déné, Algonkians, and Inuit of 500 years ago is the way in which they had adapted to life in a very difficult land. For most people today it is hard to imagine a life without money, stores, machines, radios, doctors, mosquito spray, and matches. Even the trappers and hunters of the modern north use clothing, guns, and motors which are made in southern Canada or in other countries.

The old-time Indians and Inuit had to make all their own tools, weapons, clothes, and houses. They were their own doctors, teachers, policemen, and butchers. Almost everything they ate, wore, or used came from close around them. With the exception of a little rough copper and iron found in a few places, the people did all their work with tools of stone, bone, antler, ivory, shell, and wood.

The hunting peoples developed great skill in snaring, trapping, and hunting the creatures on which they depended. Some of their inventions are still unmatched in the modern world for usefulness and beauty. The skin-covered kayak with all its equipment, the birchbark canoe, the domed snowhouse, the double insulating suit of furs, the block-and-tackle made of ice or ivory, and the webbed snowshoe — all these are of excellent design.

Like all peoples of the world the northern tribes found ways to bring beauty and variety into their lives. They tattooed their bodies and embroidered their clothing with beads of horn or soapstone, with the quills of goose and porcupine, with moosehair or strips of weasel skin. Some made toothmark patterns on birchbark containers. Some people painted their skin tents and shirts with paint made from red ochre or black graphite. Any possession, a wooden bowl, a horn dipper, or a knife, might be decorated in some way. Painting, carving, embroidery, tassels, fringes and beads, dyeing, and bleaching were all used.

Under the conditions of life in the north before Europeans came, the Inuit and Indian people learned certain ways of behaving which they had to work out in order to survive. For thousands of years their customs worked well, but some of them are quite different from those of industrial people.

The hunting people could not plan too far into the future. They could not store food for more than a few weeks ahead, and at any time sickness, accident, bad weather, or the movements of animals could spoil their plans. Having no control over nature, they learned to wait with patience until the tide turned, the weather improved, or the herds came by. They learned to accept disappointment and hunger calmly, for losing one's temper did not help.

Because the world around them could not be changed and had always been the same, old customs were followed and old people's wisdom was not challenged. It was bad manners to ask many questions, to try to change people. People learned by doing things and by observing, for there were no books. They knew a great deal about wild creatures, the weather, and all the things which today we call geography, zoology, and other names.

Houses, clothes, and tools were only a means of staying alive in a way of life without money. They had to be left behind or carried when travelling, and they could always be replaced. There was no point in saving or collecting things which could not be used. For most northern people there were three kinds of possessions: those of a person, those of a family, and those of a community. Things, however, possessions, were not as important as sharing. The main purpose in life was to be with other people.

Most northerners during their lifetime would meet only a few hundred people, and many of these would be their relatives. The kind of relationship or kinship was very important and many rules existed for it. Among so few people there could be hardly any secrets, and the good and bad points of everyone's character were known to all.

In their limited world of creatures and people, all men and women belonged, felt very much at home. They had to learn to get along with each other with as little argument as possible, especially during the long dark winters. When troubles arose, things had to be settled within the group. Next to death, the worst punishment, the worst thing, that could happen to anyone was to be cut off from one's own people.

Survival

Except for certain seasons and in some favoured regions the hunting peoples of the north lived a few jumps ahead of starvation. They were part of nature's balance which included all living things from caribou moss to whales. In this interdependent world of eatables and eaters there were limits to the numbers of all creatures, including humans.

The life of the people required good health and endurance. Everyone from an early age had to play a part in getting food, travelling, and other tasks. The main burden of supplying food fell on the men hunters, and each man could only support a limited number of dependents.

Under such conditions it was always difficult and often impossible for families to support the badly crippled, the mentally disabled, or people whom old age had made infirm. Women had to travel and carry loads through summer flies and winter blizzards. It was almost impossible for them to feed, warm, and carry two infants at the same time.

For all these reasons the population was controlled in the only way possible, by the same means used in ancient Greece and other parts of the world. Abnormal babies, one of twins, unwanted girl babies, were killed at birth by suffocation or exposure to cold. Very old people were sometimes left to die when their families moved on, and often asked their children to leave them or strangle them.

Such customs were a grim necessity to people without the mental hospitals, orphanages, old folks' homes, and birth control of modern times. When hunger no longer called the tune, they were gladly abandoned. When the explorer Ross met the Netsilik people a century and a half ago, he saw Iliktak, an old man who was being pulled on a sleigh by his family across a difficult land. Early in this century Chief Robuscan of Abitibi carried his very heavy crippled wife on his back in their travels for almost twenty years.

Trade without money
Although the northern native people were self-sufficient for necessities, life could be made more pleasant by trading. There were always things which could not be found within one's territory and things which other people made different from or better than one's own.

Among the various minerals which were exchanged, soapstone was important. It was used for cooking pots, oil lamps, beads, and (in the southeast) tobacco pipes. Copper was the only metal that could be hammered into knives and ornaments without being heated. It was found near the White and Copper rivers of Alaska, along the Coppermine River, and in central Victoria Island. People whose territory contained copper bartered it to neighbouring tribes.

A little iron was to be found in shapes that could be made into tools, and this was traded. The Mackenzie Inuit had some iron tools long before Europeans came to this continent — perhaps these were obtained in trade from Asia. Most often, iron was used with pyrites or flints to strike sparks for firelighting. Firelighting stones were traded, and so were the hard stones which could be made into cutting tools — flint, chert, slate, and obsidian.

There were other "raw materials" too. The ivory of walrus and occasionally from fossilized mammoths was valuable for making icepicks, harpoon heads, buckles, and similar tools. The horns of musk-ox made good icescoops and cups. Antlers made picks and clubs. Bird feathers of many kinds, weasel skins, the claws of bear and wolverine, and the bills of loon and raven were all in demand as good-luck charms and ornaments.

Some things were made and sold in manufactured form. People who lived near a good supply of birchbark or soapstone, for instance, often became very skilled at making things of these materials. Usually the completed articles were lighter to carry and brought the maker a better price. The Algonkians used to exchange furs for corn and tobacco grown by the Hurons or the Mandans of the plains. The Indians of the northeast coast made ornamental beads from certain seashells and these beads, called *wampum*, were sold in such numbers that they became a kind of money.

The tribes of the Pacific coast also made beads of shells which in English are called dentalia and serpula. These were popular in the northwest, especially among the Kutchin people, who used them almost as money. The northern Pacific coast people caught the oily oolichans or candlefish, and would take the oil from them over the mountains in cedar boxes, in the hollow stalks of seawrack, or in animal bladders. The inland Athapaskans would exchange furs for the oil and for bundles of dried clams.

Depending on the region, a variety of other things were made for sale — blankets of woven strips of rabbit skin, nets of hide or willow bark, ochre powder for paint, bags of seal oil, dried meat, wooden bowls, sled-runners, mats of rush and willow, canoes, snowshoes, lamps, bowls, moccasins, and sealskin boots. The Mackenzie Inuit and the Cree Indians made pottery, and some was sold to neighbouring tribes. Sinews for bowstrings and for sewing thread were dried, cleaned, and sold.

To many Inuit who lived beyond the treeline, wood was the most valuable item of trade. Those who lived nearest the trees or near a river or sea current which carried driftwood would sell to less fortunate neighbours. At Akilinek on the Thelon River Inuit would meet to cut wood and exchange other things. Another well-known trading place was Barter Island, where the Mackenzie and Alaskan Inuit would meet. At such times news and gossip would be exchanged, and there would be games and dancing.

Often two groups would learn something of each other's language in order to trade. The Kutchin and Inuit of the Mackenzie did this, and so did the coastal Tlingit and their inland Athapaskan neighbours. Between the Tlingit and the Tagish, Tutchone, and Teslin peoples there were permanent trading agreements. One family would trade with another, man to man, woman to woman, boy to boy, and girl to girl. Marriages were arranged to make the system safe, and eventually the Tagish and Teslin people changed their language to Tlingit.

Traded goods passed from hand to hand, tribe to tribe, for hundreds, sometimes thousands, of miles. The old barter system still goes on all over the north, but modern goods are included. A white whale may be exchanged for a barrel of gasoline or a rifle for a canoe.

Fights and feuds

Most of the time the hunting peoples were too busy finding food to fight each other, and groups stayed out of each other's way. But like all human beings they did quarrel about all sorts of things. One of the most common causes of trouble was wife-stealing. The best hunters tried to keep several wives, always trying to get wives by persuading them to leave their husbands or by kidnap and murder.

Another cause of trouble was that sickness was often blamed on witchcraft by someone outside the family, and the relatives of the sick person would try to take revenge. People who were not relatives, especially complete strangers, were always treated with suspicion, and the slightest misunderstanding on either side could result in fighting. Once someone was killed, the relatives were supposed to seek revenge, and such feuds were known everywhere. Only in the Mackenzie and Yukon region, however, where conditions permitted large villages, did fighting become large-scale and organized.

The Inuit have many stories of duels, and of special training by men before they set out to challenge enemies. One man practised shooting arrows into the wind and beat his foes by making them fight during a storm. The Inuit of Ungava tell stories of being chased by Naskapi Indians who had just obtained guns. The Inuit placed sharp splinters of caribou legbone upright in the snow or moss, and the points pierced the moccasin-clad feet of the Indians. The Teslin people were once being hunted by Tahltan enemies, but the Tahltan chief had relatives among the Teslin band. At his advice the Teslin people wore their snowshoes back to front and the Tahltan chief persuaded his followers that they had missed the trail and should go home. Because women were most likely to be captured, rather than killed, there are many stories of escape from the enemy. There is the story of a Tagish woman who left a trail of bird-down from her clothing for her tribesmen to follow. Other captured women would be made to carry the spare weapons of their enemies, but would trample the arrows into the snow and drop axes into rivers whenever they had a chance.

A Kutchin woman, Upsen Vey, captured by Inuit, cut holes in their kayaks, all except one, which she used to go upriver toward her people. She expected the Inuit to repair their boats and follow her, so she pulled her kayak up a log and into the woods, leaving no sign. She watched three kayaks go up the river after her, counting them by putting sticks in the ground. When three kayaks had gone back down river, she continued on to her people. She had been the wife of two Inuit, and when she got home she married two Kutchin brothers.

Two Algonkian women were once captured by Iroquois and made to guide the enemy canoes. While the Iroquois men slept, the women steered toward a big waterfall and swam to safety just before the canoes went over to destruction. The contact of people through fighting, and especially the exchange of women, was an important way of spreading customs and languages from tribe to tribe.

The better the living conditions, the more organized was the fighting. The Yukon peoples, especially in the south, had small wars with rules observed by both sides. The Teslin people once trained for several months to attack the Tahltan, and the warriors toughened themselves with exercises and cold baths. A priest or medicine man was hired to seek the help of the spirits. When the Teslin were filing down a mountain to attack at dawn, each man held the spear of the man in front so that no noise would be made. Once some Kutchin men persuaded the Mackenzie Inuit to pay them in furs, ivory, and oil for the killing of a friend. He was not dead, however, and when the Inuit recognized him they killed three Kutchin, including him.

Armour was worn occasionally by the men of all tribes. It was made of heavy doubled or tripled hide, and in the western regions it was covered with resin and sand to make it tougher. The western peoples also used another kind of armour made from flat bones or parallel sticks tied together. Shields of wood or thick hide were used by most Indian tribes. Some special arrows, spears, and knives were used for fighting, and the Kutchin used extra-strong bows for attacks on the Inuit, but often hunting weapons were used. The Athapaskans used heavy bear-clubs made of wood or antler, with a sharp point or pick. To make them even heavier they would soak them in grease, and these were the weapons the Kutchin used to batter down Eskimo snowhouses.

Warfare among the northern peoples was common, but seasonal and small-scale. It usually consisted of surprise attacks rather than all-out battles, and it included many actions of crime and punishment which modern society would deal with by police, courts, and jails. There were no full-time soldiers, and until guns were brought to the north, bands were rarely wiped out or driven from their territory.

Stories of the people

Everywhere in the world before modern ways began, people told stories for fun, to teach their children, and to pass along the his-

tory of their group. Most folktales tell of giants, dwarfs, and magic
as well as of ordinary daily life. They change as time goes by, but
often there is a central idea which does not change for hundreds of
years, and is about something that actually happened.

The stories of the northern people show the close bond between
hunters and nature. In these tales people, animals, and rocks may
talk to each other and take each other's shapes. Some of the
stories contain teaching for young people about the rules of behaviour and manners. They point out that it is good to be patient,
truthful, calm, quiet, unselfish, and uninquisitive — some of the
things admired by the Indian and Inuit people of the north.

Not all of the stories were full of magic and history — the Naskapi people have for instance a special name for stories about
everyday happenings, or tales made up on the spot. These are
called *tubadjimun* stories. The legends which deal with heroes in
the half-magical world of long ago are called *attenogan*. Here are
some examples.

The girl who married a dog   One of the oldest stories in the north
is known in various forms among both Inuit and Indians. It is also
found in northern Asia. The most common Inuit version is about a
girl called Uinagumasuituk, "the girl who didn't want a husband".
Her father makes her marry a handsome stranger who is really a
dog in disguise. Some of their children are human and they become Inuit. The others are like dogs and become the other human
races. Later the girl is pushed from a boat by her father but she
clings to the side. He cuts off her fingers, which become whales,
walrus, seals, and other sea creatures. She sinks down to become
Sedna, Nuliajuq, or Takkanaaluk, the goddess of the sea. The Naskapi and Dogrib people also have stories of a woman who marries
a dog, and the origin of the Dogrib people is explained in this way.

The orphan boy   Another tale known everywhere among Inuit is
about an orphan boy who is badly treated. He is made to sleep
with the dogs, has the poorest of food and clothing, and is lifted up
by his nose until his nostrils grow very wide. Kautjayuk is the
boy's name, and by various magic happenings he grows very big
and strong. He kills three polar bears with his hands, and finally

kills all of his tormentors, sparing only those few who were kind to him. There are many Inuit stories about orphan boys who survive hardship to become great men, and similar ones are told by Déné and Algonkian peoples.

The flood   Many peoples in different parts of the world have stories about a great flood. The story told by all the Déné and Algonkians varies only a little all across the north. In this story a hero builds a raft or canoe to save himself and some animals during a great flood. When the water has stopped rising, he asks various water animals such as the otter, beaver, and muskrat to dive down and find land. The muskrat comes up almost drowned but holding some mud in his paws. Soon the land appears, and a fox, a wolf, or a wolverine is sent around it to find out its size.

The joker   All North American Indians have stories about someone long ago who was part bad and part good, a mixture of hero and villain. Sometimes he would be in the form of a fox, a wolverine, or a jay, sometimes a man. In the Cree language there are many tales about a practical joker, called Wesatkedjak. One of the best-known stories of the joker, which is told by Inuit too, is about the time when the bear had a long tail. He is tricked into dangling it through a hole in the ice for fishbait, but it freezes and breaks off.

In a related set of stories the joker himself gets into trouble. After being entertained with magic tricks by other animals or people, he invites guests to his tent to show off his own skill. All his magic goes wrong, however, and he ends up each time in a mess.

The musk-ox boy   The eastern Athapaskans and the northern Algonkians have a similar story of a tiny boy whom an old woman finds in the droppings of musk-ox. (In the Athabaska region the animals are bison.) The boy is cared for by the old women, whom he calls grandmother, and grows to be a hero who uses his power over the oxen to help his people.

Many stories are told of strong men, great runners, and fighters. Ya Moga was such a hero among the Hareskin people, and the Igloolik Inuit have their counterpart in Ayuki.

Drum, song, and dance

As with most sides of native life, stories, song, poems, and speeches were not considered very different, and the art of using language well was highly valued. Most of the chiefs could make excellent speeches without any preparation or notes. One great speech which is still remembered by the Dogrib people was made by their chief Edzo, who persuaded the Yellowknife people to make peace, using words of great power and beauty.

Like all people, the northern hunters had songs for sad times and happy, for the end of a good hunt, to go with games, to mock enemies, or to welcome visitors. There were lullabies, love songs, religious songs, and songs to brighten long journeys. In some regions songs could be owned by their maker, who could pass them down to his children or give them as a gift to friends. Without their tunes most of the songs are good poetry. Here is one example, part of an Inuit song translated into English:

Glorious it is to see
The caribou flocking down from the forests
And beginning
Their wanderings to the north.
Timidly they watch
For the pitfalls of man.
Glorious it is to see
The great herds from the forests
Spreading out over plains of white.
Glorious to see.

Glorious it is
To see long-haired winter caribou
Returning to the forests.
Fearfully they watch
For the little people
While the herd follows the ebbmark of the sea
With a storm of clattering hooves.
Glorious it is
When wandering time is come.

The human voice was the main musical instrument in the north and there were many ways of singing. One of the most unusual was the "throat-music" of the Inuit women, which sounds like breathing, or bird calls made in rhythm.

Although rattles of skin or wood filled with pebbles were used among the Déné and Algonkians, the main musical instrument of the north was the drum. The drums (still used in places) were flat and circular, varying from one to four feet in diameter. The covering was of thin skin, usually caribou, and the drum was held in one hand, beaten by a stick in the other. The drums of the Inuit were covered only on one side; the drums of the Indian people often on two sides. Similar drums are used among many far-northern people of the world.

The dances of the hunting peoples were usually accompanied by drumming and singing. Among the Déné and Algonkians there were dances of welcome and of peace. All the tribes had dances describing the hunt, with the actions of the hunter and the movement of animals such as the shambling bear or the strutting male ptarmigan.

Northern games

Of the hundreds of games played by the northern peoples, only a few can be mentioned here. There were games of strength such as rock-throwing, finger-pulling, and wrestling. Other games such as long-jumping and high-jumping tested agility. Some Inuit played at the high-kick and did acrobatics on a tight sealskin line.

There were endurance games too. Long-distance running was popular among the Déné and Algonkians, on foot or snowshoes, and in Inuit boxing each man took turns at striking his partner on the temple or shoulder. Another Inuit game was the tug-of-war between two men with string looped around their ears.

Whole villages would play at football or handball with a blown-up bladder or a skin stuffed with moss. The northwestern people played the Alaskan game of blanket-toss, using a large walrus or moose skin. There were contests of skill such as archery and club-throwing. Most of the contests and tests of strength were taken lightly within the band, but could be more competitive and serious

Inuit games.

against other bands or tribes. Such games were often a means of testing the power and friendliness of strangers.

Gambling was popular among the Indian tribes and some of the Inuit. One of the Indian games is a version of one played all over the world. One team guesses who is holding certain carved bones under a cover. In other gambling games the players had to guess the number of sticks in a bundle, or call the colours on six painted dice tossed on a plate. The gambling games were often accompanied by a special song, and in the old days a player might lose his tent, his canoe, and even his wife.

People of all ages, particularly Inuit, played another game with an ancient history in the world, "cat's-cradle" or string games. The various figures were often accompanied by special songs and stories, and the elders knew hundreds of different ones. There were also many varieties of "hole-and-pin" games. In one Inuit version called *nugluktak* a bone drilled full of holes is hung from above, and the players try to stick long needles into the holes as the bone twirls around. Then there were games to make people laugh, such as face-pulling contests.

One Inuit game called *inugait* consisted of putting together a tent, its furnishings and people, all represented by seal bones which were fished out of a bag by a loop of string. "Pick-up-sticks" was played everywhere, and among the Inuit and Naskapi, particularly, dolls were made for the little girls. Boys would receive miniature bows and arrows early in life, and learned to hunt small animals or birds for the family food supply. Some Inuit men built tiny kayaks, complete in every detail, in which their sons could practise on shallow ponds.

Leaders and followers

The most important part of social organization among all the northern hunters was the family. Each person knew most of his relatives, even the most distant ones. If someone needed help for hunting, in a fight, when sick, or for building something, he was almost certain to call on relatives. Generally speaking, people obeyed their older relatives and gave orders to the younger ones. There were special relationships — some relatives were not supposed to be alone together or to speak directly to each other, but others were expected to be very close and to tease each other. People did not call each other by name, but always "grandfather", "sister", "cousin", or whatever the relationship was.

Among the smallest groups the oldest active hunter of the family was usually the leader. When several families came together the various leaders would form a sort of council to decide important matters. If the whole tribe gathered, the leaders of each band would form an informal tribal council. Among the Cree such leaders were called *Okimau*, and among the Inuit, *Issumatat*.

In general, leaders were men or women of proven wisdom and skill, and the group followed their decisions. Often one man would be the leader during a communal hunt, another during a fight with enemies, and still another during a long sledge or canoe journey. Some people were all-around leaders who stood out because of their strength, wisdom, and skill in magic. Such a person might become the main chief of a band or a whole tribe, but even then his followers could disagree or just move away to live elsewhere. Although most of the leaders were men, women of strong character sometimes had power over a band or tribe. The Kaska, the

Kutchin, and the central Inuit each have had famous women leaders.

There were no policemen, courts, or judges in the old days. In
most cases fear of the criticism of the majority was enough to
make people behave.

The health of the people

In the north before Europeans came, the hunting peoples were in
general strong and healthy. There were troubles such as arthritis
and rheumatism, but no diseases such as influenza or measles. Only
a few Algonkian people used tobacco, and there were no sweet
things to destroy teeth. Many babies died because of difficult conditions and lack of medical knowledge. Those who lived, however,
were healthy. When European sailors and workers first came to
Fort Churchill, the Indians were shocked at the number of hump-
backed and bandy-legged strangers.

Daily life involved a great deal of exercise for people of all ages,
and fat people were very rare. Women worked hard, especially
among the Déné tribes, where women carried loads of over a hundred pounds when travelling. Among the Algonkians, the southern
Déné, and the Mackenzie Inuit, sweat baths were taken in special
lodges heated by hot stones. The northern Indians bathed in snow
inside their tents in winter, and the western Déné boys would
have to jump into the water through holes in the ice.

There were two main divisions of nursing or medical knowledge. Troubles such as cuts and broken bones, or digestive pains,
were understood quite well and treated by skilled people. Other,
more difficult sicknesses of the mind or body were blamed on magic, and were usually treated by the shaman or medicine man.

Fits of hysteria were common, as among all northern peoples,
especially during the long dark days of winter. Usually the patient
was tied up for everyone's safety until the fit had passed. Perhaps
because of the meat diet, nosebleeds were frequent among the
Inuit. Sometimes bleeding was done on purpose to relieve headaches. The Inuit and Kutchin would cut the patient's skin above
the eyebrows for this, and the Naskapi used sharp bone needles.

For stomach troubles and similar pains there were medicines
made from leaves, berries, treebark, roots, and some kinds of

earth. Spider webs, poplar bark, and puff-balls were used to stop bleeding from wounds. New seal blubber, spruce gum, and lemming-skins were used on cuts as both antiseptic and poultices. Although it is not a medicine, during times of starvation, hungry Inuit children were given a kind of chewing gum made of eider-duck down mixed with blubber and blood. Algonkians gave Jacques Cartier's crew spruce tea to cure them of scurvy.

Sometimes quite difficult operations were performed, as when two Kutchin women mended a man's broken knee cap. Using flint knives they cut back a flap of skin away from the bone. Then they put small pegs of caribou bone into holes drilled at each side of the crack in the kneebone. The pegs were pulled together by a lacing of sinew and the skin sewn back in place. The patient fainted several times with pain and was revived by having little hot water bottles of moose skin placed on his hands, but the knee mended perfectly. Among the forest peoples broken limbs were sometimes set in rolls of green birchbark which dried and hardened to hold firmly.

In the case of an arrow wound Athapaskan women would probe out the arrowhead with a willow wand and would leave the wand in the wound, pulling it out just a little every day so that the wound healed on the inside first, instead of just at the skin with infection inside. Among the Copper Inuit a man's leg was amputated with stone knives. The cut was sterilized by fire and the skin sewn over the stump with sinew thread.

There were many ways of treating the sick by magic and prayers. The Naskapi and Cree medicine men would sometimes conduct a ritual in a special tent which would move mysteriously and was called the "shaking-tent". Inuit shamans used a method of diagnosing called "head-lifting". The patient would lie down and the shaman would lift the patient's head slightly with a skin loop. The shamans knew a lot about human nature and were able to mix common-sense advice with their magical treatments.

The spirit world

The peoples of the north lived according to the weather, the seasons, and the movements of wild things. All around the people were strong forces which they could not explain — water, winds, snow and ice, the sun, moon, and stars, and the cycle of birth and death.

To people so close to nature it was natural that all things, including the wind and water, had life and spirit. The Algonkians believed in one great spirit whom they called Manitou, but there were other spirits in their world too. Like the Inuit and the Déné they believed that each person could have a helping spirit to call on in times of trouble, usually in the form of a bird or animal. Among the Déné each person was believed to have his own power or medicine, given by the guardian spirit. This power was called *ekonze*.

Among all three peoples there were men and women who possessed special religious powers. These powers were usually obtained by long periods of living alone and fasting so that the secrets of the spirit world would be revealed. Young people who showed promise were trained by the older medicine men and women. The shaman or medicine men often used a special language and had various ways of performing rituals to be in touch with the spirits. Some of the most famous shamans were believed to be able to make caribou or other wild things come toward hunters from far away.

Certain creatures such as the dog who shared men's lives, the bear who most looked like a human, and the clever raven were important in the old religion. The Cree people particularly cared for the bear spirit, and among the Mistassini Cree a bear's skull would be specially placed in a tree, looking over water. Its hide would be kept unused for a year out of respect for the dead animal. Some Eskimos too would leave offerings by the bones of a polar bear they had killed. Once a famine among the people around Great Slave Lake was blamed on a hunter who had driven an exhausted caribou through deep snow to his tent, beating it with a stick and so offending the caribou spirit.

The medicine men regulated the religious life of the people by a system of rules which today are called *taboos*, a word from the South Seas. There were taboos made out of respect for the animal spirits. Naskapi hunters, for instance, were not supposed to give the bones of beaver to their dogs. Netsilik Inuit did not sew or make things close to their fishing weirs, and Inuit women almost everywhere were forbidden to sew caribou skins in snowhouses out on the sea ice during the dark months. It was taboo for Inuit to eat the meat of land and sea animals at the same meal. In Labrador a knife used for cutting up whales had to be bound with seal-skin, not caribou sinew.

Many taboos were concerned with women, because the birth of children was such a powerful mystery and because men wanted to keep women in second place. No Indian women were allowed to step over a hunter's legs as he sat near the fire. Dogrib women were not allowed to eat the delicacy, moose nose. Chipewyan women had to break their own snowshoe trail just after having a baby, instead of following the tracks of the band.

Many troubles such as bad weather, sickness, and poor hunting were blamed on the breaking of taboos. In such cases the shaman would often advise gifts to the offended spirits, movement to another place, or some sort of fine or punishment. Often the taboos were based on sound principles of health or conservation, and most peoples of the world, even in modern time, have similar customs.

Many people of the world believe that the human spirit can live on in a new body if the old body dies. In various forms the northern hunting peoples made this part of their religious life. The Kutchin have a name, *natli*, "the returning one", for those who have lived another life in the past. The Inuit often found it natural to give the name of a dead relative to a newborn child so that the name and the soul could continue as one. Such a child may often be called "grandfather" or "auntie" by its older relatives, because it has the soul of the dead loved one.

Summary

This has been an outline of a way of life shaped by the northern forest or barren land. Despite the differences among Inuit, Déné, and Algonkian, between coast and mountain-top dwellers, the hunting life made for a certain way of looking at the world and other people — a way which is still strong today. Now we can examine more closely the three great culture groups and the tribes they embraced.

3 A VARIETY
OF PEOPLES

Despite the differences in land form, climate, and growth within the great arc of subarctic forest from Yukon to Labrador, a certain general type of human culture was formed there. The Déné and the Algonkians shared this way of life, and choosing one of their most useful creations, we will call them the *Snowshoe Peoples*.

For most of the Snowshoe Peoples, caribou was the most important source of food and clothing, though every other possible source was used. In the mountains of the northwest sheep and goats were hunted; musk-ox were within reach of the tribes closest to the barrens of the Yukon and Northwest Territories. Wood buffalo roamed the southern fringe of the forests west of Hudson Bay. Moose lived throughout the western belt, and in places there were elk or deer.

Fishing was usually second to caribou hunting in its importance but was more important to some groups. Bear, beaver, porcupine, muskrat, and marmot were all valuable, and the hares snared by women and children were a great standby during times of poor hunting. Each summer there were migrating waterfowl, and always ptarmigan. Eggs, shellfish, roots, lichens, bulbs, and the sweet sap of the birch tree gave variety in food.

Animals were hunted with bows and arrows, spears, deadfall traps, and snares. Even the great moose were snared by strong skin ropes which caught their antlers among the trees. Almost all the tribes used the "driving" method of frightening caribou along lanes of brush fences into pole compounds. Moose and caribou were lured, especially at mating time, by calls and rattles and were speared from canoes while swimming.

Fish were caught in gill nets made of rawhide strips, willow bark, or root fibres which had to be kept moist. Bone or tooth hooks were used for jigging. In summer a variety of traps and weirs were made with baskets, poles, and stones, and from these fish were taken by dip-nets, spears, and gaffs.

Throughout the northern forest, meat was either roasted for eating or boiled in containers holding water brought to a boil by putting in hot stones. The containers were made of birchbark, woven roots, animal stomach, or hide. Often a hide was lowered into a hole in the ground to hold the water, stones, and meat. After a good hunt extra meat was usually dried and cached up high during the summer, or stored frozen in winter. Sometimes dried meat was pounded up with fat and stored in hide bags as pemmican. Fish were split and smoke-dried in summer or frozen in winter; berries and roots were dried for storage.

Tent covers, clothing, and some canoe covers were made of scraped and cured hides, sewn with animal sinew. Ropes and strings of sinew or strips of hide were used for snowshoe lacing, snares, bowstrings, and tumplines. Strips of fur, especially that of the hare, were woven or loop-twined into blankets and ropes. Except among the most northerly tribes, coats were usually made with separate detachable sleeves, and men wore loincloth and leggings rather than pants. A great variety of tools were made of stone, wood, antler, and beaver teeth for skinning, carving, scraping, pounding, drilling, and all the tasks of people who manufactured everything themselves. The pointed awl and small crooked knife were two of the most important northern Indian tools.

All the tribes built several kinds of house or tent, depending on the size of dwelling needed, the season, the length of stay, and the materials available. Dome-shaped tents were used everywhere, covered with bark or hides over bent saplings. Rectangular cabins of poles under bark, hide, or brush were also used. Winter tents were covered with hides on which the fur was left and banked with moss or snow. The most common dwelling everywhere was the cone-shaped tent or tepee. A hide-covered tent for about 15 people would be covered by 30 to 35 caribou skins, heavy ones at the bottom, light ones at the top. Often two houses or tents would be built with their doors facing a shared open fire.

Snowshoes, like bark canoes and toboggans, are part of the popular image of the northern Indian, and were essential to life in the old days. The styles varied from region to region and people could tell the tracks of a stranger's snowshoes or the outline of his canoe. Each tribe used two or more designs of snowshoe for different winter purposes and snow conditions.

The northern people preferred to live in large groups of several hundred whenever good fish runs or caribou kills permitted, but for much of the time, especially during the end days of winter, they split up into little bands of two or three families, always in touch with each other in case of trouble. They used many signs to stay in touch, some local, some shared by many tribes. Smoke signals, peeled and notched poles, forked twigs, stones, and bark were all used to tell of a way to good hunting, to ask for help, to announce death or birth.

Both the Athapaskan and Algonkian peoples separated boys and girls as they approached adulthood, and gave them special training. Girls were kept apart from all other people at this time, attended only by older women. This separation would last for several months, or over a year in some cases.

The Algonkians

One explanation of this name is that it was first applied to Micmac Indians who were "*algomekig* — at the fish-spearing place". Although there were many Algonkian peoples, including the Blackfeet of the plains, in this book we are concerned with the northernmost tribes — the Cree and Naskapi — and to a lesser extent their southern neighbours, the Ojibway and Montagnais. In general, the life of the forest Algonkians became simpler and harder from south to north. The Ojibway and Montagnais of the south had gardens,

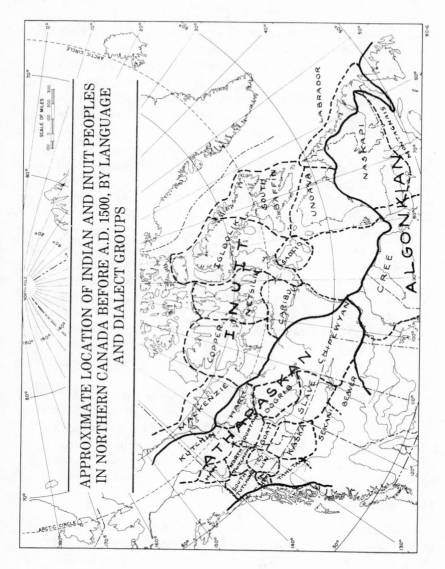

APPROXIMATE LOCATION OF INDIAN AND INUIT PEOPLES
IN NORTHERN CANADA BEFORE A.D. 1500, BY LANGUAGE
AND DIALECT GROUPS

maple syrup, wild rice, and direct trade with the corn- and tobacco-growing peoples between the Great Lakes. The Cree and Naskapi country went far beyond such comforts and included the windswept "land of little sticks".

The customs and beliefs of the Algonkians differed from those of the Déné. The Algonkians worshipped one great spirit, Manitou, although other spirits were important, especially that of the bear. Sweat baths were used for health and religion, and the shamans used the shaking-tent ceremony. The Cree, especially, feared a half-human monster called the Windigo which roamed the woods seeking people to eat. Perhaps this belief was connected to cannibalism, which occurred at times among all northern peoples during starvation, and was regarded with horror. Among the important figures in the Algonkian spirit world were the Four Winds, who were brothers, the Great Hare "Nanabozho", and the Horned Serpent.

Marriage among Algonkian people was usually arranged between first cousins, and even chiefs rarely had more than two wives. Life for Algonkian women was hard on the whole, but they were treated with more equality by the men than their Athapaskan sisters. The southeastern Cree and Montagnais had family hunting grounds with known boundaries, presided over by a senior hunter, and passed from father to son.

The Naskapi   The land of the slim, proud people Naskapi is the high interior of Quebec and Labrador, where rivers rise to flow north, south, east, and west to different seas. To the south and in the valleys the forest is heavy, but most of the land is rocky, covered with lakes and rivers. The trees are small and scattered among wide stretches of tundra and swamp. In winter it is a bleak and windswept country, and at all times of the year the Naskapi people of old had to work hard for their living.

The name Naskapi was given to the tribe by their closely related neighbours, the Montagnais, but the Naskapi have their own name for themselves, *nenenot*, "the people". Probably they were never a large tribe, perhaps 1,500 at the most. Their remote territory did not attract Europeans at first, and the Naskapi kept their ancient way of life much longer than most Indian tribes in Canada.

Three great caribou herds migrated in northern Quebec and Labrador between the tundra and the forest, and Naskapi life revolved around the caribou hunt. The caribou spirit was important in their religion, and ceremonies such as *mokosjan*, when the marrow of caribou bone is eaten, are still observed. No travelling or hunting was begun by the Naskapi without prayer or ceremony. The wolverine, Kwikwatsiau, was a chief character in their legends and stories.

When a Naskapi youth married he usually lived with his bride's parents for one year, doing "bride-service", contributing to the larder of his new relatives. Besides the usual Algonkian dwellings, the Naskapi sometimes built a large type of tent for several families and for winter dancing. It was rather like two halves of a tepee set well apart and joined by a long ridgepole, the whole tent being covered with caribou hides and often floored with split logs. For their oval tepee the Naskapi often used caribou skin in three overlapping layers, which were not sewn together and which could be taken off quickly. The Naskapi canoes were high-ended, and like the Montagnais their snowshoes were very wide and circular. In spring a special sled, the *tatilabinak*, was used to haul canoes to open water. Naskapi women wound their hair on small, flat boards, and mothers carried their babies in a moss-bag rather than the usual Algonkian cradle board, the *tikenagan*. Like those of the Inuit, the winter coats of the Naskapi had fur inside, were sometimes worn in sets of two, and had hoods attached. Headbands of fur or hide were common, and caps of hide were worn by both men and women.

One of the most distinctive customs of the Naskapi was the decoration of their caribou skin clothing with designs in red ochre and greasepaint, put on with special pens and stamps of bone or antler. For tattooing they rubbed colouring into a series of small cuts made by a stone knife, rather than using a needle and sinew.

The Cree   The name "Cree" comes probably from a French version of the name of one part of the whole tribe, "Kristineaux", but it is now well known. Five hundred years ago, the home of the Cree people reached from the east side of James Bay, across the rivers that flow north into Hudson Bay, and beyond the north end of Lake Winnipeg, around the present site of Nelson House.

Within this wide territory, pottery and other traces of Cree life have been found up to a thousand years old. Probably there were at least 15,000 Cree-speaking people when the first Europeans arrived, with differences in dialect from region to region. Usually the tribe is spoken of as two main groups — the Woods Cree of the west and the Muskegon or Swampy Cree of the east. There is now a third division, the Plains Cree, but they emerged after Europeans came.

The Cree people tend to be taller than their Naskapi-Montagnais cousins, and this is especially true of the Great Whale River band. Their country is close to the treeline, and their old way of life was much like that of the Naskapi. Like them they used a balancing-stick, held in both hands, when walking on snowshoes and pulling a toboggan by means of a chest-strap. One custom of the Great Whale — Kanaaupscow people (which may have been common to other Algonkians) was the use of special "fins" of wood shaped in a half-circle and held in each hand while swimming.

The Mistassini and Waswanipi Cree live around southeast James Bay. Some of their present customs and equipment are of Montagnais origin, but no one can say just when the mingling of people occurred. Other Cree, the Swampy bands around the south coast of Hudson Bay, have mingled with Ojibway culture. Some of them moved north to be independent of the Ojibway about the time when Europeans first arrived.

The Cree of Hudson Bay and James Bay lived near the migration routes of geese and other waterfowl and made great use of this food supply. Those who lived near the Churchill River were north of the best stands of birch trees and the best growths of swamp-reeds. Instead of the reed mats of their southern kin they used hides for tent floors and covers and made cooking pots of soapstone as the Inuit did. Their hooded clothing and the crescent-shaped knives used by women may have been a result of Inuit influence.

On the whole, the country of the western Woods Cree gave a better living than other Cree territory. The barren ground caribou herds reached them at the southern end of their migration. There were also woodland caribou, elk in the central highlands, moose, and woodland buffalo. At the time when Europeans arrived, a few of the woodland people had begun to spend part of the year on the grassy plains to the southwest, hunting the plains buffalo.

Within the Cree tribe as a whole the women excelled in embroidery, using moosehair, bird quills, and porcupine quills. Geometric and flower designs were sewn onto clothing, tumpline headbands, arrow quivers, and medicine bags. The Cree and Naskapi were the only Algonkians to tattoo themselves. Cree women were sometimes tattooed at the corners of the mouth, but men were tattooed on the face, legs, and body.

Although the Cree did not have as elaborate a religious life as the Ojibway, they had similar customs, including secret societies to which most of the old men belonged. Medicine bags containing charms against bad luck and evil were carried by all men. The dead of the tribe were remembered each year at a special feast.

The Cree people were always regarded by early European observers as high-spirited, handsome people, fond of ceremony and admirers of the art of speech-making. The custom of tobacco smoking in pipes of soapstone spread among them from the St. Lawrence region, and the Cree made it a part of all their religious and social life.

The Déné

In what is now Canada lived about twenty tribes whose people spoke dialects of the Athapaskan or Déné language. No sharp differences existed between the tribes in custom or language, just a gradual change from tribe to tribe. The Tutchone of the far west find it difficult to speak with Chipewyans of the eastern border of Athapaskan territory. One division of the Athapaskans of the north can be made along the line of the Mackenzie Mountains. West of this line the tribes share a mountainous homeland and were influenced by the non-Athapaskan coastal people.

The Déné had stricter customs concerning the training of young people than those of the Algonkians. For the Chipewyan and other peoples near the tundra, life was hard enough without much extra discipline, but the mountain tribes had special training for boys. They were separated under the leadership of older men and were toughened for fighting or hunting. They would swim in icy water, sleep out naked in the cold, go without food for days, and run long distances. At night they were made to sleep with straight legs so that they would grow into good walkers.

The separation of girls was also strict and lasted up to three years in some tribes. Girls approaching womanhood had to wear a basket or hood which covered their whole face and head. It was usually made and put on by the sister of the girl's father and was meant to protect hunters from the gaze of the girl. When the band moved, the girl would have to make a separate trail, helped by an older woman.

The northern Déné, both men and women, wore nose ornaments, though tattooing was generally limited to a few lines across the cheeks. Face paint was worn by the men of most tribes. The coats and shirts of Déné men were usually made with long pointed tails at back and front.

The strongest men and best hunters among the Déné kept several wives, and the shortage of wives for younger or weaker men was a cause of much trouble. A man could win his neighbour's wife if he beat the other man at wrestling, and one women is known to have been won and lost ten times in one evening.

The canoes of the Déné, especially those of the Yukon, were mostly flat-bottomed, low at bow and stern, partly decked. Some snowshoes were made far longer than the Algonkian types, and often snowshoes were made of unsquared or unsplit branches.

Just as the Algonkians feared the Windigo, the Déné feared the Nakkan or Naghan. In English these beings are called "Bushmen", and they differ in description from tribe to tribe. They were men from other tribes who hid in the woods to steal a wife, outlaws who lived alone, or, according to some tribes, supernatural creatures who tried to kidnap women and children.

The Chipewyan   The most easterly group of Déné are the Chipewyan. This name comes from the Cree word *Chipwayanewok*, meaning "people of the pointed skins". This was said either because of the pointed Chipewyan coattails or because beaver skins were dried in a particular way.

The tribe probably numbered about 3,500 when first met by Europeans. Their territory was the edge of the woods surrounding

the tundra of the Keewatin and Mackenzie districts. The Yellowknives lived north of and around the east end of Great Slave Lake,
the Lakehead people lived north of Lake Athabasca, and the
Caribou-Eaters, the largest group, occupied southern Keewatin
and a little of northern Saskatchewan and Manitoba.

During the summer migration of people following the caribou,
groups of two or three hundred Chipewyan might gather. When
two related families met after a winter apart, it was the custom for
the two groups to sit several yards away from each other, silently.
One old person from each family would then in turn recite all the
deaths and misfortune of the winter, while the women wailed.
When this was ended, everyone would rise to meet each other, men
greeting men, women greeting women, and to exchange gifts together with good news.

Chipewyan men were named after the seasons, places, or animals, but women were always given names which included the
word for one animal, the marten, *tha*. Religious and social life
among the Chipewyan was fairly simple, but girls were separated
from boys at the age of eight or nine and thereafter lived very hard
lives. It was common for women to carry loads of over a hundred
pounds on their backs in summer or by toboggan in winter.

Although most of the northern hunting peoples were unconcern-
ed with calculation and accounting, the Chipewyan language has
several counting systems, using tens, fours, threes, and so on. Calculation, particularly of gambling odds, was a well-developed part
of Chipewyan culture.

Caribou were the central element in Chipewyan life, and the
people closest to the treeline would follow the caribou onto the barrens each summer. Dogs would drag the tent poles, which were
made into snowshoes for the return south in the fall. The Chipewyans were the only tribe to make right and left foot snowshoes
with one straight side.

Some customs of the Chipewyans may have been learned from
the Inuit whom they occasionally met near the treeline. Such ways
included the use of hooded and fur-trimmed parkas, the eating of
raw meat, and the occasional use of double-edged paddles for canoe-
ing. Their usual paddle had a longer, narrower blade than the Algonkian type and could be used for poling.

The Slaveys   Between Lake Athabasca and Great Slave Lake, and part way down the Mackenzie River, lived several groups of Déné people. They were not organized or identified as a definite tribe, and very little is known about their customs other than their general Déné ways.

Being south of the main caribou herds they relied much on moose, and for lack of caribou skins, they often made winter houses of brush, banked around with snow. When moose hunting a hunter might follow his prey for days on long, light snowshoes, wearing light clothing and carrying only a few arrows.

The men often wore skewers of bone through their noses in the Kutchin style, and their shirts or coats had pointed tails like those of most Déné.

The small and separate bands of Slavey people were not warlike, and the more agressive Cree called them *Awokanak*, which means "timid people", or slaves. Another explanation for their modern name is that it is a mispronunciation by Europeans of the name given to the Slaveys by the Beaver tribe — *Tsade*, which also means "timid people".

Only after Europeans came, were the Slaveys considered a distinct "tribe".

The Dogrib   The Dogrib tribe has been named after a legend in which a dog is an ancestor of the people. Their prehistoric territory lay between the Great Slave and Great Bear lakes from the Mackenzie forests to the open tundra. They normally formed four bands, totalling probably close to 2,000 people.

Caribou were the main item in Dogrib hunting, though musk-ox lived on the edge of their territory long ago and were hunted at times. Like the Chipewyans, the Dogribs had a custom when a boy killed his first fox, caribou, or other animal. His fellow hunters would pull off his clothes, saying "be lucky".

As among other tribes it was not good manners for Dogrib people to call each other by name, but to say "my niece", "my uncle", or whatever a relative might be, or "father of so-and-so", "daughter of so-and-so", to someone not related. According to early European accounts, Dogrib women had higher standing than the women of most other Athapaskan tribes. The first white traders wrote of the pride with which young Dogrib husbands would display the needlework of their wives.

The Dogribs have always had a reputation for liveliness, a fondness for games and dancing. In one of their peace dances men would face each other in two lines, holding their bows with the strings away from them to show friendship.

The Hare people   The country of the Hare tribe in the days before the fur trade was the forest north of Great Bear Lake and west of the lake to the Mackenzie River. They were never numerous, probably less than a thousand people living in six or seven small bands.

Caribou herds migrating both north and south of the Great Bear Lake were hunted, and the Hare people killed musk-ox on the barren grounds. On the whole, however, the tribe did not travel far east onto the tundra or north into the coastal home of their enemies, the Inuit. They made heavy use of small animals and fish and were named the Hare or Hareskin people because of their frequent use of the skins and meat of the arctic hare.

The general way of life of the Hare tribe was very much like that of the Dogrib and Chipewyan. Like them their clothing included hairbands of hare or caribou fur. They did not ornament their bodies or clothing very much; they occasionally built rectangular winter houses like the Slavey; and their arrows were longer than those of neighbouring tribes. It was the local custom of their medicine man to hang by ropes from trees or tent-poles when trying to talk to the spirits.

On the whole the Hares avoided fighting and were friendly with the Kutchin and Dogrib tribes. They clashed occasionally with the Yellowknives and Inuit and exchanged raids with the Mountain tribe whom they called the "Bad People".

The Mackenzie Mountain people   In the mountains between the valleys of the Yukon and Mackenzie rivers and along the valley of the Liard lived three tribes who have often been called the Nahanni Indians. Not much is known about the life of these tribes in pre-European days, especially the two most northerly ones. From north to south they were the *Mountain, Goat,* and *Kaska* tribes, who were related by language and custom.

The former hunting grounds of the Mountain and Goat peoples included the upper parts of the Pelly and Ross rivers in the Yukon, but they were driven east by the Tutchone. They hunted woodland caribou, using compounds and snares, and set snares among the rocks high in the mountains for mountain goat and big-horn sheep.

Like the Kutchin, the Mountain and Goat people built boats of moose hide for downstream journeys, using as many as eight skins for each boat. When in need of a temporary toboggan they used the legskin of caribou or moose. This type of toboggan was called a *tifreiwiltho*. They used snowshoes up to six feet long for use in fresh snow and shorter ones for packed snow.

The Kaska were the most numerous of the three mountain tribes, grouped in five bands around the head of the Liard River. They were of Athapaskan language and life-style, but traded often with such coastal Indians as the Tahltan and Tlingit. From them the Kaska adopted a system of two clans, named after the wolf and raven and the custom of holding potlatch feasts. The women learned the coastal art of weaving sheep wool and goat hair into blanket cloth, and adopted the custom of attacking dummy enemies while their men were away fighting the real ones.

At the time when the first Europeans visited them, the Kaska had a powerful woman chief. She led about 400 people and defied the powerful Tlingit chief "Shakes" in order to save the lives of the trader-explorer Campbell and his men. She has been called the "Nahanni Chief", but her real name is not known.

The Kutchin   The word Kutchin means "People", and was used by each of the ten or so bands who lived in what is now Alaska and Canada. One such band for instance were the Tukudh or Takudh-Kutchin, "People of the Slanting Eyes". This was translated by French-speaking traders as Loucheux, the name commonly used now for Kutchin people.

The Kutchin tribe totalled probably more than 3,000 before the coming of the European fur trade. Down the Yukon River they traded and at times fought with the Tanana and Koyukon Indians and had contact with the Alaskan Inuit. On the northern Yukon coast and in the Mackenzie Delta they met their chief enemies and occasional trading partners, the Mackenzie Inuit, whom they called by the rude name of *anakrei*, which means "enemy feet", but sounds like "excrement" in Eskimo.

Certain customs of the Kutchin were similar to those of the Inuit. Women sometimes carried their babies inside their coats instead of the usual moss-bag or scoop-like Kutchin birchbark baby carrier. The headbands of the men were of Inuit style, and their leggings wide, like the trousers of the Inuit. Kutchin bows were often made in several parts bound with sinew as the Inuit did, and sleds with high framed runners were used, similar to those of Alaskan Inuit. The canoes of the Kutchin resembled those of the river Inuit of Alaska, and travelling men sometimes made a kind of dugout snowhouse, glazed by fire, called a *zohlkan*.

The most common kind of Kutchin dwelling was the dome-shaped tent of caribou skins stretched over red-painted spruce poles. The winter house, with furred skins was called *nivase*, and the lighter summer type *ditrije*. The clothing of the Kutchin was heavily fringed, and men in particular wore decorations of quill and dentalia shells. Both sexes wore headbands, fur caps, and winter hoods. Men wore their hair in a large greased ball at the base of the neck, covered with bird-down and with feathers inserted. Women wore round nose ornaments of bone, stone, or shell, and men wore bone skewers. Men's faces were heavily painted with black charcoal and red ochre, and each carried a knife with a distinctive forked handle, common also in the southern Yukon.

From the coast tribes the Kutchin adopted a system of social clans uncommon among the eastern Athapaskans. The system included a division into three clans, the Natsai, "Dark People", whose sign was the crow; the Tsitsia, "Fair People", whose badge was the wolf; and the Tendjeratsia, "Halfway People", who had no badge and were of low standing. Some families grew rich in dentalia shells, wolverine skins, caribou compounds, and other things of value to the Kutchin. Rich men gave potlatch feasts, but usually only as funeral ceremonies.

The Kutchin were perhaps the strongest of all Athapaskan tribes in their independence, fighting spirit, and love of excitement. In their northern mountains they have been able to preserve much of their old culture and independence up to the present day.

The people of the southern Yukon   The country of the southern
Yukon territory is in the form of a rough basin or hollow between
mountain ranges and is drained by the Yukon River system. The
Athapaskan-speaking people who lived there about 200 years ago
shared a common language and general way of life. They, like
other Athapaskans of the western mountains, preferred houses
roofed with bark to the hide-covered tepees more common among
the eastern tribes. They had a variety of food sources, including
the salmon runs which were fairly dependable as a winter standby.

Perhaps because of an easier living compared to that of the
tribes east of the mountains, the southern Yukon people were
more numerous and developed a more complicated social system.
They spent more time in organized fighting over trade, territory,
women, and insults real or imagined. Of all the surrounding tribes,
the Tlingit people of the coast had the greatest influence on the
southern Yukon Athapaskans. They would come over the steep
coastal mountains by way of the Chilkat, Chilkoot, and Taku
routes. Being warlike and organized, they forced the inland tribes
into permanent trading agreements. The coastal system of division into nobles and commoners, wolf clan and raven clan, was
adopted by the inland tribes, whom the Tlingit called *Gunana*.

Those tribes closest to the Tlingit were the most changed and
became "middlemen" in trade with the tribes beyond them. The
Tagish and the Teslin peoples eventually gave up their language
and today speak only Tlingit. The T'atlowa T'lan, "Flat-Place
People", who lived near Hoatchai in the southwest, were closest to
the Chilkat Tlingit, and like them became fearsome fighters. The
farther people lived from the Tlingit, the less common were the
potlatch ceremony, the importance of the clans, the class division,
and the use of "coppers" as special tokens of wealth. Trade and
fighting, both an important part of life in the southern Yukon,
decreased in the same way north and eastward.

The Chilkat Tlingit control of trade in the southern Yukon was
challenged unsuccessfully by the Hudson's Bay Company and was
really ended by the events of the Gold Rush. During the long
"rule" of the Chilkats, the Northern Tutchone were the only tribe
to resist. About 1847 the wife of Tlingit Thlin, a Tutchone chief,
was insulted by a Chilkat trader, and Tlingit Thlin killed the Chil-

kat and four of his slaves. All trade with the Chilkat was stopped and Tlingit Thlin became a rich trader himself until Han and Tana-na enemies destroyed his goods.

The flood of gold-seekers from all over the world after 1878 was so immense and rapid that it swept away the tribal life of the Indians of the southern Yukon. Compared to what is known about other northern tribes, very little has been written or remembered of their old ways.

The Inuit

It is likely that before Europeans arrived there were about 22,000 Inuit in what is now Canada — slightly more than at present. The most obvious link between the various groups was the language. Despite some variation between east and west, the first interpre-ters from the Keewatin to visit the Mackenzie Delta and Ungava Bay were able to speak quite well with the Inuit of these wide-apart regions.

Although the Inuit made the best of whatever country they lived in, and some lived well inland, the sea and its wildlife were a major force of the Inuit culture. Many of the features of Inuit life well known to modern readers were the result of life by the sea and in a land of long winters and few trees.

The kayak was used by all Inuit, snowhouses by almost all, as well as dogteams, and special clothing which made life possible in the winter spaces. The double winter suit of caribou fur, the wa-terproof kayak jacket of intestine, waterproof boots cunningly sewn, birdskin and fishskin clothing, the baby-carrying pouch in women's coats — all were developed to perfection by Inuit women.

Clothing varied in design from tribe to tribe, and patterns were made by inserting patches of differently coloured skins. Some northern Indian people used tattooing to decorate their faces and bodies, but none as much as did the Inuit. The tattoo marks were made by pulling a bone needle through the flesh, threaded with sinew or hair dipped in lampblack or plant juice. Another method was to prick a series of holes with a sharp bone. The design of women's face tattoos was the same almost everywhere, lines ra-diating from the mouth over the cheeks, chin, and forehead. Some

Nulumaluk Inurana, leader of the Liverpool Bay band
of Karngmalit (Mackenzie) Inuit, 1865.

of the tattoo designs had social and religious meaning, such as the memory of a dead relative or success in whaling.

Unlike the Snowshoe People, the Inuit had few special customs to mark the time when boys and girls grew up, and training in toughness for boys was provided by daily life. As a boy grew, however, his first bird, seal, or caribou was always a reason for a feast or small ceremony.

The custom of bride-service was common to most Inuit groups, and there was a complicated system of adoption in which almost all families gave or received children. Each large community of Inuit built its *qaggeg*, a big snowhouse, loghouse, or other winter dwelling. In it were held dances, especially the great midwinter festival where masked and disguised clowns supervised events.

One of the most important and distinctive items of Inuit culture everywhere was the *kudlik*, the stone lamp used for cooking, light, and heat. It had animal fat for fuel and a wick of moss. The *inuksuit*, stone figures built to guide travellers, to frighten caribou into ambush, or for other reasons, were another feature of Inuit culture.

In all small rivers along which arctic char migrated, the Inuit built stone weirs or traps and speared the fish with a pronged spear, the *kakivak*. Despite many similarities in the Inuit way of life across the Arctic, changes from region to region were greater than among the Snowshoe Peoples, and it is best to describe the life of the Inuit tribe by tribe.

The Mackenzie Inuit   Where the Mackenzie, Kugaluk, and Anderson rivers flow into the Arctic Ocean lived the most different of all the Inuit tribes, people who had strong links with the Alaskan cultures. There were about 2,500 of the Mackenzie Inuit, divided most of the time into five main bands. Their territory contained both woods and barrens, caribou, musk-ox, and the occasional moose. At sea were whales, walrus, and seals, and altogether the region was one of the richest inhabited by Inuit.

The Mackenzie people hunted the great baleen whales out at sea, but one of their main sources of food, hide, blubber, and bone was the belugas, or white whales. Each summer these would come into the Mackenzie River and the Inuit would gather to hunt them. At the village of Kittigazuit as many as 1,000 people might meet. With a line of kayaks the men would herd the whales into shallow water to be killed. Up to 200 whales might be taken in this way, the biggest ones weighing a ton each. In addition to the usual Inuit fishing by spear and jigging, the Mackenzie people used nets of skin line set on poles in the riverbed.

With such a supply of food and fuel the Mackenzie tribe was able to live in large bands for much of the year and to have an elaborate social life. Their winter houses, each named after its location, were roomy places built of upright logs covered with dirt or turf. At whaling time or other seasonal gatherings, drum dances were held, and people would play at *nalukatuk*, bouncing high from a stretched walrus skin held across posts by a ring of Inuit.

Both men and women wore short coats without flaps or aprons, and knee-length pants. The skirts and cuffs of the coats were trimmed with fur in the Alaskan style, and the fur around women's hoods was of long wolverine hair which stood out in a ruff around the wearer's face. The women wore their hair in a high pile, and their hoods were made very roomy to accommodate the hairstyle. Men's hoods were made of caribou or wolf-head skin, with the ears left on.

The kayaks of the Mackenzie men were unlike those of tribes in the east, being smaller and having a high, pointed bow and stern. Men who killed a bear wore *tutut*, ornaments of stone or ivory fastened through their cheeks. When girls and boys reached the age of twelve or thirteen, their teeth would be filed down with sandstone, and the boys would have their cheeks and ears pierced ready to receive men's ornaments. The Mackenzie Inuit were the only tribe to mark the growing up of boys and girls in this way.

Most Inuit were sturdy and muscular in build, but the Mackenzie people were bigger than average and boisterous by nature. They would go far upriver to hunt, to obtain stone for their knives, and to meet the Hare and Kutchin Déné. They fought and traded with the Déné and adopted from them the custom of wrestling for wives.

The Copper Inuit   To the east of the Mackenzie people lived the tribe whose territory centred around Victoria Island, and who have been named after the copper to be found there. There were probably about 1,000 people in the six or seven bands of the Copper tribe.

Occasionally they hunted at the treeline and very rarely would meet the Hare or Yellowknife Déné. They were mainly a people of the open tundra and the sea and were experts at sealing on or through the ice. When European visitors first arrived, they were living in snowhouse villages rather than winter houses of stone and sod. For part of the summer the Copper people would scatter into small groups to wander overland, fishing or hunting caribou and musk-ox.

The Copper Inuit clothing was of the general Inuit style common to all except the Mackenzie tribe. In the local Copper version coats, hoods, and sleeves were short, and the women's coattails long and very narrow. For dancing the Copper men wore small caps with the beaks of loons at the top, and tassels of weasel skin. Another special custom was the shaving of men's foreheads.

The Netsilik Inuit   Eastward from the Copper tribe lived the Netsilik people, who were named after a lake into which seals sometimes swam — Netsilik means "there are seals". The seven small bands of the tribe lived on or near King William Island. The channels and bays of their country were icebound for most of the year, and they were perhaps the most expert of all tribes at seal hunting on the winter or spring ice.

Their kayaks were long and narrow, and their clothing was of the central arctic style with pointed hoods on the coats, short fringed flaps on the men's coats, and long wide flaps at back and front for the women. Women would often braid their hair around two long sticks called *tuglirak*, using strips of dark and light skin for the binding.

Although the Netsilik people travelled inland occasionally as far as the Thelon River for wood, their meetings with Déné were very rare. They were strong and aggressive people, and also had a reputation for magic which made them feared by their neighbouring tribes.

The Caribou Inuit   Inland from the west coast of Hudson Bay is the district we now call Keewatin. Here lived about five bands who are collectively called the Caribou Inuit. Two-thirds of them had little or nothing to do with the sea, and the rest relied heavily on caribou, doing most of their sea hunting during the summer.

The inland people used long narrow kayaks covered with caribou skin and built their sleds very roughly with hardly any curve upward in front. With only caribou fat for their lamps, they often lived without heat in their snowhouses and cooked outside on fires of moss and willow.

Like their Netsilik and Igloolik neighbours, the women wore headbands of bone or copper across their foreheads, plaited their hair on *tuglirak*, and wore the hoods of their *amaut*, baby-carrying coats, extra long.

Their country adjoined that of the Chipewyans to the southwest, and southward along the coast they met the Cree. From these tribes, whom they knew by separate names, they may have learned the art of quill embroidery and developed it to a high degree.

The Sadliq Inuit   On Southampton Island, known as *Sadliq* in the Inuit language, lived a small tribe about whom very little is known. They seem to have been avoided by the mainland tribes and were looked down upon for their crude living habits and simple ways.

They wore bearskin clothing more than most Canadian Inuit, used flint-headed weapons more than other tribes, and buried their dead in shrouds of caribou skin. The men wore their hair long, and sometimes coiled it in a large ball worn over the brow. They built houses of stone, turf, and whalebone, and one man who had no kayak with him paddled out to meet the first foreign explorers on a float of three blown-up sealskins.

The Sadliq people were wiped out quite suddenly by foreign diseases, and the last survivor died in 1948.

The Igloolik Inuit   One tribe occupied a large territory reaching from the northern limit of the Caribou people to the north of Baffin Island. They had no name for themselves as a tribe, but we may call them the Igloolik people after a place in the centre of their country.

The Igloolik people, like the Netsilik and South Baffin tribes, are often called Central Eskimos. They lived equally from sea and land, but were close to the largest walrus herd in the Arctic. They were expert at hunting these great beasts, and the large baleen whales which were less numerous.

Having a meat supply greater than that of most tribes, the Igloolik people were able to keep large dog teams even before guns were introduced. They lived in houses of stone, whalebone, and turf, but moved into snowhouses out on the sea ice for part of the winter. In the fall they sometimes made transparent houses of iceblocks, with sealskin roofs.

Like the Netsilik and Caribou women, the Igloolik women wore high boots and stockings with square pouches on the outside of each leg. Families moved frequently within the wide tribal territory, and in general their culture was richer and more varied than that of neighbouring tribes.

The South Baffin Island Inuit   The people of Baffin Island from Clyde Inlet in the north to Cape Dorset in the southwest did not form one tribe, but lived in about seven main locations, each group related to its nearest neighbours. Their country was divided by high mountains, great bays, and inland plains, without a central meeting place. Cumberland Sound had the greatest population, and there was occasional contact between the Cumberland Sound people and the Igloolik tribe by way of the large inland lake Netsilling.

The South Baffin people dressed rather like the Igloolik tribe, but the men's coats were shorter, slightly slit in front, and without flaps. Women rarely wore their hair with *tuglirak* sticks, but in coils or braids, and the forehead-band was not common. Before foreigners came, the Baffin women wore trousers and boots like those of the men, rather than the older style of short pants worn with high boots.

They were an all-around people, hunting every species of wildlife though there were no musk-ox on Baffin Island. A few families might live inland by the two great lakes, but only for a season or two. The west coast with its mud flats was rarely visited. The people who lived along the southern coast of Baffin Island had contact with those to the south across Hudson Strait. They crossed by ice or water along the islands which they called *tutjat*, stepping stones. Sometimes families would drift across the strait on rafts of ice or driftwood. On the other side they would visit friends and obtain new wood from the Ungava forest with which to make kayaks or umiaks.

The Ungava Inuit   The people of Ungava and Labrador are usually grouped together as the Labrador Eskimos, but there are differences in dialect and customs around the long coastline. In pre-European days the differences were greater, and it seems better to divide the people into two large groups roughly along the line of the Leaf River.

About ten bands lived around the east coast of Hudson Bay, the south coast of Hudson Strait, and the west coast of Ungava Bay, though they did not form one tribe. In those days the caribou migrated north to Hudson Strait, and people often went inland to hunt and fish, especially in summertime. Some families would stay inland for a whole summer or longer, living mostly on caribou and fish. They would use a special small round lamp, burning caribou fat, and would make candles of caribou tallow poured into the skin of goose legs.

Perhaps because of the supply of wood from the south of their region, and the lack of drifting ice during the summer, the Ungava people made great use of umiaks rowed by women, as well as kayaks, and often visited the chain of offshore islands.

The people of the tiny and barren Belcher Islands were expert with kayaks, and because caribou were few they made frequent use of birdskins for clothing. They used male ducks for men's clothing, female for women's. Long grass grows well along the coast of Hudson Bay and the women there used it to weave beautiful baskets. Mats of willow were also used by the people of this coast for bedding or for hunters to lie upon out on the ice.

Near James Bay and along the Leaf River the treeline was the boundary between the hunting grounds of Inuit and Algonkians. For the most part the two groups avoided each other through mutual fear.

The Labrador Inuit   Like the Inuit of western Ungava and southern Baffin Island, those of Labrador lived in over a dozen bands from Ungava Bay to the north shore of the Gulf of St. Lawrence. Each band knew its neighbours for over a hundred miles on either side, but there were no definite tribes.

The Labrador region was the warmest of all Inuit territories, with the longest season of open sea. The bands lived on the coastal strip of tundra, but could reach the forest within a few minutes or at the most a day, depending on location.

Until the Europeans came, walrus, whales, and caribou were plentiful all along the Ungava and Labrador coast, and the people of the Labrador coast in particular enjoyed a fairly rich and varied way of life. The Atlantic codfish was a source of food not available to other Inuit, though the Labrador people did not rely on it heavily until European times.

Like the Mackenzie Delta people the Inuit of southern Labrador were able to live in large groups, and were still moving southward around the coast when Europeans first arrived. They crossed to Newfoundland and traded with the Beothuk Indians there for hardwood bows and arrows, or for the wood to make them. The Inuit also met Naskapi, Montagnais, and occasionally Micmac people from across the gulf, but their movement south was unwelcome to the Algonkians.

Before the storm

During thousands of years as we have seen, people and ideas moved across the north until three great language families emerged, each with its subdivisions or tribes.

Within the limits set by nature and their tools of stone, bone, or wood the tribes lived as fully as they could. Their dancing, hunting, fighting, and building left little mark on the land. The effects of tribe on tribe, the movements from region to region, came slowly, and each group or tribe developed a way of life which suited local conditions.

Perhaps things would have remained much the same for further thousands of years, but a much different kind of human arrived. "The hairy men from the east", as one Algonkian chief described them, crossed the Atlantic and moved across the north like a slow flood that lapped at every tree and tent, camp and cache, changing all it touched.

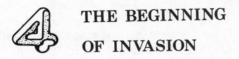 **THE BEGINNING**

OF INVASION

Some thoughts to carry

The whole time during which northern native people were seeing
their first foreigners is called by historians the *contact period*. Altogether this period lasted about 400 years, beginning near Newfoundland and ending near Victoria Island in the Arctic less than a
century ago.

What should these foreigners be called? First there is the
problem of origins. We cannot say "white men", because some
were black. European is not accurate, because eventually
some were African or Asian, and after several hundred years
many were Canadian or American. Some of them lived all their
lives among native people and cannot be called "strangers", or
"newcomers". Words like "Euro-Canadian" and "non-native" are
clumsy; in fact any term we choose will be open to debate. Let us
settle for *foreigner*, in the sense of people who are born — as
most still are — outside the north.

The invaders came by ship over the Atlantic, Pacific, and Arctic oceans, by foot and canoe along many trails and rivers. There
were slow steady advances like that of the fur trade, and sudden

sweeping inrushes like the Yukon Gold Rush. Sometimes ideas
and things went ahead of the foreigners, so that by the time they
arrived in person many changes had been made.

One thing to keep in mind is that during the centuries of contact and invasion *the foreigners changed* as much as, perhaps more
than, did the native peoples. The first foreigners to arrive had
guns, sailing ships, and other advantages, but in many ways they
were primitive. They rarely washed, their medical knowledge was
poor, and many of them had the ill-health and poor physique of
people from crowded, filthy cities.

The foreigners of the early centuries of contact believed in witchcraft and tortured people for religious reasons. They had not yet
discovered how to use steam or gasoline power. Those Labrador
Inuit who met the Portuguese explorer brothers Corte-Real in
1500 were probably very much like the Copper Inuit who met
the explorer Stefansson in 1910. Their clothing, language, experience, and thoughts would be almost the same. Between the
Corte-Reals and Stefansson, however, were 400 years of tremendous scientific and social change.

History cannot be divided up neatly into separate sections, because each happening mingles with others like streams of water
running together. In the case of the invasion of northern Canada
there was a definite beginning by way of the St. Lawrence River
and Hudson Bay. We will make that beginning into a chapter,
and then follow north and west in chapters to come.

Sails from the east

Scandinavian Vikings may have come to Baffin Island and Ungava
almost a thousand years ago, but we cannot be sure. We do know
from their writings that they met Dorset Eskimo and/or Beothuk
Indian people in northern Newfoundland about the year 1008.
The Vikings stayed only a season or two, and traded a little with
the natives. As was to happen many times later, different languages and different customs caused fighting, and there the contact ended.

A few British ships may have been seen along the Atlantic coast
a century or two after the Vikings, and after the year 1400 fishing

vessels from several European countries began to come each summer to the fishing grounds around Newfoundland. Year by year the fishermen and whale hunters built more huts and fish-drying racks along the coast, all the way up to the mouth of the St. Lawrence River. They mingled with the Inuit and Indians, but as always trouble began. If one Portuguese fisherman stole a Beothuk girl, her people might blame the foreigners. If one of the Inuit stole an English rowboat, all Inuit might be blamed and attacked. One side, the foreigners, brought no women, and tried to take them from among the Indians and Inuit. The natives for their part tried to obtain boats, axes, and other valuable foreign goods, and to protect their hunting grounds.

After the year 1400, the various coastal nations of Europe were growing fast, full of energy to invent new things and to explore the world. Their kings wanted to be powerful, to conquer other countries, and to help the Christian Church to spread everywhere. European explorers were sent by their kings and queens to claim new lands and find gold, slaves, or other wealth. France claimed the lands around the St. Lawrence River, and England claimed Newfoundland.

The explorer Cabot in 1498 bartered Venetian earrings and a sword to Labrador Algonkians and netting needles to Inuit. Many of the explorers kidnapped native people to take back to Europe. The Corte-Reals for instance in 1500 and 1502 took 60 Naskapi or Montagnais people to Portugal. One Inuit man kidnapped (with his kayak) by Martin Frobisher from Baffin Island gave an exhibition for Queen Elizabeth I, hunting royal swans on the palace pond. In 1606 the Inuit of southern Labrador fought the English captain Knight, and in 1704 the French commander Courtemanche, and many were killed. In those days few foreigners considered it wrong to kidnap people or to claim the country of Inuit and Indians.

As England concentrated on Newfoundland, the French moved up the St. Lawrence River. In 1535 Jacques Cartier found Iroquois living at Hochelaga and Stadaconna, now Montreal and Quebec. By 1603 when he visited again, the Montagnais had displaced the Iroquois along the northern shore. The enmity between Iroquois and Algonkians became an important factor in the history of New France.

The St. Lawrence fur trade

The mainland settlements of the French did not develop as their king had hoped. Farming by French families grew slowly, and the fur trade became most important. The hatmakers and clothmakers of Europe found that they could make fine things from beaver, otter, and other furs. Such garments became fashionable, and there was a great demand for furs. The Indians used very few furs themselves, and were happy to exchange furs for foreign goods. Soon the Indians and foreigners were both bound together in the fur trade, which spread west and north. It became the central part of Canadian history.

On to Hudson Bay

The British, in their search for a sea route to Asia, discovered Hudson Bay, and in 1610 Henry Hudson made the first trade with a Cree man in James Bay. This man, whose name is forgotten, must have been brave, for he approached the strangers' ship alone and exchanged his furs for a knife, a mirror, some buttons, and a hatchet.

The French traders Radisson and Groseilliers reached James Bay by land in 1660, and a few years later they helped the British to begin a trading post at what is now Rupert House. By 1717 the Indians of southern Hudson Bay were able to trade at several posts between the Churchill River in the west and the Eastmain in the east. For 50 years such trade was interrupted by war between the French and the British.

The Indians might find a fort in British hands one year and in French the next. Each foreign side tried to win over the Indians with gifts or threats. Both the French and British forts were attacked at times by Indians whose wives had been taken, or who had waited for weeks at the forts, neglecting their hunting, for supply ships which did not come. There were acts of kindness too on both sides, when Indians brought meat to hungry foreigners, or when the traders fed Indians during times of poor hunting and sickness. The western Hudson's Bay Company forts attracted Indians from far away, and in 1694, while Fort Nelson was in French hands, a float of 300 canoes, Assiniboine, Ojibway, and Cree, came downstream to trade.

People overwhelmed

During the first two centuries of foreigner invasion the displacement of tribes and the fighting involved everyone. Each group of foreigners and each tribe of Indians or Inuit was attacked, and attacked others in turn. Slavery was common in those days, and thousands of southern Indians were brought to the St. Lawrence colony as slaves. The northern peoples were affected too, and a count taken between 1720 and 1743 shows Naskapi, Montagnais, Cree, and Eskimo slaves in New France and Newfoundland.

The French colony was founded among the Huron tribe and the Algonkian tribes of the St. Lawrence. These tribes traded their furs to the French, and passed along furs from surrounding tribes. In the same way the Iroquois tribes traded first with the Dutch, then the British settlers on the Hudson River farther south. The tribes closest to foreigners became "middlemen". A Huron for instance might exchange a beaver pelt for a French axe in Montreal. Later he might exchange the used axe for three beaver pelts from an Ojibway Algonkian near Georgian Bay. The "middlemen" Indians were able to get foreign goods in this way without actually trapping furs themselves, and they tried to prevent any meetings between foreigners and the farther tribes.

Even before the foreigners came, the Iroquois had begun to form a very powerful organization of five tribes. The French had helped both the Hurons and Algonkians against them, and they wanted revenge. They also wanted to control the fur trade of the north, and armed with guns obtained in trade they began wars which, becoming entangled with the wars between France and Britain, lasted a hundred years. It is interesting to imagine how different history would have been if all the native peoples had united to deal with the Europeans.

Although the Hurons lived in a way similar to the Iroquois and were as numerous — about 20,000 each — they were no match for the Iroquois war parties. The Hurons were weakened by foreign diseases, and they had become dependent on French officials and missionaries who taught peace. By the year 1650 the Hurons were defeated. The Iroquois encircled the French colony and raided into the north, reaching James Bay, Lake Mistassini, and Lake St. John. Their attacks are still remembered with horror among the

Cree, Montagnais, and Naskapi people who call the Iroquois *Nottaway.*

Despite the struggle with the Iroquois the fur trade spread. Many Frenchmen preferred the adventure and freedom of the woods to the hard work and limits of farming. They learned to canoe and snowshoe and often married into Indian families. With the explorers and missionaries they pushed inland north and west, always guided by the Indians whose language they had learned.

The Micmac tribe became the most powerful of the coastal Algonkians. They raided the Montagnais and helped the foreigners to wipe out the southern Labrador Inuit and the Beothuk Indians of Newfoundland. Both these tribes fought bravely to keep their lives and territory, but they had no guns. Year after year men, women, and children were killed or driven into hiding like animals. The last Beothuk, a woman called Shanawdithit, died in 1829, and by that time the Inuit who survived had moved north along the Labrador coast. In 1756 the Inuit had agreed to a peace treaty, but this forbade them to visit Newfoundland, part of their ancient homeland. It did not stop foreigners from coming to Labrador.

The history of the first European arrivals was not all sad and blood-stained. The Micmac and Iroquois Indians adopted many of their captives, including foreigners who grew to love and prefer the Indian way of life. There were friendships, marriages, and much peaceful trade between all the peoples. The foreigners learned how to dress, hunt, and travel in the native way, and in turn the Indian and Inuit people adopted foreign tools, clothing, and habits. To this day European Canadians of the Belle Isle region use the *kamotik* sled of the Inuit, and both Naskapi and Inuit boys play with crossbows, called *pititshitayak* by the Inuit, *passigan atshapi* by the Naskapi. There were happy times like the day when the trader George Cartwright taught Shadluvinik and his band of Inuit at Cape Charles to play leapfrog, or when Atuiuk and Tuglavinak went fox-hunting on horseback in England.

The exchange between peoples, however, was bound to be one-sided. Foreign diseases wiped out whole villages of native people. For every marriage of an Eskimo or Indian man to a foreign woman there were hundreds of native women married to foreign men. Hunting failed as animals were trapped or shot in great numbers. Of all the eastern tribes the Naskapis were the least affected, but even they had been drawn to mingle with Montagnais at the coast or pushed farther north by wars and foreign settlers. Diseases found their way to the most remote Naskapi camps, and they could no longer live without some foreign foods. The James Bay Cree and the Labrador Eskimos were even more affected. Their old independence had gone, and the foreigners with their smallpox and brandy, guns and blankets, laws and religion, had come to stay.

5 THE DAYS OF THE BEAVER

The fur trade has been the life of the northern Indian people for so long that no one can remember any other life. The first foreigners brought goods which were more exciting, more labour-saving, than those of the ancient native trade. The Indian people everywhere welcomed the new trade, but they could not foresee the great changes that were to follow every needle, knife, and gun.

Trade through Indian eyes

To the foreign traders the important thing was profit — money to spend on *their* kind of life, far away from the northern forests. But for the Indian hunters and trappers the trade was a part of everyday life, a way of improving, not replacing it. Trade was personal, social, political.

The time of exchanging furs for trade goods was a time to visit, gossip, and play games. It was a time to make plans, to smoke peace pipes, and to make agreements which were rarely broken. It mattered just as much *whom* you traded with as what you traded.

In the beginning when the Indian people were still independent and traders were competing, the fur trade was made to suit native ways. Each group of Indian middlemen profited from its neighbours, and played rival foreign traders against each other. It did not take long for the hunters to learn the various qualities of steel, blankets, liquor, and other goods. They learned by heart the price-lists of the traders and would not accept any changes.

One trading chief warned the trader at York Factory about 1750 not to use a sawn-off ruler when measuring cloth, not to put his thumb in the scoop when measuring out gunpowder, and not to water down the brandy. The chief asked for a good trade because the winter had been hard. Both sides, foreign and Indian, used tricks when possible, and the trader had to be on guard against torn skins cleverly patched and mended. Some of the Kutchin knew how to darken land-otter skins and stretch the tails to make them look like the expensive sea-otter. Some Montagnais young men stole from the foreigners the skins they had just traded and sold them again the next day.

The Chilkat Tlingit traders would demand from their Athapaskan customers furs piled as high as a gun muzzle in exchange for the gun — an old trick of the foreign traders. Some middleman tribes grew rich enough just passing other people's furs to the foreigners for a profit; they themselves did not bother to trap. Some began to specialize in supplying meat for the many fur posts and canoe brigades. In 1780 the Assiniboine plains dwellers burned the grass around the Hudson House post so that the bison would stay away from the post. In this way the post people could not hunt for their own meat, but had to buy from the Assiniboine.

In general, however, the northern hunting tribes stayed independent as long as they could. The Indian way was to travel light and to share things. Once people were comfortable, no promises by the traders, or higher prices, could get them to increase "production". The Naskapi and Chipewyan hunters, whose territory was hard to reach, were the particular despair of foreign traders and would live for long periods without visiting the posts.

Four faces of the fur trade

Although there were many different kinds of foreign traders during the long days of "King Beaver", four main groups brought trade and changes to Indian peoples.

For almost 200 years the *Moravian missionary traders* of the Labrador coast were visited by Naskapi and Montagnais people. These German priests gave no brandy and were not interested in moving inland to increase their trade. Their main purpose was to Christianize the Inuit, and their influence on the Indians was steady and slight.

Even before the Moravians were the French *Compagnie du Nord* and many free traders. The French alternated with the British for control of the Hudson Bay trade, and carried trade into the northern woods from Labrador to Saskatchewan. Their canoes moved into tribal lands, and their traders learned to live as and with their Indian customers. They prepared for actual trading by giving gifts such as needles or a little brandy.

The great influence of the French traders in the west was their development of canoe travel, using and improving on Indian methods to make long, fast journeys. The *voyageurs* often took Indian wives, and their children were brought up in the fur trade. When the official French trading ended in 1763, the waterways to the west and north were already the home of many French woodsmen and French Catholic Métis. In 1776 a group of independent French traders, travelling up the Churchill River, met Lake Athabasca Chipewyans coming downstream and bought their furs, which had been intended for Churchill and the Hudson's Bay Company.

The third and most important group of foreign traders was the British *Hudson's Bay Company*. For many years the Company held from the British kings the "right" to trade, and in fact govern over most of what is now Canada.

For over a hundred years the Company traded only from its strong forts at the mouths of rivers flowing into Hudson Bay. Explorers were sent far inland to bring in new tribes, but it was up to Indian people to bring their furs (or other people's) to the coast. Many fine furs were lost to the French and other free traders who moved inland, and the costs of furs that came to the coast were pushed high by Cree and Chipewyan middlemen.

One custom begun by the Company was the naming of certain leading Indian men as Trade Captains or Trade Chiefs. These men were usually respected leaders who set the terms of trade for their whole band of followers. When a trade chief and his party arrived at a fort, he would be greeted by gunfire or cannonfire, perhaps by a drum or flute band if the fort were a big one and the chief important enough.

The chief and his sub-chiefs would be given uniforms, medals, sashes, and other gifts according to rank, and would be invited to smoke and drink with the chief factor or governor before trading began. The rest of the band would wait until the signal was given, then trade their furs through a small window in the loghouse, for the Company was on guard against attack.

After 1763 and the end of French government in Canada, a group of British and American free traders began to take over the old French canoe routes to the west. They competed with the Company, and in 1769 when the Company post at Fort Albany wanted ten beaver skins for a gun, one pedlar, as the free traders were called, offered the same gun upriver for only six skins.

By about 1770 the pedlars had arrived in the Athabaska region, and began to fight among themselves for trade with the Indians. Finally some of them joined to form the North West Company. The Nor'westers, as they came to be called, were the fourth strong influence upon the northern Indians.

Brandy, beaver, and pemmican

To meet the threat of Nor'wester competition, the Company moved inland, and there were soon two lines of trading posts along the canoe routes from Hudson Bay to the Mackenzie and the Rockies. These were days of bitter competition, with the companies like opposing armies, with a few free traders, with the Indian tribes taking sides, and all seeking profit from furs.

At this time the great canoes made their long, fast journeys carrying supplies west and furs east. Their crews, mainly French, Métis, and Indian, paddled and portaged long hours, eating mostly pemmican. This Indian food that fuelled the fur trade was made of flakes of dried meat pounded to a paste with fat, and sometimes berries. When sewn into bags of hide the *pimikehegan* would harden and keep for months, sometimes years.

Everything was valued in beaver pelts, and each blanket, axe, gun, or wolverine skin would be priced as so many "made beaver".

Trade chiefs were appointed by both companies, and each side showed newly met Indians how to clean and prepare pelts for the foreign market. Gifts were given to try to make the tribes want more goods and bring in more furs.

Whisky, brandy, rum, and other liquor was given to or sold to the Indians. Some hunters often liked it so well that traders had to give it in order to get furs. Alexander Mackenzie, the Nor'wester, was at Great Bear Lake in 1805 and wrote: "Eleven Red Knives arrived with the Little Chief with provisions and peltrie — I gave them 6 quarts of mixt rum and one fathom of tobaccoe."

Later the Company, having no competition, was able to reduce the use of liquor, but at Fort Chimo in 1840 Naskapi Indian visitors to the post were given rum — none was given however to the Inuit, and the custom was never begun with them. For the Indian people the coming of liquor was one of the worst parts of the fur trade, for it destroyed pride, independence, and common sense.

Waves of people

The guns that came with the fur trade helped to set in motion a great movement of people. As guns changed the lives of the tribes from east to west, horses brought by Spanish soldiers far to the south made their way up to the great northern plains. The Blackfeet, the Sioux, and the Plains Cree developed the colourful plains culture so famous now, and everywhere the tribes of plain and forest moved against each other like waves when a stone hits water, or like crowding caribou.

When Iroquois power ended, many Iroquois adventurers joined the canoe brigades of the fur trade and travelled as far as the Pacific. Louis Aruihunta was the Iroquois steersman of a trading boat that reached the Anderson River Inuit in 1857. In 1814 Iroquois trappers were being blamed for a shortage of beavers near Fort Chipewyan.

Around the Company posts English, Scottish, and Irish men with Indian wives, mostly Cree, fathered a new people, the *Métis*. Along the inland routes French-Cree, Ojibway, and Saulteaux Métis dominated. The two groups moving and meeting by the Red River became a new nation, a new power in the land.

Gerry Potts, the amazing plains scout, Gabriel Dumont, and Louis Riel are famous in history, but they were not of the northern forest. It was those restless French-Métis buffalo hunters who moved north and west who stayed in the mainstream of the fur trade. As hunters, trappers, canoemen, scowmen, wagon drivers, and interpreters they moved into the Mackenzie Valley, often ahead of the foreign traders.

François Beaulieu is one of the best known of these men. In 1789 he went down the Mackenzie River to the Arctic Ocean with the explorer-trader Alexander Mackenzie. His son François II was a fearsome fighter during the dark days of fur-trade strife, and took wives from about eight tribes to help him control the local trade. François II died in 1872 at the age of 101 years. His son Etienne, "the King", Beaulieu was a leader in many ways, and for several years operated a meat supply post at the eastern end of Great Slave Lake.

The Cree empire

Just as the Iroquois had once set off a wave of movement among the tribes, the Crees became the main force for a hundred years. Their country encircled the trading posts of Hudson Bay and was reached by the canoe traders of Montreal. They were active and numerous and, when armed with guns, set about defending and extending their control of the fur trade.

Being close to the posts, they learned much about foreign ways, and their women married foreign men. Moses Norton, who became governor of the Company post at Churchill, was an English-Cree Métis. In 1765 he reported that Crees could buy an axe from him for one beaver skin, then take it upstream to sell to Chipewyan or Blackfoot for ten beaver! They would buy a new gun for 14 skins and sell it to their Assiniboine friends for 36 skins.

Some Crees moved east to become the Mistassini and Tête de Boule, but the main movement was westward. By 1730 the Company trader at Fort Albany was complaining that war with the Dakotas had stopped the canoes from reaching him and had emptied the Winisk and Severn country of people.

In the forest the Crees displaced the Chipewyans, and on the plains they pushed back the Gros Ventres Sioux and the Blackfoot, fellow Athapaskans and former allies. The Naskupa, Assiniboine Sioux, were Cree allies, and moved westward with them on the plains. Behind them followed the Ojibways, close relatives of the Crees, and lords of the great canoe routes.

The Crees raided down the Mackenzie River, and in 1789 Mackenzie found a paddle left by Chief Beardung and his Cree war-party the year before. The Great Slave Lake Athapaskans have a story about a women captured by Cree — in Slavey she is called G'umbah, "The Ptarmigan". In Chipewyan she is called Thanadelthur, "Marten Shake". Each tribe's story is roughly the same.

The woman is taken by Crees to a foreign trading post. There she manages to speak to the traders and tell them that some of the "pelts" carried by the Crees are really bundles of the scalps of her people. The traders give her a gun and other things, and tell the Crees to let her go back to her tribe. Two men of her tribe find the tracks of her Cree snowshoes and do not believe at first that she is one of them. Later they go back to her people and she marries both of the men. In such stories the Cree are called *enna*, the enemy.

Gradually the Cree territory became over-trapped and over-hunted. The Cree people became involved with and mingled with the foreign traders until their tribal strength and independence was lost. Foreign diseases killed many of them, and settlers invaded their hunting grounds on the plains. The frontier of the fur trade passed beyond them, and surrounding tribes obtained guns with which to fight back. In 1885 chiefs Big Bear and Pound-Maker led some of the western Cree in a last fight, together with the Métis, for the old free life. They were defeated, and with the sad, heroic story of Manitou-Wayo, "Almighty Voice", ten years later, the sun set on the Cree "empire".

Chipewyan power

In a smaller way the Chipewyan people repeated the Cree story. Before 1714 Cree guns had kept the Chipewyans away from York Factory, the Hudson's Bay Company post at the mouth of the Nelson River. In that year first one Chipewyan woman, then another, escaped from her Cree captors and after great hardship on the barrens, came to Governor Knight at the post.

*Slave Woman, who made peace between the
Chipewyan and the Cree in 1715.*

The second Chipewyan woman was called Slave Woman by the
foreign traders, and her real name is not known. She was a strong,
brave person who scolded the Crees for their cruelty even at the
risk of death. In June 1715 she agreed to go with William Stuart
and 148 Crees to find the Chipewyans and bring them to trade at
the coast.

The weather was very bad, and travel from east to west meant crossing many rivers and going around lakes or swamps. There was sickness, and the party divided into smaller groups. Stuart's party once went eight days without food, and found the bodies of some Chipewyans who had been shot by Crees while coming to trade. At this point the Crees with Stuart were afraid to go on, but Slave Woman persuaded them to wait for ten days while she went on alone.

On the tenth day, just as the Crees were about to leave with Stuart, she came back with 160 of her people. She interpreted and persuaded until her voice was hoarse, and finally the two sides had a feast of friendship. Ten Chipewyan men returned to York Factory to learn to be trading interpreters and agents.

In 1717 Governor Knight founded Fort Prince of Wales, which was later called Fort Churchill. Slave Woman had asked that her brother be made a trade captain so that he could deal with the Yellowknife Chipewyans. She wanted to continue to visit other Athapaskan tribes to make peace, even if it meant leaving her family. She died of sickness, however, at the new fort. Because of the peace she helped to bring, the fur trade moved quickly north and west.

There were no handy river routes leading from Chipewyan country to Churchill, and for many years the Ethen Eldeli (Caribou-Eater) Chipewyan men would leave their women, children, and old men at Nueltin Lake rather than risk the rough and hungry journey to the coast. Once they had guns, the Chipewyans became middlemen, buying furs from their Yellowknife kinsmen and other Athapaskans. In 1766 three brave Dogrib men managed to reach Churchill, but on the whole the Chipewyans kept other Indians and Inuit away. They pushed south into "moose country" and west beyond Lake Athabasca.

One of the best-known men of this period was Matonabbee. He was born in 1736, the son of a Chipewyan man and a captured Cree woman. After his father died, he was adopted by the Métis, Governor Moses Norton of Churchill, and grew up as a hunter and interpreter for the Company. He was a great traveller, and helped to keep the peace between Crees, Slaves, and Chipewyans. In 1765 he went with Chief I-dot-le-aza to visit and trade with the Copper Inuit.

From 1770 to 1772 he guided Samuel Hearne of the Company to the mouth of the Copper River. Hearne hoped to begin regular trade with the Inuit there, but an older chief urged Matonabbee and the other Chipewyans to kill all the Inuit, and this was done.

For his help to Hearne, Matonabbee and his six wives were given many presents by the Company, and he received the empty title "Head of all Indian Nations". In 1782, a French Navy captain captured the Churchill post and took Hearne prisoner. When Matonabbee heard the news he hanged himself, and during the following winter all his wives and children starved to death.

Akaitcho and the Yellowknives

The Yellowknife Chipewyans of the northwest had been looked down upon and mistreated by their southern kinsmen. In 1782 an epidemic of smallpox almost wiped out the Caribou Chipewyans, and since both guns and trade had come to the Yellowknives, they became the most powerful group in the region. In 1790 a trading post was opened at old Fort Providence (later called Fort Rae), and the Yellowknives prospered.

One chief was followed by about half the Yellowknife people, and controlled a large trading area. His older brother Keskarrah had travelled with Matonabbee, and one of his sisters was married to the Métis leader François Beaulieu II. The chief's name was Akaitcho, "Big-Feet".

When the British navy explorers Franklin and Back arrived in his territory, Akaitcho helped them greatly at the cost of hardship for himself and his people. During a very bad winter at Fort Resolution, Akaitcho tried to keep up the spirits of both Indians and foreigners, and set an example by hunting constantly.

The Yellowknives oppressed the Slave, Hare, and Dogrib tribes for over 30 years, but in 1823 the Dogribs began to fight back and retake their old hunting grounds. Between the success of the Dogrib revolt and the urgings of foreign explorers and traders, Akaitcho was persuaded to make peace. As he grew older his power declined, but he always commanded respect, and in his old age he and his oldest wives were carried by young men in litters whenever the band moved.

In the years which followed, the Yellowknives began to mingle with other tribes, particularly the southern Chipewyans and Dogribs. The few survivors of the old tribe died in an influenza epidemic in 1928 and the story of the Yellowknives ended.

The deadly friend

Perhaps the most serious change brought by the fur trade was the increased killing of wildlife. String fish-nets and steel traps increased the kill, but the gun, so welcomed by the tribes, changed everything. People such as the Chipewyans had needed about 150 caribou each year to feed, clothe, and equip an average tent-family of eight. The same sort of estimate could be made for any group in their balance with wildlife.

First with muzzleloaders and later with carbines both Indians and foreigners attacked the seemingly endless supply of wildlife. They killed for furs, for meat, for tongues and livers alone, and for the fun of it. As one area was stripped of wild creatures, people moved to another, and that too was soon emptied.

In 1712 starving Crees looted the fort (then in French hands) at the mouth of the Severn River. To prevent such incidents, the Company would provide food at the posts for Indians trading or waiting for supply ships. In the fall of 1771, 4,500 extra fish and 1,000 extra geese were stored at Fort Albany in addition to the winter's food for the post staff. Such hunting, however, cleaned out a wide area around the posts. At Churchill in 1770 a thousand Indians waited for supply ships, and winter had come, with grave danger to all, before the ships arrived. At Fort Selkirk in the Yukon in 1851, and in other places, the same thing happened, and in 1844 many waiting Hareskin people starved at Fort Good Hope.

By 1750 the eastern elk around the St. John River in Quebec were wiped out, and the Montagnais people had to move. By 1780 there were very few caribou left around Fort Severn or Fort Albany. The Lake Mistassini herds disappeared about 1885, and by 1910 the great western Ungava herd, which had ranged from James Bay to Hudson Strait, had gone.

One hundred and fifty Naskapi people starved to death in 1892 while waiting by the Koksoak River for a herd that did not come.

All through the 1800s groups of people died of starvation in northern Quebec and Labrador. The beaver, foundation of the fur
trade, grew scarce everywhere.

The unbelievably huge herds of plains bison were slaughtered
and the wave of destruction rolled north. The beaver were almost
all gone from around Lake Athabasca by 1820, and guns were
sounding all the way to the Arctic Ocean.

Some of the northern posts sent out meat to feed the Company
people in places where wildlife was scarce. Although there had
been starvation around the post 20 years earlier, Fort Good Hope
in 1864 shipped out 200 barrels of dried caribou meat in addition
to 3,000 skins of beaver, marten and fox, bear, wolf, musk-ox, and
a few birds.

Peace and power

In 1821 the North West Company joined the Hudson's Bay Company, and a year later the British government confirmed the
"right" of the Company to control most of Canada.

Slowly the control or monopoly of the Company, missionary influence, and a general weariness of trouble brought peace to the
tribes. Liquor ceased to be important in the fur trade, though it
had become too much a part of trade to stop altogether. The Company was able to place its posts to suit itself rather than to head
off competition.

The northern Indian people settled down into definite small
territories, each with its trading post. By this time the supply system to posts was fairly reliable, and the Company staff had much
experience in living in the north. They could survive without Indian help if necessary, but the Indian people could no longer live
without the ammunition, flour, matches, and other trade goods.

If Indians concentrated on trapping and hunting for furs to
trade, it often interfered with the seasonal round of meat-hunting
and fishing. Some travelled to the posts to meet the supply boat
just when caribou hunting was best, and often suffered as a result.
The Slave Lake people began to move onto the bleak barrens in
winter after fox and musk-ox but stayed near the post all summer
— a reversal of the old custom of going to the barrens in summer

and wintering in the forest. The system of giving credit for fall supplies became more common. Some Indian men, through bad luck, lack of skill, or disinterest, went deep into debt. Traders kept records on each trapper and graded him according to the furs he brought in. A man might be a first-rate hunter, leader, and parent, but if he did not bother to trade furs the traders would rate him lowly.

Gradually Indian people became more and more dependent on the trading posts. Even in 1717, 109 "home" Indians, Crees of Fort Albany, were given a daily ration of oatmeal while waiting for the geese to come north. With the thinning out of wildlife everywhere and the shift from meat to fur, debt and rations became more and more part of Indian life.

Although it was Indian custom for those that had to share with those that had not, relief rations placed the Indian receiver more and more in the power of the trader. Relief became a sad and shameful necessity that caused bitterness on both sides.

Fur trapping was done best by small family groups, and the old tribal hunting bands disappeared in many regions. The trade chiefs became less necessary, and those that continued were chosen more by the Company than by the people. By the end of the fur-trade days foreign traders, missionaries, policemen, or other officials had taken much of the leadership from the Indian people. Decisions about travel, crime, ownership, and even marriage were being made for native people, not by them.

Side effects

We have looked at the main sweep and changes of the fur trade days, but there were many small changes, many side effects. For one thing fur was not the only item produced for the foreign trade. Horn was bought for combs and ornaments; isinglass for preserving eggs came from sturgeon fish. Animal fat and scent glands were used for medicines and cosmetics. Even the bones of the vanished bison were sold for fertilizer. Moccasins, mitts, snowshoes, and other Indian things were sold, the beginnings of a tourist trade.

Some of the trade goods were new, and their use had to be learned by Indian people. Some Kutchin men wore tobacco as a charm for a while. Other people tried to eat tea or make porridge with it at first. Chief Daklowedi of the Yukon carried his first flour and lard many miles before someone explained how they should be used. New uses were found for trade goods, and mirrors were used to flash in the sun and attract deer or were sewn into clothing as ornaments.

As glass beads replaced the native bird or porcupine quills, there was a great blossoming of beadwork on clothing and equipment. Blankets became part of clothing as well as bedding, and later the famous duffle cloth became standard lining for mitts and moccasins. Netting twine, ice-chisels, fiddles, sewing machines, canvas, and kerosene all became part of Indian life.

Supplies were never certain in the north, particularly early in the trade days. When some Chipewyan got their first guns they ran out of gunpowder and converted the gunbarrels to spears and ice-chisels. In 1832 some Dogrib hunters had no guns, but carried powder and bullets to supply the gunners and thus share in the kill. People learned to make bullets of stone, to mix leaves or bark with tobacco, to split matches into two or four, to patch tents with flourbags.

"Women's Lib" came to the north as Indian women watched foreign men doing work such as carrying water, chopping wood, and keeping house. They saw that foreign men and women behaved differently together, and those Indian women who married foreign traders found their lives easier and safer on the whole. Women were needed to prepare the skins on which the fur trade depended, and gradually their position changed.

Customs and fashions travelled with the fur trade. The long needle-nosed Athapaskan snowshoe spread eastward. The "liberty caps" of the French Revolution became the tribal wear of Naskapi and Montagnais women. Northern trappers almost everywhere east of the Rockies adopted the tweed caps of old-time Scottish fishermen. The holiday dresses worn by some Mackenzie River women at the annual Inuvik games are of a style a century old.

There were special demands in trading from tribe to tribe. In 1899 for instance, the Hudson's Bay Company at Fort Chimo stocked birchbark for the Naskapi Indians who had no good bark in their territory. One coloured fox skin would buy enough bark to make a canoe. When the Loucheux of the Mackenzie first began to trade, they wanted beads above everything else, and the traders also sold them pictures of wolves and ravens as symbols of their clans. Moose hides bought from the trappers of Norway House were and are sent north to be sold to Inuit.

Furs from five regions

Although the general history of the fur trade was the same for all the northern tribes, each part of the north has its special character and its own history. Very roughly there are five parts or regions in which northern Indian people supported the fur trade.

Northern Quebec and Labrador

From Lake Kaniapiscau and its neighbours in the centre, rivers flow in every direction to the sea, like the spokes of a giant wheel of water. This land has been lightly written of in history books, but it has much to tell.

You can learn of the polar bear that reached Nitchequon over 300 miles inland, of the mountain sheep killed near Lake Petitskapau though none are supposed to exist in the east. There are dark tales like that of the Hannah Bay massacre for which the Uncle and his companions received that sentence (given only to Indians and Inuit) of banishment to a far country. There are, too, the inland lakes where ranger seals live.

Before 1800 the Hudson's Bay Company, the Nor'westers, and various summer free traders struggled for furs, fought, and sometimes starved in the Mistassini and Eastmain country. Otherwise there were only the coastal posts of Labrador, James Bay, and the St. Lawrence. The Algonkian peoples wandered from coast to coast and one day in 1798 three canoe loads of Naskapi arrived at Nemiscau, a thousand miles by water from their starting point on the coast of Labrador.

Cree men helped the foreigners who mined mica for the Company on the Eastmain coast, and until 1823 they killed white whales for the traders in Great Whale River. Some helped to tend the horses and cattle that were kept at the James Bay posts. With the

Chief Tooma of the Naskapi, at George River in 1905.

end of the trade war in sight, the Company began to explore the possibilities of trade inland.

John McLean opened Fort Nascopie in 1818, on the George River. Years later his Naskapi companions brought him, dying, to the new Fort Chimo post. In 1819 Mistacoosh and three companions took the trader Clouston inland by way of Seal Lakes, and similar journeys followed. Posts at Nitchequon, Indian House Lake, and last in 1916, Fort Mackenzie, tapped the none-too-full treasure house of Ungava.

In 1904 the Revillon Frères company opened several coastal posts, but these were bought by the Hudson's Bay Company after 32 years of competition.

By 1880 dog-teams were being used, but the Algonkians still relied mainly on the old ways — canoe, man- or woman-hauled toboggan (with otter grease on the bottom in very cold weather), or backpacking, with a piece of folded birchbark on the forehead to stop the cut of the tumpline. Canoe brigades ran inland to supply Fort Mackenzie and Mistassini. Three Cree men, Edwards, Matoosh, and Jolly, were bow-, middle-, and steers-men in the last of the great freight canoes to work in Canada. Their journey inland from Rupert House took five weeks upstream, two weeks down, During the days of Fort Mackenzie men like the Montagnais Dominique Gregoire carried mail over 500 miles overland from the fort to Seven Islands.

Modern ways came slowly to this region of barrens and hunger. The great Naskapi leaders Ostinetsu and Camoquist wore their red-dyed leggings and blue loincloths long after other Canadian Indians were all in pants. In 1920 many of the Crees trading into Rupert House used only bows and arrows, though this was due to poverty, not choice. From 1920 to 1945 Mandayoh of English River survived alone with bow and arrow following the death of his wife.

By 1929 the yearly number of beaver taken around Rupert House had dropped from 2,000 to just 4. That was a time of great hardship, especially for the coastal Cree people who had grown dependent on the trading posts. All of the Katapaituk's 13 children died, 10 out of 12 of the Blackned's, and many more. Hunters could not afford ammunition, eight families shared one canoe, and people lived on porcupine, suckers, and the yellow inner birchbark.

The Company cut down credit to a limit of $50 per year, and at this point James Watt, the post manager at Rupert House, began the program which made him an unforgettable part of Indian history. When Robert Stephens and Andrew Whiskeychan found the last beaver house inland on the Pontax River, Watt "bought" the beavers and showed the people how one pair of beaver could multiply to 288 in ten years if left alone.

Gradually Watt and his wife Maud got Indian support for their conservation scheme, and officials of the Quebec government backed them up. By 1951 there were preserves totalling 187,100 square miles, and by 1956 the average family income from beaver furs at Mistassini was $1,200.

James Watt also began the canoe factory which is well known today and an emergency whitefish fishery. For his work he is called Amisk Okimau, "the Beaver Chief".

Unfortunately the officials of the Company at that time were reluctant to support his schemes. The Watts were given a hard time, and after James died Maud was helped by the Crees. First the people gave her $343, collected from families who were very poor. Later Chief Robert Moore and the other men of Rupert House collected $2,000 in beaver pelts for her.

After World War II ended in 1945, fur prices went down and life again became difficult for most of the Ungava Indian people. The canoe brigades stopped and most of the inland posts closed. A railway was built inland to the new mining town of Schefferville in the heart of the old Naskapi hunting country. In 1958 the Fort Chimo Naskapi moved to Schefferville at the suggestion of the government, and now the huge James Bay Development threatens to end the fur trade and the bush way of life.

The swampy land

Around the southwest coast of Hudson Bay lies the swampy lake-strewn forest that is the old heartland of the fur trade. Its story has been told in other books and other chapters of this book, so we will pass over it quickly.

During the quiet century of Hudson's Bay Company rule, there was a movement north of Ojibway people into lands vacated by the Crees. Bands of people, sometimes from two or three tribes, settled in areas around the main posts such as Fort Albany, Trout Lake, Oxford House, and Brochet.

For a long time York boats carried supplies from Norway House to other Manitoba posts. The Robinson brothers and other Indian carpenters made these 30- to 40-foot boats of whip-sawn lumber. After 1900 many European men who liked the northern life began to work as freighters, taking supplies by canoe and scow to various posts and mining camps.

After the treaties were made, traders began to travel with the annual treaty party in order to get the Indians treaty money, and there was much competition when free traders came from the city just at treaty time. One of the best-known free traders around Oxford House was Old John Hire, who had several posts. A Cree Treaty Indian of Moose Factory also traded, and had three posts while fur prices were high.

Despite the gradual movement of mining, railways, logging, and other industries into the region, most of the people lived from trapping, hunting, fishing, and tourist guiding until World War II.

The Ethen Eldeli (Caribou-Eater) Chipewyans occupied the northwestern end of the region from Reindeer Lake to the barrens. Chief Kasmere was one of the most colourful characters around the turn of the century and learned the language of the Keewatin Inuit. He would visit them and play the *udzi* gambling game for sled dogs. He had a strong cabin on a hill by Kasmere Lake, with windows facing each way. When Inuit passed on their way to the Brochet post, Kasmere would charge a toll of fox-skins before letting them pass.

Silty river country

From Lake Athabasca to the Rocky Mountains is a great region of rolling hills and flats where silty rivers in deep valleys run to join the Mackenzie. By 1785 the first trading posts had come to the Indians of this region. Cree and Métis adventurers went down the Mackenzie, and after them the foreign traders. By 1805 there were posts as far north as Fort Good Hope, which served the Hare, Kutchin, Mountain, and even Inuit peoples.

One common story among the Mackenzie River people is that of a hunter who saw strange chips of wood floating downriver, not those made by a stone axe. He went upstream and met foreign men who gave him a steel axe and other gifts. In the Hare version this man is Tooseego, "Dry Loon".

The early days of trade were full of fear and confusion. Foreign traders employed gangs of bullies to force the Indian bands to trade with them. They kidnapped women as slaves or to force payment of debts, and bribed the tribes with whiskey. Tribes as far west as the Sekani fought each other, and Deadman Island in Great Slave Lake was named when Beavers massacred Dogribs there. In 1823 Chief White-Eyes of the Nahanni River Goat tribe avoided Fort Liard for fear of attack by Kaska or Slavey men.

Disease, hunger, and uncertainty made the tribes desperate, and their anger was turned on the foreigners. About 1813 a prophet at Fort Chipewyan called upon his followers to stop using dogs as beasts of burden, as they were man's relatives. He also wanted the foreign traders driven out so that other and better traders could replace them. Between 1800 and 1821 four trading posts in the region were burned by men of various tribes, and some of the foreign people killed.

Edzo

Not long after the fur companies came together the Dogrib people had won a victory over their Yellowknife oppressors. Four Yellowknife men came boldly to visit the Dogrib chief Edzo and to challenge the Dogribs to fight again. Edzo was weary of war, but the four men threatened until they were killed. Edzo decided to visit the Yellowknife chief Akaitcho and arrange for peace.

With his wife and four men relatives, Edzo canoed near the Yellowknife camp and hid his wife, telling her to return to the tribe if he did not appear after three days. He and his companions then carried on and hid across the water from Akaitcho's band. At night Edzo went alone to the tent of Kaw-tay-wee who had married Edzo's sister. She fed him and hid him under the sleeping skins. When Kaw-tay-wee came in, he listened to Edzo's plans.

Next day Kaw-tay-wee asked a friend to go by canoe over the lake to hunt, but the friend saw the smoke of the Dogrib fire and turned back, saying he had forgotten his skinning knife. He warned Akaitcho, who came with many men to where the Dogribs sat by their fire. Akaitcho was angry at first and threw his knife near Edzo's feet, but finally Edzo convinced him to make peace, and the two tribes met for a feast at Gutson Gatee, "Raspberry Lake".

With peace the tribes settled again, though the old boundaries had changed. The wooden York boats and great blunt scows with sweepers replaced canoes on the supply routes, and many Indian or Métis men worked on the pole and trackline or ran the horse-drawn carts on the portages. Madame François Houle was a colourful Métis character of the time, a strong woman, dressed in deerskins with a knife at her belt, bossing the rough-tough scowmen of the Liard River.

Around the posts and missions some Indian families began to keep gardens, and in 1872 Chief Shawcla and six other Slavey men bought cattle at Fort Providence to drive back to their village. One Dogrib family around that time had a tame moose that pulled loads on a plains-style *travois*.

By about 1890, a new group of people, mostly Dogrib, but with a few Hare, Mountain, and Yellowknife members, came to occupy the country just south of Great Bear Lake and to be called the Satudene.

In 1870 the government of Canada took over control from the Hudson's Bay Company and by 1900 other traders had arrived in the northwest. By this time too there were steamboats on the rivers, and by the 1920s trappers, both foreign and Indian, were flying supplies to camp and furs to market. Game laws, trapping laws, and treaties brought an end to the good or bad old days in the country of the great northern lakes and silty rivers.

Kutchin country

The Kutchin or Loucheux people of the Porcupine, Peel, and Mackenzie rivers had received iron spears and other Russian trade goods by way of the Inuit before the foreign traders came down the Mackenzie. When the first Fort Good Hope was built (it was later moved upstream) some of the eastern Kutchin traded there. One of the best known was Cecilia, the woman leader of the Arctic Red River Nakotcho people during the late 1800s.

In 1840 the Peel River post was founded, later to be called Fort McPherson. Vitsinets-uti, "Father of Painted-Face", became the first of a family line of trade chiefs for the Tatlit group. The Inuit began to come upstream to trade, and in 1841 one family travelled with Loucheux hunters up the Rat River.

Relations between the Inuit and Loucheux remained touchy however, and in 1852 the Loucheux massacred many Inuit at Separation Point. Two Hudson's Bay Company workers, Hébert and McKay, were held responsible for this, as one of them shot the Inuit leader just after the Inuit had fired their arrows into the sand of the riverbank to show friendship. The two were sent out of the country, but peace was long delayed by the killings.

John Firth was for 52 years the manager of the Peel River post. He was a strong, quiet man who kept the peace as well as possible during the stormy days of Inuit-Loucheux fighting, the Gold Rush, and the whaling fleets. He married a half-Loucheux girl, Cathy Stewart, and their 12 children were the first of a well-known family in the region. On one occasion Firth saved a young Loucheux girl from forced marriage to the great Yukon Chief Saveak, who was then 64 years old and had many wives. Firth arranged a feast to keep the chief busy while the girl escaped with her parents.

Before the Canadian traders reached the mountain country of the Yukon Kutchin, men like Chief Hatoudiau of the Porcupine Tukudh people would trade Russian, other foreign, and native goods. He used to visit Fort Good Hope to buy iron tools which he then traded to the Inuit of Herschel Island, or to the western Kutchin.

Such native traders resented competition and in 1826 the explorer Franklin had been threatened for trading with Inuit. When Fort Yukon was built in 1848 at the mouth of the Porcupine River some Kutchin were angry because they lost their control of trade. The new system was soon accepted, however, and improved on the old one. Beaver replaced wolverine as the most important skin, and beads gradually replaced the dentalia shells which had been used. The *hyagua* shells, as they were called in the Chinook trade language, continued as money for years. One bundle of shell-strings, called a *naki-eik* in Kutchin, was worth 24 beaver. A seven-foot string of shells was worth two and one-half beaver.

One of the best-known chiefs of the Yukon River Kutchin was Saveak, "Bright Sun-Rays", who later took the name Sahne-uti, "Father of the Runner". He had more than ten wives, and became the most important trading chief in all the Kutchin territory. The last trade chief of the Tukudh band was Assak, and the Vunta people were represented by Oltei and Tetcukavitak.

Francis Tuttha Thsuga, "Small Nipples", was the last trade chief on the Peel River. He would steer each of the moose-hide boats through the worst rapids on the spring trip to the post. Before reaching the post the oars were painted red and everyone would put on his best clothing. A cannon would be fired from the post as they approached, and the landing was followed by days of feasting. The last such trip was made in 1923. His son Francis was the first elected chief in 1905.

In 1867 the United States of America bought Alaska from the Russian government, and Fort Yukon was moved several times up the Porcupine River. After 1894 Old Crow became the trading centre for the Yukon Kutchin, and as in other regions life began to revolve more and more around the posts. Sled dogs came into use, and the old double-ended "women's sleigh" disappeared in favour of toboggans with steering handles. After 1900 steel traps displaced the log deadfalls and the flat Kutchin canoes, *thrui*, were covered with canvas instead of bark. Canvas tents replaced hides, and log cabins took the place of the "moss houses" of the post.

Between 1900 and 1947 wartime and peacetime variations in fur prices brought about movements of people down to the Mackenzie Delta when beaver and muskrat were paying well, and into the hills while marten skins were high-priced. Free traders moved into the country, and a Kutchin trader opened his store, still operating, at Old Crow.

The bush life continued for most Kutchin until the 1960s, and there is still respect for former expert trappers like Lazarus Sitichinli, Thomas Njootli, and Moses Tizya. Some still trap, and Chief Hyacinth André at his Tree River camp in 1970 got 65 lynx. His wife in that year snared 500 rabbits which she sold in Inuvik.

People over the mountains

The Indian peoples of the mountainous southern Yukon and northern British Columbia were the last to see the pale-skinned traders enter their lands. They were no strangers to foreign goods, however. The strong and stocky coastal Tlingit, the Chilkat, and Chilkoot Indian traders had been carrying Russian goods over the high passes for almost a hundred years. The Athapaskan tribes closest to the Tlingit were dominated by this fierce and arrogant trading tribe, bound to them by formal trade agreements and by marriage. The Tagish, Atlin, and Teslin had even changed languages, and now spoke only Tlingit. The coastal Tlingit carried their trade as far as Fort Liard.

In 1838 the Russian-American Trading Company who had long operated on the northwest coast handed over its "rights" to the Hudson's Bay Company for ten years in exchange for a yearly payment of 2,000 sea-otter skins.

In 1838 Robert Campbell of the Hudson's Bay Company went up the Liard River to look for new trading country, and was befriended by a woman chief of the Kaska tribe. She led about 400 people, and warned Campbell that the Tlingit chief "Shakes" controlled trade all over southern Yukon and northern B.C. Several times she saved the lives of Campbell and his men and on one occasion her followers pulled down Shakes' tent, thinking that Campbell was in danger while inside it. When some of Campbell's trade goods were stolen, she had them returned, and another time she spat in the face of a hunter who threatened to harm the Europeans. She has been called the "Nahanni Chief" but her real name is not known.

Tlingit Thlin and his son Hanan were the chiefs of the Pelly River, and they were hostile to Campbell when he first appeared in their country in 1842. On his next visit they decided to help him, and one old man gave Campbell furs, for he had gone lame after attacking Campbell and wanted Campbell to remove his curse.

Farther down the river Chief Kon-It'l befriended the Hudson's Bay Company man, and Fort Selkirk was built near the junction of the Pelly and Yukon rivers. The Chilkat Indians of the coast were afraid of this invasion of their trading territory, and in 1852 the Chilkat Chief Mustah came down by raft from the mountains to challenge Campbell. With the help of the Tutchone chief Tsartrish, Mustah and his followers drove Campbell's party from the post and burned it. In his writings Campbell mentions how Chief Kon-It'l helped him after the fight, but the chief told his children some more details. He saw the smoke of the burning fort and when he went upstream to investigate, he found Campbell tied up in a canoe stuck on a small island and cut him free. In gratitude the trader gave the chief the right to use his name, which became the English name of the family.

The Hudson's Bay Company withdrew from the southern Yukon because of Tlingit hostility and the difficulty of travel over the mountain barrier. The Athapaskan tribes preferred to stay with the Tlingit traders rather than help the foreigners who were poorly supplied with goods. Little by little, however, the power of the Tlingit declined, and when a Tlingit trader insulted the wife of Chief Tlingit Thlin, the chief stopped all Tlingit trade with his people until peace was made on his terms. Still, in 1881 the Tlingit traders were active, and a Tagish boy who had bought from them a pair of rough shell earrings refused to sell them to an American explorer for a shotgun, a thousand cartridges, a gold watch, two sacks of flour, and a stove.

Gradually the combined influence of European traders, explorers, and prospectors destroyed the power of the Tlingit traders. By 1900 the Gold Rush brought thousands of Europeans and the trade of southern Yukon almost disappeared. It revived when the Gold Rush ended, and Enainta, "Watches the People", was spokesman for the Kaska of the upper Liard River when traplines in British Columbia were chosen and registered.

The beaver story ends

For over 300 years the furs of beavers, mink, marten, wolverine, weasel, and many others flowed from the northern Indian lands as the trade rolled westward. We have seen how some ancient Indian ways survived those days of change. Rabbits are still snared, though with wire, not sinew. Moccasins are still a favourite winter footgear, and the special small Indian bear dogs are still kept by the Tahltans in the west and the Nemiscau Crees of the east.

Families still camp on the trapline and hang pelts on their bent wood frames, while inside the tent the baby in hammock or *tike-nagan* hears lullabies in an Indian language, and the sweet smell of spruce tips on the floor mixes with the good smell of cooking meat or bannock. Maxwell Paupanekis of Norway House, Thomas Boulanger of Berens River, and John Tetso of Fort Simpson have written about their lives as trappers during the last fifty years, and their books carry the true flavour of experience.

Few young Indian or Métis people now want the cold, loneliness, and hard work of the trapline, and its rewards are often small in terms of money. In some countries where furs are sold there is an outcry against the cruelty of steel traps, and each year more trapping regions are invaded by construction work, exploration, and other activities. Some government people are trying, however, to make fur trapping a more steadily paid and professional kind of work. There may be a return of native people to the woods if this is done, but the important days, the great days of the fur trade, are over.

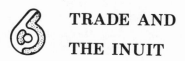 **TRADE AND
THE INUIT**

Trade and other foreign influences came to the Inuit in a variety
of ways. In Labrador the Moravians were both missionaries and
traders. The whalers traded, and to a lesser degree, so did the explorers. The fur companies, expanding slowly from the Indian
lands, finally spread throughout the home of the Inuit.

The Labrador coast

In the early 1750s, during the period of French power, the Inuit
of Hamilton Inlet hunted whales and seals for sale to the French
traders. Farther north, people would hunt over the watershed
into Ungava Bay, returning each fall to trade with the French.

The British also alternately fought and traded with the Inuit of
southern Labrador, but disease, fighting, and intermarriage
changed the pattern of native life enormously. After 1771 the
Moravian mission obtained permission from the British government to establish stations along the Labrador coast north of
Hamilton Inlet. They began a new way of life, part traditional,
part European, based on community trading posts.

At each mission station the Moravians opened a trading store which was not intended to make a big profit, but to pay for the cost of keeping the missionary and his family, the mission buildings, and relief which was given during hard times to the Inuit from the mission stores. Only useful goods were bartered: guns and ammunition, European clothing, tea, netting twine, nails, and so on. Some tobacco was traded, for it had become a part of Inuit life, but the missionaries sold no liquor. They were afraid of the results if Inuit visited traders farther south who sold rum and expensive useless trinkets and used every possible means to prevent such trade. Credit was given at the mission stores, but real money was rarely used in the northern Labrador coast until after 1940.

The Moravians used their stores in a deliberate plan to change Inuit ways, to teach them to survive in a world of growing European influence. They introduced seal-nets and encouraged basket weaving and ivory carving. They organized fisheries for salmon, char, and cod and bought other products of Eskimo labour. By about 1850 the Inuit were firmly tied to a new yearly round of activities:

Christmas — Easter	fur trapping
April	caribou hunting
May and June or July	seal hunting
July and August	char and salmon fishing
August and September	cod fishing
October to Christmas	netting seals

The table on the following page, with the amounts in quintals, barrels, casks, tierces, and other old measurements, shows the variety of goods produced for sale by Inuit to the Moravian stores.

Soon after the Moravians were established, however, other Europeans came to complicate the scene. Settlers and a few free traders came to live here and there along the coast, and the Newfoundland cod-fishing fleet began to call each summer. The fishermen sold the Inuit many things, including wooden boats which soon replaced umiaks and kayaks of skin. About 1831 the Hudson's Bay Company built a few trading posts in northern Labrador, but the Moravians controlled most of the trade for the next hundred years.

Exports of the Moravian Church and Missionary Agency
from Labrador, for the years 1883, 1893, and 1903
(from MacGregor, 1907, p. 350)

Articles	1883 Quantity	1883 Value	1893 Quantity	1893 Value	1903 Quantity	1903 Value
codfish	2689 qtls	7,140	2994 qtls	8,185	4035 qtls	21,149
trout (char)	579 brls	2,870	787 brls	3,720	798 brls	4,788
skin boots	632 prs	490	230 prs	437	3224 prs	5,849
seal oil	313 cks	11,185	194 cks	6,120	353 pns	7,200
cod oil	3 cks	35	3 cks	118	41 pns	910
cod liver oil	7 cks	640	6 cks	375	3 pns	96
furs	16 cks	2,925	6 cks	1,720	11 pgs	7,000
dry seal skins	13 cks	200	—	—	5 pgs	100
salted seal skins	14 cks	425	8 pgs	190	7 pgs	200
reindeer skins	36 pgs	1,625	72 pgs	1,000	5 pgs	800
straw work and curios	—	200	2 pgs	60	15 pgs	150
feathers	—	—	4 pgs	15	12 pgs	150
salmon	37 tcs	407	5 tcs	84	6 tcs	50
Totals	—	$28,142	—	$22,024	—	$48,442

Quantities are shown in quintals, barrels, pairs, casks, tierces
puncheons, and packages.

Fair and wise as the Moravians were in their dealings, they
could not control the changes that took place, and even their own
plans made the Inuit dependent on the missions. The fishing fleet
began to fish closer to shore and at times the Eskimos' fishing
places and their gear were taken. More and more European settlers came to live near or among the Inuit, trapping, fishing, and
hunting as they did. Labrador became one of the few places in
Canada where foreigners and natives lived in the same way on
equal terms.

There were changes in the outlook of the Inuit, who had former-
ly looked down on cod fishing, but became dependent on it. Some
Inuit began about the year 1800 to hunt inland from Hopedale,
Nain, and Okak into Naskapi territory, and Naskapi or Montagnais

people, attracted by trade and the new peace, moved to the coast.

To operate a trapline required a dog-team, and with the help of rifles, seal-nets, and fish-nets the Inuit were able to feed large teams, whereas only a few dogs had been used in the old days. Between 1861 and 1876 the number of Inuit-owned dogs went from about 220 to 720. The settlers also had teams, and the result was ever-increasing use of wildlife.

Ever since Shadluvinik in 1792 killed a bird at 100 yards with his first musket shot, rifles had been used with terrible effect. Between 1800 and 1850 the people of Nain and Hebron shot caribou for their sinews alone. Seals grew scarce, salmon even more so, while walrus and polar bears almost completely disappeared. Even the coastal forests were cut back as settlers and Inuit built houses and heated them with wood-burning stoves.

All through the 1800s there were periods of starvation. From 1860 to 1880 the Moravians cut down on credit at their stores to teach responsibility, but riots resulted. After 1900 the price of codfish went down and life became very hard indeed for both Inuit and their settler neighbours. Despite the hard times, however, one of the Nain Inuit in 1900 was the first fisherman to put a motor in his boat.

In 1925 the Moravians leased all their stores to the Hudson's Bay Company, and for the next few years high prices for fox furs brought some improvement. In the 1930s however, the great depression brought fishing and trapping almost to a standstill. In July 1942 the government of Newfoundland took over all the northern stores as a welfare measure, but by that time the wealth of the land had gone.

The Moravian trade system was bad in that it changed the old scattered and independent way of Inuit life. It was good in that it prepared the Inuit for what was to come. In general, however, the history of the Labrador coast was like that of the Indian fur trade, the whaling period, and the whole period of foreign contact. Furs, fish, meat, oil, and ivory poured from the land and sea to make fortunes for merchants far away. In return the northern people had their world turned upside down and much of the land made lifeless.

Hudson Strait

The channel between Baffin Island and northern Quebec, especially the northern part which had the least ice, was the gateway between Europe and western Canada. In 1611 Inuit at the western end of Hudson Strait traded and fought with Henry Hudson's mutinous crew. From that time on, passing fur-trade supply ships, explorers, and whalers stopped in the Strait to take on water, to shoot the sea birds which nested in myriads on the cliffs, and to trade with Inuit bands. It was not until the 1920s, however, that permanent trading posts came to the Strait.

In 1697 La Potherie, a French commander, offered some Inuit of Nottingham Island a puff at an Indian peace pipe — something unknown to them. By 1817 trading was a regular habit, and one ship's officer write down this exchange.

One sealskin coat — one steel knife
One pair sealskin pants — one needle
One pair sealskin boots — one saw
One wooden eyeshade — one bullet
One pair birdskin gloves — two buttons
One fishing spear — one file

Hudson's Bay Company instructions to their ships' captains in 1798 warned the captains to be on their guard against the Inuit who were friendly but well armed and unpredictable. There were some fights caused by both sides, but on the whole the Inuit were anxious to trade and lit fires on shore to attract the ships or paddled out up to twenty miles offshore in umiaks and kayaks. The Sadlimiut who met Captain Lyon on the coast of Coats Island in 1824 were seeing their first Europeans.

The Inuit men, women, and children would spend hours or days on the ships bartering clothes, eggs, meat, and tools. As often as the seamen cheated with broken penknives and mouldy tobacco, the Eskimos would pick pockets and make off with anything loose around the ship.

Rum was sometimes drunk, and was called *imiarluk*, "Strong water", by the Inuit, but more often the visits were enlivened by singing and dancing on both sides.

North from "the bottom of the Bay"

The arc of fur trading posts between Churchill in the west and
Richmond Gulf in the east stayed unchanged for a long time,
unable to expand north along either the west or east coast. The
posts were in Indian territory, and north of them was a no-man's
land with a history of fighting. The Inuit distrusted the foreign
traders, whom they blamed for arming their Indian foes with guns.

Guns and other goods were traded north from James Bay and
west from Labrador to the Ungava Eskimos. It was not until 1830
that the Hudson's Bay Company moved its operations north. Posts
were established at Fort Chimo and at George River for both the
Eskimo and Naskapi trade. Small sailing boats called sloops sailed
from Fort Chimo to the Eskimo camps of Ungava Bay for trade
but no other posts were built until after 1900.

During the early days of the Fort Chimo post one of the Koartak
Inuit came down by dog team to trade. On his way home through
the woods outside Fort Chimo his dogs, bunched together on the
narrow trail, met a Naskapi man pulling his toboggan. The Naskapi,
for fear of the dogs, leapt clean over them, and grabbed the Inuk.
Both men looked into each other's frost-rimmed faces, afraid, thinking of all the terrible tales each had heard about the other's people.
Then the humour of the situation struck them and they both sat
down to roar with laughter, after which they shook hands and went
their ways.

In 1756, shortly after the massacre of about 40 Eskimos by a Cree
war-party north of Churchill, two Eskimo men were persuaded to
visit Churchill by ship and were returned home with many gifts.
In 1774 the trader Graham trained young Inuit men in the use of
guns. Trading ships and explorers travelled north along the Keewatin coast during that and following years, and gradually trade goods
began to pass from Churchill north, while furs and ivory flowed
south. Peace came between Indians and Inuit after about 1790,
and by 1866 the people of Eskimo Point had learned the tricks of
the fur trade well enough to have become middlemen who insisted
on handling the trade of the tribes farther north for the usual profit.
As the Padlermiut Eskimos of Keewatin obtained guns they moved
southwest into territory formerly occupied by the Chipewyans. By

1900 they were visiting the trading post at Brochet, 150 miles south of the Manitoba border and well within Indian control.

As the Indian fur trade and foreign exploration flowed northwest from Churchill, contact was made with the Inuit of the Mackenzie Delta. At first they were suspicious of the European traders. One party killed five men of the North West Company below the Ft. Norman Rapids in 1799, and the first European explorers of the Delta coast were often attacked by Inuit who wanted metal tools and other loot.

In the early 1850s the Inuit began to visit Fort McPherson. The Hudson's Bay Company opened Fort Anderson, nearer to the coast, especially for trade with the Inuit; but after five years in 1865 the post closed, for an epidemic of scarlet fever had almost wiped out the Anderson River band. The Mackenzie Delta Inuit continued to use Fort McPherson, with growing peace between them and the Loucheux, until 1921, when a post was built at Aklavik.

Interpreters plus

As the fur trade expanded from southern Hudson Bay a group of Inuit played an important part as guides, interpreters, and ambassadors or peacemakers. Some of them travelled great distances across the north — paddling, rowing, or snowshoeing — and passed through Indian territory at a time when this was dangerous for Inuit.

One of the most important of the trade interpreters was Tatanoyuk, or Augustus as he was called by Europeans. He was born about 1795 at Roes Welcome Sound on the Keewatin coast and worked for the Hudson's Bay Company as an interpreter speaking Cree and English. From 1820 to 1822 he was interpreter for the navy explorer Franklin in the Mackenzie Delta. At that time he had a companion Junius Hiutiorok, also of the Keewatin coast, but Hiutiorok died not long after the trip.

Tatanoyuk worked with several explorers along the northwestern arctic coast, and became well loved and respected. In 1830 he went to Fort Chimo to help set up the new trading post there. In 1834 he returned to Churchill to set out again for the Mackenzie as a member of an expedition led by his old friend Lt. Back of the

Royal Navy. Tatanoyuk was travelling north of Fort Resolution with two other men, Iroquois and European voyageurs, when he was parted from them by a storm and died. As Augustus he was included in the book *Ungava* by R. M. Ballantyne.

Ouligbuck was a friend of Tatanoyuk, born about 1800 on the Keewatin coast. He accompanied Tatanoyuk on Franklin's second expedition to the western Arctic, and worked hard as a boatman while he learned English and several Indian languages. In 1827 he returned to Churchill where he harpooned white whales, made canoe paddles and fish-nets, and even weeded turnips in the post garden.

In 1829 he went with an older man, Moses, to join the trader Nicol Finlayson for the opening of Fort Chimo. Ouligbuck stayed there for over six years, and in 1836 he went with his wife and children to help the explorers Dease and Simpson in the northwest. His last expedition was with his son William on Dr. Rae's journey to Committee Bay, and he died at Churchill in 1852. In 1961 the Canadian Government mapmakers named Ouligbuck Point, near Cape Parry in the western Arctic, in his memory.

William Ouligbuck, son of Ouligbuck, was born at Fort Chimo in 1831, and through his travels with his father William learned to speak about ten languages. He was with Rae on the expedition to the Boothia Peninsula, 1853-54, and worked at times for the Hudson's Bay Company as a caribou hunter, harpooner, and interpreter. Most of the time, however, he preferred to live as a hunter. He died in 1896, but between him and his father, they had travelled the arctic coast from Point Barrow, Alaska, to the Labrador coast.

Another important Eskimo during the days of exploration and fur-trade expansion was Albert One-Eye. He was born at Eastmain in James Bay about 1824. He was very popular with his own people and with the Europeans and was hired as an interpreter and general worker in 1842. In 1848 he agreed to go with Sir John Richardson's expedition to the Mackenzie Delta, and probably saved the lives of the European explorers by explaining their presence to the Mackenzie Eskimos. Like Tatanoyuk and others he was able to communicate quite well with the western Eskimos despite a distance of 2,000 miles between the dialects.

In 1849 he went with Dr. Rae by boat down the Coppermine River, but the boat was steered badly through rapids and Albert was accidentally drowned near Bloody Falls.

There were many other Eskimo people who helped to spread peace and trade — one of them was Attasi, a Labrador woman who spoke the Naskapi dialect of Algonkian. She came to Fort Chimo and was of great help in arranging things between Europeans, Eskimos, and Indians.

The days of the whale

Long before Europeans came to the arctic seas, some of the coastal Inuit were expert hunters of the great whales which they called *arbvit*. They would hunt the giant creatures, which grow to 60 feet long, from kayaks and umiaks with harpoons, lances, and floats of inflated sealskin. Even now there are the big white bones and skulls of whales around the remains of Inuit villages several hundred years old.

The arbvit are called by several names in English — right whales, Greenland whales, or baleen whales. Baleen grows in a whale's mouth in long thin strips which are used to trap the tiny sea creatures on which the whale lives. It is a springy material rather like plastic, and the Inuit used it for bows, combs, and sled-shoeing.

The ribs and jawbones of a baleen whale can be twice as high as a man, and were used for the rafters of houses or for sled-runners. Enough oil can be melted from the blubber of a whale to fill a hundred oil drums. Altogether a large whale could provide enough food, fuel, and other things to keep several families and their dogs for a whole year.

Before Europeans discovered how to use mineral oil for lamps and machinery they depended on whale oil. The baleen also became valuable for making things, especially the springy corsets worn by women during the 1800s. When this fashion was most popular the baleen from one whale could pay for the cost of a year's voyage by a whaling ship and its crew. The baleen and oil from two or three whales might pay the cost of the whole ship, with some profit left over.

By the year 1590 about 350 European ships were hunting whales near the pack-ice between Greenland and Baffin Island. The Hudson's Bay Company tried whaling in Hudson Bay near Marble Island from 1764 to 1782, but gave it up as unprofitable. By that time the Scots and Americans were the main whaling people, and they gradually explored beyond the pack-ice. Whalers reached Pond Inlet in 1820, Cumberland Sound in 1840, and Roes Welcome Sound in Hudson Bay by 1850.

Most of the ships going to the Baffin Island coast were Scottish, and most of those to Hudson Bay were American. Some of them tried to return home at the end of each summer, but others would stay until the ships were frozen in. In spring they would hunt whales by small whaleboat from the edge of the ice. When the ice melted they would cut a way out to sea for their ship.

For the sailors, life was cold, dirty, rough, and dangerous. Many ships were caught in the ice and crushed or abandoned, and many men died in ship or boatwrecks, or of scurvy due to a poor diet. The wise sailors adopted the clothing and the food of the Inuit. In the fall of 1900 a whaling ship was wrecked on the Ottawa Islands of Hudson Bay. Although some local Inuit and some Aivilig Inuit who had joined the crew offered fresh meat to the European sailors, they refused it. They killed their captain who tried to ration the biscuits and salted meat from the ship. All the sailors died except one called Bob Stewart, who went to live with the Inuit and later became a trader.

Sometimes the Inuit and whalers fought each other. A ship was sunk by some Ungava Inuit because its crew killed too many caribou, which were very scarce then. The captain and half his crew from a wrecked ship were killed by Ungava Inuit for trying to kidnap women. At Kuuvik near Richmond Gulf some whalers terrorized the Inuit until the women promised to make mitts for them. They made special mitts with no thumb piece, and tied them tightly around the whalers' wrists. The whalers were then helpless and their guns were taken away.

On the whole, however, the Inuit did not object to the arrival of whaling ships and sailors. They believed that the land, sea, and animals were free to anyone. In the beginning too, neither Europeans nor Inuit could foresee the terrible effects of diseases on the

Inuit or the wiping out of so much wildlife. The Inuit welcomed
the whaling fleet which meant trade, excitement, and more security. Although the Inuit supplied most of the meat to the ships,
there were times when hunting was poor and they could get biscuits, salt pork, and canned meat from the ships' supplies.

The whaling ships gathered most often at Pond Inlet, Cumberland Sound, and Roes Welcome Sound, and passing ships called
frequently along the north shore of Hudson Strait. At first the
whalers and Inuit were not prepared for trading, and the Inuit
would sometimes take off most of their clothes to exchange for
knives, rope, wood, and other things. Often the ship would lose
anything not locked up or nailed down because the sailors would
trade all they could. The sailors would also exchange their own
clothes for furs, ivory, or Inuit clothing and sail home half-dressed.

Gradually the ships' captains prepared for trade as well as whaling, and by 1900, when whales were becoming scarce, all ships
carried trade goods. The *Eva*, the *Frances Allyn*, and other ships
carried Scottish shawls, telescopes, fox traps, smoked sunglasses,
dominoes, sledge planks, mosquito-netting, violins, and many
other things to sell. The prices were often very high, and in 1906
a police patrol found that a gun worth $10 was given in exchange
for musk-ox skins worth $750. A box of cartridge primers worth
eleven cents was exchanged for a musk-ox skin worth $50.

Another way in which the Inuit could obtain trade goods was by
working for the whalers. Money was not used, but the Inuit would
be paid in guns, ammunition, canvas, and so on. If a man worked
for a whole season or more he might be given a 30-foot wooden
whaleboat by the homeward-bound captain. Whole families of Inuit
sometimes signed on as "ships' natives". They would live on or
near the ship, eat some meats with the crew, and receive whatever medical care was available. Their work would include hunting, sewing, and piloting.

Inuit men were hired as boatcrews and harpooners, particularly
during the last 20 years of eastern arctic whaling. Malliki and Aud-
latnark of Roes Welcome Sound and Angmarlik of Cumberland
Sound were well-known whaleboat skippers, though there were
many more. Other Inuit families visited the whaling ships occasionally to trade or to do part-time work such as moving oil barrels

or carrying blubber by dog-team from the ice-edge to the frozen-in ship. Sometimes families would camp near the carcass of a whale stripped by the whalers, living from its meat and trapping the foxes which gathered there.

Even bands of inland or central arctic people journeyed to meet the whalers. In 1904 one family sailed by whaleboat from Baker Lake to Repulse Bay and back again — a voyage of a thousand miles — to visit the whaling ships. Altogether the effect of the European whalers on the Inuit was enormous. The tribes were mixed as people moved to visit the ships or were carried all over the coast on board them. Many Inuit were taken to the seaports of Europe, Canada, and America, and brought back new languages, fashions, and ideas. One of the first was Inuluapik of Cumberland Sound, who went with Captain Penny to Scotland and later guided him on his "exploration" of the Sound.

New words were adopted into the language of the Inuit. "Sailor" became *seealar*, a follower; "flour" became *palaugak;* and "Portuguese" became *puatigee*, meaning a brown-coloured person. The Scottish sailors, dirty from stoking steam engines or boiling whale blubber, became known as *pauktut*, "greasies". The European whalers were too lazy to learn Inuit names, and made up their own such as Aivilik Dick, John L. By 'n' By, and Wager Dick. Some of these names are still used by Inuit for dealing with Europeans, though they use their Inuit names at home.

Some of the whaling captains brought their wives with them and Inuit women learned knitting, baking, and other European women's skills. There were very few such wives, however, and many whalers took temporary Inuit wives. Many eastern Inuit are partly descended from foreign whalers as a result.

American square dances and Scottish reels were adopted by the Inuit and displaced drum dancing in some areas. In Hudson Strait women took to decorating their *amauts* or parkas with coins from sailors of many countries, and the plaid shawls became popular, especially in northern Quebec and Keewatin. The whalers sometimes played European football on the ice, and this was blended by the Inuit into their own game. One foggy day in 1875 a polar bear suddenly joined a football game, chasing the sealskin ball, but soon had the field to himself.

Whaleboats which could last a lifetime and could be sailed against the wind replaced skin umiaks and increased the summer travelling range of Inuit families. These boats and the rifles which changed hunting methods were among the most important things introduced by the whalers.

Although the whaling fleet brought good things, the ships and men carried diseases which destroyed many Inuit. In 1899 for instance, the ship *Active* left three sailors to set up a shore station at Cape Low on Southampton Island. The germs these men carried wiped out all but five of the Sadlimiut tribe, and other Inuit were brought to the island. In 1895 the ship *Terra Nova* found 30 Inuit dead at Dexterity Bay on northern Baffin Island after a visit by other whalers. By about 1900 the whole population of Inuit had been reduced by diseases by about one-third the original number.

Another great change brought by the whaling fleet was the disappearance of wildlife. Baleen whales were almost wiped out by about 1915, and very few are seen even now. Wherever the whaling fleets were based, the caribou, musk-ox, and walrus were hunted out of existence. During the winter of 1886 the crew of the ship *Abbie Bradford* ate about 150 caribou, and other ships took similar numbers. In 1903 the *Eva* took 350 musk-ox skins.

Musk-ox and caribou were sometimes killed just for their furs far inland, and the meat was left to rot. In the excitement of owning rifles some Inuit killed many more caribou than they could eat. Whales and seals which had been taken by harpoon were now shot and half of them sank before the boat reached them.

As baleen whales grew scarce and the price of baleen fell, the ships' captains began to try every way of making the voyage pay. They hunted white whales, narwhals, seals, bears, and walrus. In one summer about half a million seals were killed. Even falcons were taken to be trained as hunting birds in Arab countries. Together with the killing of wildlife in Labrador, Quebec, and Keewatin around the fur-trading posts, the slaughter of the whaling period was tremendous.

A few whaling companies tried mining, and Inuit were employed with Scottish miners digging mica at Lake Harbour from about 1900 to 1912. Some shore stations were built for the fur trade, and some Inuit became storekeepers. Ilatnak of Fullerton began a trading career when he took trade goods by dog-team from the ship *A. T. Clifford* and sold them for furs around the Keewatin.

By 1908 a plastic substitute had been found for baleen, and the price of baleen fell. Mineral fuels were taking the place of whale oil, and in any case the whales were almost all gone. The last whaling ship visited Hudson Bay in 1915, and a chapter in history was over.

European whaling in the eastern Arctic had made many people rich in other countries. In the north it had brought death and disaster to many people, and changes which could never be turned back. For ten years or so after the end of whaling the Inuit suffered shortages of things they had come to need — ammunition, matches, tea, and so on. People who had built their lives around whaling now had to turn to fox trapping, which was an uncertain business, or to hunting, in a land where animals had become scarce.

Western whaling

American whalers discovered the Bering Strait fishery about 1850, and the first two whaling ships wintered at Herschel Island off the Yukon coast in 1890. Each spring after that a fleet would leave San Francisco to hunt whales north of the Mackenzie Delta. When not cruising, the ships would gather at Herschel Island or at Baillie Island 260 miles to the east.

The crews of these ships were a mixed lot of Europeans, Africans, Japanese, Chinese, Arabs, and men from all over the South Seas. The Inuit of Bering Strait in Alaska were expert whale hunters, and had learned the European way as employees of the whaling fleet. Some of them moved to the Mackenzie Delta with their families and became known to the whalemen as "Masinkers".

Other Alaskan Inuit, the inland Nunamiut, moved to the coast and eastward, hunting to supply the whaling fleet with meat. Many of the Mackenzie Inuit, who were called the "Kogmollicks" by the whalers (from the Inuit word for winter house and really the name for the Copper Inuit), also worked for the fleet. The effect upon the Mackenzie people of the whaling days was overwhelming. Before the arrival of the ships they had always gone upriver to Fort McPherson or other posts to trade, leaving behind many of their people. Now every man, woman, and child was placed in contact with other Inuit from Alaska and with men of many countries of the world. The sailors were a rough and wild crowd, so that Herschel and Baillie islands had terrifying times of drinking, crime, and violence.

The Mackenzie Inuit learned new customs and new languages but they died in hundreds as liquor caused murders among them and diseases swept through the villages. The measles epidemics of 1900 and 1902 were very bad, and smallpox took many lives. By 1910 only about 130 Mackenzie Inuit were left out of a population that had once numbered 2,000.

Just as in the eastern Arctic, the whaling captains took trade goods, twenty to thirty tons per ship, to barter for meat, Inuit clothing, ivory, and furs. Even the Loucheux Indians visited Herschel Island to trade, and the Hudson's Bay Company posts inland lost business. The whalers could bring their goods more cheaply by sea than the "Bay" could by the long river route. The whalers also gave credit, which was then rarely given by the fur companies. From the whalers the Inuit could buy a greater variety of goods such as record players and furniture. By 1900 some Inuit were placing orders for expensive modern rifles and whaleboats. Although the whalers were a wild and sometimes brutal crowd, they treated the Inuit more as equals in many ways than did the fur traders and missionaries.

About 1900 steel fox traps were introduced by the whalers, many of whom began trapping furs themselves in the winter months. But the number of whales had been greatly reduced. As in the east, walrus, seals, caribou, and musk-ox had been driven away or killed off, and when whaling ended shortly after 1900, the life of the Mackenzie Inuit had been changed beyond recall. In 50 years of western whaling 30 million dollars worth of whale products left the Delta region, at the cost of almost all the native Inuit and much of the animal life of sea and land.

The years of the fox

The fur traders move north   During the period of baleen whaling

the Hudson's Bay Company and other fur traders did not try to
expand their operations north into Inuit territory. In the west,
after the short-lived Anderson River post, the Inuit had to travel
inland to Fort McPherson. From Churchill north along the Keewatin coast there was no post, though sloops and schooners were
sent on trading cruises. In 1879 one Inuk called Captain Mukko had
obtained a large schooner called the *Soowoomba*, with which he
traded and hunted around Chesterfield Inlet. In Quebec the Inuit
travelled to the posts at Great Whale River or Fort Chimo, and
there was some sloop trading along the coast.

For years the "frontiers" of the Hudson's Bay Company and the
whaling fleets overlapped in the Mackenzie Delta, Keewatin, and
Ungava. For Inuit in either the fur-trade region of Ungava Bay or
the whaling region of Baffin Island, the main effects were the
same — a gradual thinning out of wildlife, a mixing of foreign and
Inuit races, the death of many Inuit by disease, and a changed way
of life dependent on manufactured goods.

At the collapse of the whaling period the majority of Inuit found
it impossible to return to their former independent life. In some
cases they had forgotten how to hunt without rifles. They had become used to and fond of tea, woollen clothing, and other good
things, and in most regions wildlife was harder to find. Only the
central arctic people from Coppermine to Pelly Bay were still
hardly touched by the fur trade, whaling, or other European influence. Trade goods had passed to them, of course, and the explorer Schwatka gave the first gun to the Ukkusiksalik Inuit near
Chantrey Inlet in 1879. Even as late as 1910, however, there were
Inuit in the central Arctic who had never seen a European.

The gap left by the whalers was filled within a few years by fur
traders, accompanied by the missionaries and police, who as a "big
three" were to control the life of the Inuit for over 40 years. In
1909 the Hudson's Bay Company built a post at Wolstenholme on
the northwest coast of Ungava. In 1916 they took over the Moravian post at Port Burwell. In 1911 the Chesterfield Inlet post began, and by 1926 there were posts inland at Padlei and as far
north as Pond Inlet. Some of the coastal posts were taken over
from the whaler traders, a few of whom settled in the north.
Duval Sivutiksak, Mutch and Cornelius of Cumberland Sound, and

Berthe of Ungava were such men who married Inuit and became the heads of well-known families.

In the west, the opening of the post at Aklavik in 1912 marked the first permanent move north by the Hudson's Bay Company in 72 years. Kittigazuit followed in the same year, and Herschel Island in 1915, until by 1923 there were posts all the way east to King William Island. All Inuit now had a trading post within their territory or close to it. Until 1939 the Igloolik people had to travel long distances to the posts, for (as at Fort Ross) the ice conditions made it hard for supply ships to reach the Igloolik area. The Inuit leader Itukshardjuak used to describe his 500-mile journey to trade at Fullerton. On the way he saw his first coal in a cabin and tried to light a piece with a match. Like many other Inuit in those days, he split the scarce matches into four pieces.

Traders everywhere   From 1920 to 1930 fur prices rose sharply, and trapping became profitable. The fur of the arctic fox was especially in demand and fox trapping became the main source of income for Inuit. Up to 1946, the end of World War II, furs were the most valuable export from the lands of the Inuit.

In 1869, two years after Canada became a dominion, the new government bought all the northern lands, called *Rupert's Land*, from the Hudson's Bay Company, and other traders then had the right to do business. There was very little competition, however, until about 1920 when the high price of fur brought many new traders to the north.

Some in the west were ex-whalers like Wolki, Klenkenberg, Bernard, and Norberg, who traded from their schooners and settled in the Mackenzie area. Independent European trappers and traders moved into the northwest coast, southern Keewatin, and Ungava Bay. In the Mackenzie Delta north of Arctic Red River, over 50 trading posts came and went. There were large companies such as the Canalaska Trading Co. and Captain Pedersen in the west. Revillon Frères Ltd., a French company, built posts close to those of the Hudson's Bay Company throughout Ungava and Keewatin.

Many Inuit and part-Inuit people owned trading posts or operated them for the European companies. These included Dennis

Anuktuk, Tommy Goose, Pat Klenkenberg, and Edna and Ikey Bolt. Stephen Angulaarlik had three posts in Queen Maud Gulf and ordered as much as $40,000 worth of supplies a year.

In Keewatin, Ilatnak and others who had begun trading for whaling captains continued to make trading journeys by heavily loaded sled and large dog-team. Dick Kaumoshalik ran the "Bay" store at Wager Bay, and he and Ilatnak accompanied the manager, Jack Ogilvie, in a first attempt to cross the barrens by tractor in 1929.

Around the northern coast of Quebec there were at different times over 20 Inuit traders such as Inukpak of Richmond Gulf, Kauki of Payne Bay, Markoosie Kalingok of Mansel Island, and Nikri and Imataluk at Leaf Bay. On Baffin Island there was Mittimak, who ran the Sabellum Company post at Singiyok. Nanorak, a woman, was in charge of Captain Grant's Sinauyak post during the 1930s.

Boom! After World War I the price of fox furs went up to between $30 and $70. A blue fox fur could bring two or three times as much, and even muskrat skins were worth a dollar each during the 1920s. The high prices between 1920 and 1930 meant that if a trapper took 300 foxes (easily possible during the peak year of the fox cycle), he could earn from $9,000 to $18,000. This was at a time when most Canadians earned only $1,000 a year or less. The price of store goods was much lower than it is nowadays, even in the Arctic. Although the trapper could earn a lot of money, it meant hard work in very cold weather for him, and his wife and daughters might have their hands badly marked from cleaning hundreds of skins.

In the Mackenzie Delta region particularly, the first years of the trapping boom were exciting, and most people had a lot of money or credit at the stores. In 1917 Natkutsiak bought the *North Star*, a 57-foot schooner, from the Canadian Arctic Expedition. In 1935 two other Inuit bought a new schooner which was delivered from San Francisco at a price of $25,000. This boat was also called *North Star*, and became the "flag ship" of the Banks Island fleet. Altogether in 1926 the Delta region trappers had 39 schooners, 28 whaleboats, and 2 sloops worth over $128,000 — about one-third of them with engines.

Natkutsiak led the first group of trappers, mostly Alaskan and Métis people, to Banks Island in 1916, and it became the best fox-trapping area. In 1929 Allen Okpik and his three sons got 1,100 foxes between them, and in 1938 another trapper and his wife got 1,300, probably a world record. They received only $15,000 in that year, though ten years earlier their catch would have been worth over $70,000.

Washing machines, radios, and record players were common among the Delta Region people during the fur "boom", and the Banks Island people in particular lived in style during their summer holidays in Aklavik. Large sums changed hands during gambling games, families rented rooms at the Aklavik hotel, and one family went on holiday to San Francisco and Vancouver.

In 1925, the Danish expert on Inuit, Knud Rasmussen, arrived on his sled journey from Greenland to Siberia but found that the Mackenzie Inuit wanted $25 a day to act as guides — in other areas the rate was about $1.50 a day. In 1930 the bush pilot W. E. Gilbert flew in to Aklavik and gave rides at $10 for five minutes' flying.

In the eastern Arctic the Hudson's Bay Company introduced boats designed like Scottish fishing boats and called peterheads. These and whaleboats could be paid for in one or two good seasons' trapping, and many were bought by Inuit during the 1920s. Families who lived in areas of plentiful wildlife could live well, and in 1927 Opartok's Southampton Island band got an average per family of $2,000 and four tons of meat. One of the most prosperous groups during the 1920s was the family of Weetaltuk of Cape Hope Island in James Bay. They built log houses and several schooners up to 60 feet long, installed with engines.

And bust!   After 1930 the world of the Inuit took another turn for the worse. Some areas had been overtrapped, and both foxes and meat animals were scarce. Various laws had been passed to preserve the arctic wildlife for Inuit only, but much damage had been done. In 1928 the government asked the Hudson's Bay Company to close certain posts because they affected the migration of caribou.

With the new laws, scarcity of furs, and falling prices, the rival companies began to sell out to the Hudson's Bay Company — Revillon Frères did so in 1936, but left the country owing money to many Inuit, an act which has never been forgotten. Pedersen in the west sold out in 1938, and with the exception of mission posts like that at Pelly Bay in the 1940s, the Hudson's Bay Company was the only trader throughout most of the Arctic.

In Ungava the drop in fur prices left people unable to buy food, and game was scarce. There was a great deal of hardship and death by starvation. The Inuit of the central Arctic who had just altered their lives to depend on trapping found themselves adrift. The severe winter of 1934-35 was very bad, and many people starved to death. In regions where it took up to 12 caribou to make winter clothing for one adult, the shortage of caribou was serious, and poor fur prices meant that people could not afford clothes from the store.

At Fort Chimo, Inuit such as "Big Man" had skippered the sloops, and some became expert boat builders, using the upriver timber. From the Orkney and Scots post staff they learned to make barrels for shipping salt or smoked fish. From 1881 to 1884, 141 tons of char and salmon were shipped from Fort Chimo until the fish almost disappeared. From 1929 to 1932, this fishery was revived again using a stream trawler and refrigeration, but once again the fishing was stopped in order to save the stocks.

During the 1940s the price of muskrat pelts went up, and the people of the Mackenzie Delta were able to live fairly well. The Delta became crowded, however, with Loucheux Indians from the south, Alaskan Inuit immigrants, European trappers, and some of the Banks Island people whose fox trapping had been ruined by the collapse of the arctic fox fur market. The muskrat trappers had a special yearly round of activities, including the spring "ratting" season, when rats were shot (and still are), using .22 rifles from canoes.

Because of the competition for trapping places on the Delta, in 1948 traplines were registered, each group of trappers having the right to a certain area. The Banks Islanders could not qualify for such areas — they had formerly been rich, and the mainland people resented them hunting and trapping around Aklavik or Tuktoyaktuk.

People and reindeer

The trapping years brought about the movement of Inuit around the Arctic. The arrival of Alaskan immigrants and the beginnings of the Banks Island community were the main movements in the west. In the eastern Arctic, families were brought by the Hudson's Bay Company from as far away as Port Burwell to live on Southampton Island, and families from Port Harrison were moved on the ship *Nascopie* to Pangnirtung. At about this time, in 1934, the government agreed to a plan by which the Hudson's Bay Company would move Inuit from southern Baffin Island to Devon Island, far to the north. Twenty-two Inuit from Cape Dorset, 12 from Pangnirtung, and 18 from Pond Inlet were taken with their dogs, sleds, and boats to Dundas Harbour where wildlife was plentiful. Unfortunately, no one had bothered to check the ice conditions, and the Inuit found the ice too heavy and rough for either boat or sled travel. Two years later the Pangnirtung people were taken home, and the rest moved to Arctic Bay. In the following year some of these moved to a new post called Fort Ross, on Boothia Peninsula. Ships found it difficult to reach Fort Ross because of heavy ice, and in 1947 the Hudson's Bay Company closed the post, taking the Inuit to Spence Bay.

Such movements of people meant that relatives were left behind, and the migrants had to get used to unknown country, new sea channels, and perhaps new ways of hunting. Groups from different regions took a long time to mix in marriage or hunting partnerships. The language and customs of the Spence Bay Netsiliks and the Baffin Island immigrants were slow to mingle, and the same thing occurred in 1953 when the government moved families from Port Harrison in Quebec to live with people from Pond Inlet at Resolute Bay and Grise Fiord, well north of any other settlement.

Besides moving people to new trapping and hunting areas, attempts were made to begin other activities in the Arctic. The Hudson's Bay Company bought a herd of reindeer from Norway in 1921, and Lapp herders took them ashore at Amadjuak on the south coast of Baffin Island. The Company hoped that Inuit would learn to herd and use reindeer as the Lapps did, but the reindeer herd was not well cared for and gradually wandered away to mix with wild caribou.

In 1931 a much bigger herd was brought by the government from Alaska, and Andrew Bahr, a Laplander, was in charge of driving the 2,370 animals over 2,000 miles to Tuktoyaktuk near the Mackenzie Delta. Some Inuit helped to drive the herd, led by a man called Kaas, and it arrived in 1935. The reindeer herd is still being looked after by the government, and has not become important to the Inuit. The Lapp people settled in the Delta region and have married Inuit or other residents.

From time to time the Hudson's Bay Company, the government, and other foreign groups have had fisheries for the white whale or beluga. In Cumberland Sound white whales and narwhales were driven close to the shore by men in boats. The whales killed were skinned and their hides sold to leather companies. The blubber was melted down for oil to be used in cooking fats and cosmetics. This industry closed in 1963. In other places — Labrador, Hudson Strait, and Keewatin — whales were netted and shot, and in 1952 at Churchill one Inuk hunter killed 283 whales out of a total of 699. All the white whale fisheries are now ended except for the hunting done by Inuit for their own use.

Bannock and primus stoves

The trapping period was interrupted for some Inuit by wartime arrivals of foreigners, and each year more scientists, surveyors, and government patrols came to the Arctic. On the whole, however, the Inuit lived during the years 1915 to 1960 in a particular way which was half a return to the very old hunting way of life, and half a new life-style centred around the trading posts.

In the Mackenzie Delta region only a few of the original Inuit survived the whaling period, and they gradually mingled with the other races and Alaskan Inuit. Although the people of the Delta region tended to belong to particular communities such as Sachs Harbour, Tuktoyaktuk, Paulatuk, and Aklavik, they moved around the whole region and were more independent of police, missionaries, and the Hudson's Bay Company than the central and eastern Inuit. Most of them could do business in English and could write their own language using roman letters.

East of the Paulatuk the general pattern of the trapping years was one where a few hundred Inuit, living in roughly their old

Karngmak camp of Inuit family in the early 1900s.

tribal region, followed the seasonal rhythm of char fishing, caribou
hunting, and seal or walrus hunting. Most of them trapped enough
fox or other fur animals to pay for boats, ammunition, canvas, and
other necessities, but despite the urgings of the traders, very few
Inuit specialized in trapping.

Most of the Inuit lived in groups of several families, and visited
the trading post a few times a year. The traders, missionaries, and
policemen did most of the government welfare and medical work,
but the Inuit still controlled their own day-to-day life. Some things
became typical of the trapping years — special planks were sold
for making sled-runners, primus stoves became almost essential,
gun traps were used for sealing, and seal hooks and seal-nets were

used at times. Steel runners which were strong and good for all seasons, and primus stoves which enabled a man to leave his family and the family oil lamp behind, together with larger dog-teams, greatly increased the mobility of hunters and trappers.

The Scottish tartan shawls were adopted by the women of Quebec and Keewatin, and the knitted woollen hats with a tassel became the "trademark" of the Quebec Inuit. Almost every tent had its accordion, and almost everyone learned to play. The dances introduced by whalers and traders acquired Inuit names and became very much a part of Inuit life. Dog harnesses were decorated with woollen pompoms and in Quebec, where wildlife was scarce, rolled oats were often fed to the dogs after being cooked in the end of an old oil drum.

The Inuit of the eastern coasts used whaleboats and peterheads for summer travel, and the owner of the boat was usually the "camp boss", as group leaders were called by the foreigners. Pootoolik of Cape Dorset was a well-known leader during the trapping years, and another was Itukshardjuak of Igloolik, whose winter house had space for about 30 people to sleep. After his death his wife Atavgutarluk continued as leader and recorded the results of hunts in syllabic script.

Some Inuit worked for the police, traders, and missionaries as interpreters, guides, and pilots. Kilabuk of Pangnirtung is one of the best known, and worked for over 40 years for the Hudson's Bay Company. Panikpakutchuk of Pond Inlet and his family sailed with Larsen to the Mackenzie on the *St. Roch*. Kayak, who was on the *St. Roch*, made many long journeys guiding RCMP patrols. Partridge of Fort Chimo was well known in a line of pilots who guided ships up the difficult Kokjuak River.

To some Europeans and to many Inuit the trapping days were good days. They remember the way in which families would put on their best clothes and put new decorated harness on the dogs before dashing the last mile over the ice to the trading post. They remember the freedom of summers with tents and whaleboats, going to the islands to collect birds' eggs, and the smell of bannock in a frying pan. The movie *Land of the Long Day*, made by Doug Wilkinson with Idlaut's family in 1953, and his book of the same name show the typical life of the later trapping days.

But the price of fur changed often, and fur trading was not a dependable foundation for life. Each year the number of Inuit increased, and each year they needed more store goods. The fur trade had moved into the north at the end of a whaling period. Now as the trapping period began to come to an end the Canadian government entered the scene. Since 1900 the government had slowly increased its activities in the north, and wartime work had stepped up the pace. After about 1950 government interest in the north sharpened. An ever-growing wave of people, things, and ideas from the south swept into the Arctic. The old Inuit life had been turned upside down and the modern period began.

7 FOUR WINDS
OF CHANGE

It is difficult to separate the many kinds of foreigners, companies, and events that have affected the lives of native people in the north. The Moravians, for instance, were missionaries and traders; they did medical work and were in the north for two centuries. Some currents of northern history, however, deserve separate treatment because of the part played by native peoples. Those chosen here are the Gold Rush of the Yukon, the disease epidemics, exploration, and finally the story of the Christian missionaries.

Yukon Gold Rush

The great Yukon Gold Rush was a special part of northern history. It swept over the mountains and shattered the world of the Tagish, Tutchone, and other Indian tribes.

One's family, the salmon of the rivers, and the caribou of the hillsides — these were riches for the Yukon Indian people. A string of barter shells, a copper knife, or a village of strong houses might show the wealth of their owners, but not gold. The shining metal lay unheeded in the mountains and streambeds, while elsewhere in the world it had for centuries been the symbol of power and richness, the cause of great struggles.

Far beyond the Yukon, in Africa, Australia and California, gold had been found. Restless prospectors were exploring the world for more gold, and by about 1870 a few had entered the Yukon by different routes. One man, George Holt, was able to cross the Chilkoot Pass, so jealously guarded by the Chilkoot Indians. An Alaskan Indian gave him two gold nuggets, and the stories he told after returning south brought more gold-seekers to the Yukon.

Twenty prospectors, protected by a U.S. gunboat, met the Chilkoot chief Hole-in-the-Face, and by firing a few blank rounds from a machine gun forced the Chilkoots to open their mountain pass to all comers. From then on a steady trickle of prospectors toiled up the thousand-foot-high pass and into the Yukon River basin.

The Chilkoot, Chilkat, and related Indians, having lost their control of the inland trade, now began to make money as packers, carrying loads over the pass as they had always done. By 1898, when the gold-seekers were desperate to cross the pass, the Indian packers could make a $100 a day and more, carrying loads of up to 200 pounds across the mountains.

By 1886 over 200 prospectors had crossed the Chilkoot Pass, and others arrived by way of the Peace River and Mackenzie routes. Several traders helped to prepare the way for the Gold Rush by building supply posts along the Yukon River. Three of them were Harper, McQuesten, and Mayo. They settled in the Yukon and married Indian women. Their children were sent out to private schools in the United States, and Mrs. McQuesten became head of a wealthy family in California after McQuesten's death in retirement.

Several small gold strikes were made, each one bringing a new rush of gold-seekers over the mountains. After one such find in 1887, trader Harper knew that there were not enough supplies in the country to feed a new crowd of prospectors. He had to get out to a fellow trader, Healy, on the coast at Dyea, but it was wintertime.

Two men volunteered to go to Dyea. One was George Williams, a steamboat man, and the other an Indian whose name cannot be found in books, though he probably saved many lives. The two

men battled their way over the mountains and all their dogs died
of cold, hunger, and exhaustion. Just over the Chilkoot Pass, Williams collapsed and the Indian carried him on his back downhill
to the treeline. Some prospectors loaned him a sled and he dragged Williams 26 miles to Dyea Inlet.

At Dyea, Williams died after two days, but his Indian companion delivered Harper's message. To show how much gold had been
found, he scooped up beans from a barrel and threw them on the
store counter.

The Thron-Diuck River flows into the Yukon. Its name means
"hammer-water" because the Indians hammered stakes into the
streambed on which to hang fish-nets. To this river, one of the
best salmon streams in the Yukon, came the people who really
began the great Gold Rush of 1898.

George Washington Carmack admired the Indian way of life,
and tried to live as the Indians did. He married Kate, a Tagish
girl, and packed loads with the Indian packers of the Chilkoot Pass.
He went up the Thron-Diuck River looking for trees suitable for
poles and lumber to be sold to miners. With him were Kate and
her two brothers, Skookum Jim and Tagish Charlie.

Skookum means "strong" in the Chinook trade language which
spread along the west coast and into the Yukon. Jim got the name
when he carried 136 pounds of bacon over the Chilkoot Pass. He
was a huge handsome man, an excellent hunter and trapper. Unlike Carmack, Jim enjoyed prospecting and the hope of making a
rich strike. Tagish Charlie was a lean, active, and alert man, but
quiet.

Another prospector named Henderson met Carmack and his
relatives at the mouth of the Thron-Diuck, where they were catch-
ing salmon. Carmack, Jim, and Charlie would have gone with Henderson higher up the river, but Henderson offended them by re-
fusing to invite the Indians. They went up Rabbit Creek instead,
and made the world's most famous gold strike. Rabbit Creek was
called Bonanza Creek by the gold-rushers, and Thron-Diuck was
pronounced Klondike. Carmack, Jim, Kate, and Charlie became
rich, but although they directed many others to Bonanza Creek
they never told Henderson, who left the Yukon poor and embit-
tered.

The four discoverers staked their claims on August 17, 1896, and within two years an unbelievable horde of men, women, and children, wild for gold or adventure, poured into the Yukon. They came from all over the world, good people, bad people, actors, criminals, dentists, lords, most of them seeking gold from the ground, some from the pockets of others, and all infected with a sort of crazy excitement.

The Gold Rush doubled the size of the city of Vancouver. Edmonton grew five times bigger in a few months, and along all the routes to the Yukon, streams of travellers and tent-towns invaded Indian lands. Chinese, Japanese, Russian, English, American, and many other nationalities came north through Edmonton. Some took the Peace River route, and when Indian beartraps caught their horses they destroyed the traps. The Beaver Indians in turn pushed the prospectors' wagons down a hill at night, smashing them to pieces.

Some gold-seekers reached the Peel River, where they spent the winter of 1898 high in the mountains in cabins at a place they called Wind City. Many of them were violent men who treated the Loucheux Indians badly. Chief Francis and his people had brought meat to the hungry prospectors, had given them *tisane* spruce-tea for their scurvy, and had taken their mail to Fort McPherson. In return some of the prospectors tried to steal Indian women, and paid the Loucheux with bad bacon, crooked axe-handles, and spoiled tea.

The Loucheux of northern Yukon were less affected by the Gold Rush than the tribes whose territory caught the thick of it. George Mitchell, one of the better gold-rushers, lived with Chief Francis, whose people nursed Mitchell after he broke a leg. Mitchell feared the effect of the Gold Rush on Indian civilization, and persuaded Francis never to go to Dawson City. Francis and others who preferred beaver-hunting stayed among the eastern mountains and traded to Fort McPherson.

Other Loucheux moved close to the excitement of the Gold Rush, and about half of the Peel River people went to live with the Han tribe at Moosehide, near Dawson City. Chief Julius, nephew of Francis, was chosen to be leader of this group in 1905. The Loucheux kept their pride and toughness despite mixing with the gold-rushers. They would take meat to Dawson and enter the city dressed in their best wolverine and wolf trim, with the sled dogs in decorated harnesses.

Dawson City had 18,000 people by the summer of 1898, but never grew as wild as the whaling camps of Herschel Island, for the North West Mounted Police kept fairly good order. The Yukon Field Force of the Canadian Army provided another 200 men to control the Yukon during the Gold Rush madness.

The Yukon Indians sold meat and fish or traded other things along all the trails and rivers. They worked as deckhands on the riverboats, cutting firewood along the way for the steam engines. They worked at high wages as carpenters in Dawson, camp hunters and guides, river pilots, boat mechanics, and pool-hall handymen. Their wives cooked, did laundry, and sewed clothing or tents. Big Joe of the Pelly River led a successful strike of Indian men in 1920, and they obtained higher wages for towing boats upriver by trackline.

The Loucheux who went to Dawson became known as the "Dawson Boys". They tried all the things the city had to offer, and dressed smartly in black suits, white shirts, ties, and stetson hats and wore watch chains across their waistcoats. After the Gold Rush was over during the 1930s-40s these men returned north to take up leadership. They had more knowledge of city life and spoke better English than younger men who had grown up after the Gold Rush.

During the Gold Rush the tribes were mixed and moved. Han, Tagish, Tutchone, Kaska, and Loucheux hunted together in the mountains and took each other's meat to sell in town. One Loucheux man, Jarvis Mitchell, described a potlatch feast, open to all tribes, at Eagle. About $15,000 of goods was given away by the chief, who gave Jarvis a 410 shotgun.

There were two sides to the Gold Rush for the Indians. One was the dark side on which thousands of strangers poured through Indian lands, killing wildlife, bringing disease, alcohol, and discrimination. Many of the miners were ex-Indian fighters from the United States who had no human feelings for Indian people. Some of the riverboat captains were from the Negro slave country of the Mississippi and tried to treat Indian or Eskimo deckhands as they used to treat Negroes, but the northern people made them change.

Indian people usually travelled below decks on the riverboats, and in one dance hall a white line divided Indian from foreign women. In Dawson only one pool parlour was open to Indians, and they were forbidden to attend dances. Some of the discrimination was meant to protect Indians from the worst of the Gold Rush behaviour, but most of it was without excuse.

On the lighter side the Gold Rush gave the Tagish and Tutchone freedom from the rule of the coastal Tlingit. It ended tribal wars and brought the knowledge of the outside world all at once. The best of the miners treated Indian people simply as fellow beings, with less of the social class difference which the Hudson's Bay Company and the missionaries brought to other parts of the north.

Within three years of the Bonanza strike, the main Gold Rush ended. The finders of the gold had lived a colourful life — they went to Seattle, where Kate Carmack lost her way in the Butler Hotel and blazed a trail to her room with an axe on the stairway. She, Jim, and Charlie stopped traffic as they stood on a balcony, throwing gold and banknotes to a scrambling crowd below.

George left Kate to marry another woman, and retired in California. Kate returned to live at Caribou Crossing on Lake Tagish and died in 1917. Tagish Charlie operated a hotel at Carcross until his death by drowning. Skookum Jim, although he was treated with respect and had an income of $90,000 a year, kept on prospecting. He travelled across the north looking for another gold strike, often going without food for days. He died, worn out, in 1916.

By 1920 the population of Dawson was down from 18,000 to 1,200, and was to go lower. The valleys of the southern Yukon were littered with abandoned shovels, picks, flumes, and rotting cabins. The Loucheux returned to their hunting and trapping beyond the Ogilvie Mountains, and the southern tribes tried to pick up their old way of life. For most of them, however, the shock of the Gold Rush had been too great. They were no longer masters of their own land, but lived in the shadow of the foreigner until World War II brought the Alaska Highway and another flood of invaders.

As a result of the Gold Rush, Indian people in other parts of northern Canada, such as the Mackenzie and Quebec, have sometimes kept secret their knowledge of gold in the ground, fearing a flood of outsiders who would destroy the best of Indian life.

Invisible invader

The story of epidemics among the northern native people is not
well known. It is a tale without romance, without winners, and its
heroes are mostly forgotten. It is as much a part of the history of
foreign advances into the north as is the fur trade or the missions.
During over three centuries of imported diseases tens of thousands
died among the northern tribes.

Before the arrival of foreigners the Indians and Inuit knew no
smallpox, measles, influenza, diphtheria, or typhoid fever. They
had few colds, little or no tuberculosis, and no venereal disease.
Because of long exposure, foreigners were able to resist many of
these illnesses, but the bodies and minds of native people had
scarcely any defence against them.

Before the Moravians became established in Labrador and before
the struggle between France and Britain was over, many Inuit and
Indians north of the St. Lawrence River and the Great Lakes had
died of smallpox or other disease. Kabvik of Labrador lost her husband and other relatives in England in 1769. She alone recovered
from smallpox and returned shaven-headed to break the news to
her people, who gashed themselves with stones in their grief. In
1780 smallpox spread all over the north, reaching far beyond the
trading posts. Three-fifths of all northern Saskatchewan Indians
died, and nine-tenths of the Caribou-Eater Chipewyans.

Epidemics and famine occurred continually among the tribes.
In 1842 influenza ravaged the Labrador coast, and by 1852 scarlet
fever reached the Tutchone of the southern Yukon. From the Red
River Colony scarlet fever went north and wiped out a large Yellowknife band camped by a lake now called Lac de la Mort, "Lake of
Death". In 1865 over three-quarters of the Anderson River Inuit
died of this disease and the survivors moved west to join other
bands. In the following year over a thousand people died of influenza between Fort Simpson and Peel River, and a traveller could go
for 700 miles without seeing people along the Mackenzie River.

In 1876 whooping cough killed over a hundred Labrador Inuit,
and in 1885 a Naskapi band, stricken by scarlet fever, came to Zoar
to be cared for by the missionaries there, and left two children, still
sick, with Inuit when they returned inland.

In 1880 eight Labrador Inuit were persuaded by a German businessman, Hagenbeck, to tour Europe on exhibition. They all died of smallpox in Paris. In 1893 an American businessman took 57 Inuit men, women, and children, who had no idea of what was in store, to take part in the Chicago Exhibition. Half of them died of disease there, and the rest came home sick and penniless. In 1898 the same man persuaded another 33 people to go to Europe, Africa, and America. All died except six who returned in 1903 with diphtheria, typhoid, and syphilis which spread along the Labrador coast. A book was written about one boy who survived as a cripple. (*Pomiuk*, by W.B. Forbush, Boston, 1903.)

About 1900 a government doctor began annual trips down the Mackenzie, but despite his efforts there were continuing epidemics. Measles struck the Mackenzie in 1900 and 1902, killing 60 people at Rae, and as many in the Delta. By this time the number of the original Mackenzie Inuit was less than 400 — a fifth of the former population. Smallpox swept the Delta in 1911, and reached the western Kutchin in the Yukon and Alaska. The Birch Creek band had been wiped out by scarlet fever in 1865, and the survivors at Fort Yukon burned their houses and moved east to Rampart House. About the same time influenza killed 30 percent of the Copper Inuit. The Inuit of Herschel Island moved to Tuktoyaktuk after a disastrous epidemic of influenza in 1928.

In Labrador, despite a long exposure to European diseases, epidemics continued, and in 1918 two-thirds of the Inuit of Hebron and Okak died of influenza. By 1930 another horrible wave of influenza killed about 800 people in the northwest. The same disease stalked the Netsilik Inuit — already hungry during a terrible winter — in 1934. The sufferings of Ohowetuk's band, described by a missionary of that time, are almost unbelievable. The calendar of death continues through the 1940s and 1950s — diphtheria at Eskimo Point, typhoid at Cape Dorset, polio in Keewatin, measles in the western Arctic, influenza and measles at Fort Chimo and Frobisher Bay, and in 1960, influenza at Pelly Bay.

Tuberculosis does not attack so swiftly, but it weakens, cripples, and kills if not cured. It thrives among people who live close together under cold conditions, weakened by hunger or poor diet. All the northern tribes were affected, and by 1950 one in every five Inuit suffered from tuberculosis.

This catalogue of epidemics probably accounts for less than half the total amount of disease which continually traversed the north. Most of the epidemics happened before modern medicine, with its drugs and antibiotics, existed. In fairly recent times, sickness has attacked people far away from hospitals and doctors.

Even if the northern people had known how to nurse and treat each other, little could be done in tents and snowhouses, without taps, toilets, and laundries. In any case the epidemics usually struck down everyone — young and old, hunter and housewife. There might be no one to get food from the cache or to hunt; no one to keep fires or lamps going in bitterly cold weather; no one to control dangerously hungry dogs or to carry germ-laden refuse from crowded tents.

Disease was part of a total change which resulted in hunger or poor diet that weakened people. The European clothing which was worn for fashion or for lack of caribou skins did not keep out the cold. The deaths of so many relatives, or later their absence for years in hospitals with tuberculosis, helped to break the spirit of people already bewildered by what had happened to their world.

The year 1900 is roughly a turning-point in northern history, marking an ever-increasing spread of government services. Medical services improve continuously, and the days of the great epidemics appear to be over. The northern Indians and Inuit have increased in numbers again to about the size of the pre-foreign population.

The explorers

Most of the foreign exploration of Canada was of two kinds — the overland journeys of fur-trade explorers, and the sea journeys of people seeking a northwest passage for fur trade between Europe and Asia. The first group were involved most with Indians and have been discussed in the previous chapter. The second group travelled mainly through the country of the Inuit. Even a third group might be included, for after Sir John Franklin was lost in the central Arctic, nearly 150 expeditions, British and American, tried to find the Franklin party and their two ships.

As the foreigners "discovered" and "named" their way across

the Arctic, they were often guided by people to whom the land
and waterways were not a mystical challenge or adventure, not
new, but ancient homelands. For thousands of years the native
people had occupied their northern home, and every waterfall,
every cliff, and tiny island had its name.

Although the explorers were often brave and persistent, much
of their suffering and death could have been avoided if only they
had had the sense to learn the native way of travelling and to take
the advice of the Indians and Inuit. Sir John Franklin's overland
party suffered great hardship because Franklin did not believe
or perhaps understand Chief Akaitcho's warnings. Gallant British
Navy men dragged heavy boats over the arctic ice, poorly dressed
and dying of scurvy or starvation, while whole families of Inuit in
the country around lived their everyday life of work and play.

The fur-trade explorers almost always travelled with Indians
and adopted Indian methods, but the explorers searching for
islands and sea routes in the Arctic took a long time to learn from
the Inuit. Navy explorers were usually the first foreigners met by
Inuit, and there were some cases of fighting. Martin Frobisher
fought the people of Frobisher Bay, and 300 years later the tough
Mackenzie Inuit attacked the boats of Franklin and Richardson.
Usually, however, the meetings between explorers and Inuit were
friendly. Sir John Ross, whom the Inuit called Aglukan, was visited at his frozen-in ship by Abliluktuk of the Netsilik tribe in 1830,
and the two traded a few things.

In 1822 and 1823 two naval ships commanded by Parry and Lyon
wintered in the Igloolik region, and the Inuit saw their first pet
cats and dogs, hornpipe dances, tobacco, floggings, and other novelties. The navy discipline prevented many of the problems which
the whalers were soon to bring, and both Parry and Lyon wrote
detailed, illustrated accounts of the life of the Inuit.

In general the explorers did not change the Inuit way of life as
the fur traders, whalers, and missionaries did. They traded a little, and no doubt brought diseases with them. The many ships
abandoned in the ice or wrecked on reefs provided valuable iron
and timber for the Inuit.

Although many explorers would have died or failed without the
help of Indian and Inuit guides, very little credit was given to the

guides. Often their names did not appear in the explorer's reports, let alone on maps. Even the famous police patrols of the early 1900s were usually made with Inuit drivers. The Inuit could have made the journeys without the police, but in most cases the policemen could not have travelled without the Inuit.

Indian men and women such as Matonabbee, Akaitcho, and Slave Women have already been mentioned for their services to foreign explorers. The Inuit Augustus Tatanoyuk and Ouligbuck probably saved the lives of their employers by making peace with the Mackenzie Inuit. In 1827 Jonathan of the Labrador Inuit took Moravian explorers to Fort Chimo. He owned a two-masted 45-foot boat, and four Inuit families went along. Utakriyok, the leader of the George River Inuit, was pilot for the Ungava Bay voyage.

In 1840 Inuluapik guided Captain Penny around the great Cumberland Sound on Baffin Island. In 1902 the whaling manager Crawford Noble made the first journey by a foreigner around Netsilling Lake on Baffin Island. He was rowed in a whaleboat by the shaman and hunter Angmarlik and his wife Aseevak. Piligluit, his wife, and children were also in the party, and Katshook, Aseevak's daughter, was a child in her mother's *amaut* at the time. Today she is the head of a large Pangnirtung family.

In 1911 the German explorer Hantzsch travelled beyond Netsilling Lake to the river which bears his name. He was taken there by Ituksardjuk and Sikrinerk, and another couple, Aggakjuk and Arngnak. The whole party, including children, suffered great hunger and hardship, and Hantzsch died. Although the journey must have seemed pointless to the Inuit, and they could have easily returned to their people, they stayed with Hantzsch and cared for him until the end.

Ipilkvik and Tukkolerktuk   Of all the northern native people who assisted, befriended, and rescued European explorers, none is more important than the two who in English were called Joe and Hannah. Tukkolerktuk, which was Hannah's real name, was born in 1839 at a whaling station near Cumberland Sound in Baffin Island. She was the sister of two great leaders, Tuktu and Inuluapik. Ipilkvik, called Joe by the whalers, was about the same age and also came from a leading family.

Ipilkvik and Tukkolerktuk of Baffin Island.

Because of their ability they were invited to visit England by a merchant called Bolby. They sailed there in 1858 and stayed 20 months. They were married in England and dined with Queen Victoria. When they grew tired of being curiosities in England, they returned home. They had learned English and European ways, and Tukkolerktuk taught knitting to her Inuit women friends. She tried to stop some of the bad behaviour of the whaling crews, and kept her Victorian bonnets and dresses for special occasions. Despite their knowledge of European ways, she and Ipilkvik remained faithful to Inuit beliefs and customs, and were always first-class travellers and hunters.

In 1860, while Ipilkvik was working as a ship's pilot, the American explorer Hall came to the region. He met the Inuit couple and they became friends. He lived with them and learned their language, and made long journeys to learn their way of travelling. Ipilkvik's grandmother, Okioksilk, told Hall the Inuit story of Frobisher's landing 300 years earlier. Her account was so good that Hall was able to visit Frobisher Bay and find the remains of Frobisher's house.

Ipilkvik, Tukkolerktuk, and their daughter Pudnak.

In autumn 1862 Hall took Ipilkvik, Tukkolerktuk, and their baby son Takralikitak (Butterfly) to the United States. The baby died in New York, but the parents stayed with Hall for over a year, helping him raise money and prepare for an expedition in search of the lost Franklin party. In the summer of 1864 they were put ashore by a whaling ship in the wrong place. For nine months they travelled with local Inuit until they reached the Wager River. Here Tukkolerktuk had another baby boy. She became ill, and so did the baby, but they carried on with Hall until they met the Netsilingmiut of Pelly Bay.

The Pelly Bay people were rough and fierce. They took away the best dogs and weapons from Hall's party and challenged the men to box or wrestle. Tukkolerktuk had heard that the Netsilingmiut would hide a sharp-pointed bone in their mitts with which to kill a wrestling or boxing partner, and she advised Hall to turn back. On the way back to Repulse Bay the baby died, and according to local custom for one year Ipilkvik and Tukkolerktuk could not eat raw meat, sew clothing, or make weapons. Hall tried to recruit a party of helpers from the crews of whaling ships, and shot one man dead when trouble broke out. The other seamen would have shot Hall, but Ipilkvik had hidden all the guns. During this time Ungerdlak of Repulse Bay drew a map of Foxe Basin for Hall, which is amazingly accurate when checked with modern maps.

In March 1869 the party set out west again. There were ten Inuit with Hall, including Pudnak, a little girl adopted by Ipilkvik and Tukkolerktuk. Despite their fear of the Netsilingmiut they reached the region where Franklin had been. The Netsilingmiut Inukpuyiyuk told Hall about his meetings with Franklin, who the Inuit called Tulugak, "The Raven", and how the Inuit had fed the starving sailors as they dragged their boats south. Tukkolerktuk acted as interpreter, but while Hall and Ipilkvik were away obtaining relics of Franklin's ship she was badly treated by the Netsilingmiut.

The two Inuit and their daughter returned with Hall, who was now famous, to the United States, where they took a house at Groton, Connecticut. Hall made plans to reach the North Pole, and in 1871 they all set out on the ship *Polaris*. Hall had a great deal of trouble with the officers and the crew of mixed nationalities. He became ill, perhaps because of poison, and died on the north coast of Greenland.

The ship stayed in the pack-ice all winter, and Ipilkvik hunted for the crew, together with a Greenlander, Hans Hendrick. Hans had travelled with the explorer Kane, and the missionary Rink later made a book of Hans' life story. Hans' wife Merkrut and their four children were with him on the ship.

In October 1872 the *Polaris* drifted south into open water, but hit a mass of ice. In a panic the captain, Tyson, made everyone go onto the ice, and the ship drifted away. There were nineteen people on the ice floe, with two small boats and very little food. Ipilkvik made snowhouses for everyone, and lamps of pemmican cans, using wicks of canvas. Captain Tyson lived with Ipilkvik and Tukkolerktuk, and the three stayed faithful to each other during very bad times.

As the ice floe drifted south, only Ipilkvik and Hans knew how to hunt for seal, bear, or birds. All winter the two men hunted in cold, darkness, and danger, crouching over seal holes for up to two whole days without moving. Ipilkvik shot nine-tenths of all the seals, and saved the whole party from starvation by killing a big *ukjuk* seal and a polar bear.

The European crewmen were lazy and ungrateful. They took food away from the Inuit and made no attempt to hunt for themselves. The Inuit could have escaped over the ice as their ice floe drifted past Cumberland Sound, but Ipilkvik and Tukkolerktuk believed it was their duty to save Tyson and his crew, as Captain Hall would have expected.

Tukkolerktuk gave birth to a baby girl on the ice floe, but the baby died. They drifted on and on for almost 2,000 miles, during six and one-half months. The ice floe melted away and the whole party crowded into one boat. After four days of terrible sailing, they were picked up near Newfoundland by a sealing ship.

Although Ipilkvik had saved the lives of Tyson and his crew, the United States Secretary, Robeson, discharged him without a word of thanks, and he was not even paid in full.

Ipilkvik and his family settled down again in Groton, Connecticut. Tukkolerktuk sewed for a living, and Pudnak went to school, where she did very well. Ipilkvik soon returned north with Captain Young on the ship *Pondera*. Pudnak died in 1875, and Tukkolerktuk, weakened by the ordeal on the ice floe, died of tuberculosis in 1876.

Ipilkvik left the United States and never returned. He was guide and interpreter for the explorer Schwatka from 1878 to 1880. Three explorers who became famous — Hall, Tyson, and Schwatka — owed most of their fame, and in two cases their lives, to Ipilkvik. His training of Hall and Schwatka in Inuit travel methods was passed on to Peary and Stefansson, opening the way for a new and more successful age of exploration by Europeans.

Neither Ipilkvik's nor Tukkolerktuk's name appears on modern maps of the Arctic, though the maps bear many names of people less courageous, patient, and intelligent, far less important in the history of arctic exploration.

Inuit explorers — the journey of Kridlak   We know that Inuit had found their way into all parts of the north long before Europeans arrived with their peculiar ideas of exploration. There is one

example of a journey made by Inuit which can be called exploration. It was an adventure, a long journey made successfully at a
time when foreign explorers in the same area died after great suffering. Yet the journey of Kridlak and his people is not well
known. It was first recorded by Rasmussen and there are Inuit
today whose ancestors were with Kridlak, and who know the
story.

Kridlak was the greatest *angakok* or medicine man of northern
Baffin Island. He heard from European whalers that there were
Inuit living far to the north across Baffin Bay. From that time on
he could not rest, but thought only of finding the strange Inuit. He
conjured for the help of the spirits, and in his dreams he visited
the land far away.

Finally a group of men, women and children, filled with enthusi-
asm by Kridlak's stories, set out with him to find the people of his
dreams. From their home near Bylot Island they crossed Lan-
caster Sound and reached Devon Island. There, as the ice broke
up, they hunted all summer, killing many bears. In the fall they
built stone houses, but moved on as soon as the worst of the winter darkness had passed.

The 38 people travelled slowly, for they had to hunt as they
went, with bows and harpoons. Sometimes accidents delayed them
as well as weather and the changing conditions of the ice which
was their pathway. After two winters there was hunger and dis-
agreement. Old Okik and his family grew homesick, and lost faith
in Kridlak's vision. While Kridlak and his younger brother Paula
were fishing through the ice, Okik's party tried to kill them, but
failed. Paula lost an eye in the attack.

Twenty-four people turned back to Bylot Island, and the rest
stayed with Kridlak. The little group travelled north year after
year along the coast of Ellesmere Island, under the edges of the
great glaciers which wind down steep mountains. Kridlak believed
firmly in his purpose, and led the way with the strength of a
young man. His followers said that as he drove his dogs at night a
white flame stayed around his head.

For six more years the party crawled along the massive coast
and by the icebergs of Ellesmere. They suffered greatly from cold
and hunger, but always Kridlak urged them on. One day they

arrived at a point in Smith Sound where only thirty miles of ice separate Greenland from Canada. Kridlak chanted to the spirits and said that he could see people across the channel.

They crossed the frozen sea and found deserted houses. Travelling south they soon saw two sleds approaching, and after several centuries, the Inuit of both sides of Baffin Bay met. Each party put its weapons in the snow and there was a happy greeting. Then they travelled to the Greenland village of Pitorakvik.

The Thule Inuit, as they are now called, had experienced a disease over 50 years before, which had killed all but the young people. They had forgotten how to make snowhouses, kayaks, bows, and fish spears. All these skills were taught to them by Kridlak and his people, and the two groups mingled in marriage.

In the early 1870s Kridlak, now very old, was filled with longing to see his homeland. Most of his followers, to whom he was a mighty leader, agreed to return with him. The journey was terrible and tragic, for Kridlak died during the first winter. Without his guidance the party did not know what to do. They suffered from starvation, and some died, to be eaten by the living. After five years of wandering the survivors straggled back to Greenland and the Thule Inuit.

Today the Inuit of Thule and northern Baffin Island consider themselves one people regardless of the boundary between Canada and Greenland. In 1966 two Thule men made the 400-mile journey from Thule to Grise Fiord by dog-team. This was the first visit westwards. In 1970 some men of Grise Fiord made the journey to Thule by skidoo, and visits have been exchanged between Thule and Pond Inlet by airplane. Kridlak's journey was the result of a curiosity and determination as great as that of any foreign explorer, and the meeting of the Inuit across Smith Sound was a high point in arctic history.

The Drum and the Cross

The spirit of mission   For over 500 years the countries of Europe underwent great changes. They discovered how to grow more food on their farms, and how to build machines. Populations grew, despite wars and epidemics, and the power and energy of Europe burst out all over the world. To the Orient, to Africa, and to the Americas went traders, governors, and missionaries, each an essential part of the European flood.

During the complicated rise of the European trading nations the Christian religion had divided into many branches, but the two main ones were Protestant and Roman Catholic. The two rival faiths, English Protestant and French Catholic, were brought across the sea to join the main stream of northern Canadian history.

The French missions   The Roman Catholic church was part of the government of New France, and its Jesuit and Recollet priests were quick to travel among the tribes seeking converts. The first Indians in Canada to become Christians were Chief Menkutou and his family, who were baptized on June 24, 1610, at Port Royal, Nova Scotia.

In 1615 Father D'Olbeau opened a school at Tadoussac but the Compagnie du Nord, wanting nomadic trappers, not educated Indians, had it closed in 1621. In 1669 Father de la Brosse opened a school for Montagnais Christians at Seven Islands. As many missionaries were to do later, he composed an alphabet for the Montagnais dialect, and a dictionary in French and Montagnais. With government support the missionaries went among the Inuit of Labrador, and in 1727 the Abbé Martin requested permission to set up a seal fishery there. His superiors refused, not wanting to mix business with religion.

By canoe inland or by ship into Hudson Bay the priests increased the range of their mission. In 1731 the Naskapis of Ashuanipi Lake met their first priest. In 1684 some Crees of James Bay met Father Silvy, and in 1694 Cree people on the Nelson River met Father Marest. In 1773, however, the Pope suspended the Jesuit and Recollet orders, and by that time Protestant missionaries had begun to arrive.

The Moravian missions   We have already discussed the Moravians as traders. They were not a part of the long rivalry between English Protestants and French Catholics, and they have a special part in history because of their combined work as traders, administrators, and priests.

This German Protestant group had established missions in Greenland with the permission of the Danish government, and they obtained the agreement of the British government to open missions in Labrador. In 1752 the missionary Erhardt, together with three other priests and six seamen, landed near Makkovik. The Inuit there had been badly treated by Europeans, however, and killed all of Erhardt's party.

Jens Haven, another Moravian who spoke the Inuit language well, helped the British governor to deal with the Inuit and in turn was assisted with the opening of a mission at Nain in 1770. In the beginning Haven was assisted by Inuit such as Merkok, a woman who had been to England (kidnapped by Lieutenant Lucas in 1768), and Sikuliak, a leading hunter.

The government was happy to let the Moravians take almost total responsibility for the future of the Inuit — education, trade, and religion combined — as well as what medical help they could give. The first Inuk to be baptized was Kingmingusilk, a former shaman, on February 19, 1776. He took the Christian name of Detrus.

As the Labrador coast became more peaceful, the Moravian missionaries brought their wives and children, giving the Inuit their first example of European family life. Peace was made between the Indian and the Inuit people, and during the mid-1800s, when the hunting failed, Inuit and Indians saved each other's lives. In 1843, when the caribou were wiped out by forest fires and over-hunting, the Inuit of Hopedale fed starving Montagnais families. Between 1855 and 1860 Inuit brought starving Montagnais and Naskapi people to the coastal mission stations, and a few years later Naskapi hunters rescued a group of Inuit whose salmon fishery had failed.

By 1860 most of the Labrador Inuit were members of the Moravian church, though the Semigak family of Saglek Bay was not converted until 1933. By 1884 almost all could read in their language, from newspapers and over 20 books. Each church from Port Burwell to Hamilton Inlet had a choir, and some had bands. One custom spread to Labrador from Greenland with the Moravians, by which women wore coloured ribbons on their parkas — unmarried girls wore pink, married women blue, and widows

white. Chapel servants and lawkeepers called *kivgat* were elected
by the Inuit, and in 1903 the election of *angayukaukatigit*, village
elders, began. They were the law until police arrived in 1934. The
custom of Naluyuk Day began, and each Epiphany a small group
of men in masks and fancy dress toured their village collecting
gifts and performing. This is half-foreign, half-Inuit in origin.
Hymns were learned and school lessons given in German, and to
this day the Inuit of northern Labrador call bingo games with German numbers.

As we shall mention later, the Moravian missionaries had many
problems and eventually their private mission preserve was invaded. In 1892 the Grenfell mission was formed and began its
medical work along the Labrador coast. The trading rights of the
Moravians were transferred to the Hudson's Bay Company, and
other missionary groups, Methodist, Roman Catholic, and Church
of England, moved in among the Moravians. Today they are a de-
clining force, but their 150 years of administration were on the
whole marked by deep devotion and sound judgement. Without
the Moravians there is little doubt that the Inuit of Labrador
would have been destroyed within a generation or two.

West with the fur brigades

In England the Protestant Church Missionary Society was founded
in 1799, and at Marseilles, France, the Roman Catholic Oblate
Order of Mary Immaculate was founded in 1814. These two organizations, although not the only ones, have been the most important
in the history of Christianity among the northern tribes.

Métis Catholics of the fur brigades carried their religion westward, and in 1845 the Abbé Thibault met Chipewyans for the first
time in La Loche. By 1846 the priests at Isle à la Crosse in Saskatchewan were using the syllabic alphabet to reach the Chipewyan
congregation. A Chipewyan grammar was written by Father La
Fleche, and Joseph Touzae taught his fellow tribesmen to read.

Bishop Taché had been the first Oblate to preach to the Déné
peoples, and in 1852 he sent Father Faraud to Fort Resolution on
Great Slave Lake. Faraud had been invited by the Chipewyans
there because his medicine was thought to be strong. Denegonusye,

a Chipewyan man, became a helper to Father Faraud and converted over 300 people. He performed marriages and baptisms and became known as Yaltyiyazi, "Little Priest". A Cree-Métis and Father Mercredi, a Chipewyan Métis, were two native priests during the early days of the northwestern missions. There were lay preachers too such as Johnnie Cuhuyla, who led prayers with the Dogrib people of Rae while hunting on the barrens in 1894.

One of the first Protestant missionaries in the west was John West, who passed through Churchill and learned something of the Inuit from Tatanoyuk Augustus and Akshangnilk, both leaders. In 1820 he arrived at the Red River Colony as the Company chaplain. Henry Budd, an Indian catechist, reached Cumberland House in Saskatchewan in 1840.

James Evans was a Methodist minister at Norway House — an inventive man who soldered together a tin canoe which flashed in the sun so that the Indians called it "island of light". Many missionaries have helped to put the Indian and Inuit languages into print, but in 1841 Evans invented a system of writing called *syllabics*. It was to spread far among both Indians and Inuit, and eventually to be looked upon as a truly native thing. Evans made prayer books for his Cree followers. For his type he melted thin lead from tea chests. He made ink from soot and sturgeon oil, and paper of birchbark. For a printing press he borrowed a fur-baling screw, and the finished books were bound in deerskin covers. At first some people were afraid that the printed words were magical, and would not touch them.

In 1842 Evans visited the Chipewyan of Lake Athabasca. He was helped in his travels by two Chipewyan men, Thomas Hassel and Oig, each of whom spoke English, French, Cree, Saulteaux, and their own Déné language. While on his way to head off the Catholic mission in 1845 he accidentally shot Hassel to death, and only Hassel's mother saved him from the blood revenge which was the custom.

Peter Jones, "Kahkewaquonaby", an Ojibway Welsh Métis, was ordained in 1842 in England as a minister, and returned to preach in the Norway House region. James Settee, a Cree, preached at Lac La Ronge in 1846 and went to the Qu'Appelle Valley after being ordained in 1853.

Missionaries and the fur trade

Because the fur traders and the missionaries were for a long time the two main bringers of change to northern people, it is useful to ask how the two great foreign forces, trade and religion, got along.

In the days of New France the Church was a part of government, and in the case of the Moravians in Labrador, the missions handled trade and represented government. Elsewhere, however, the fur trade went ahead of the missionaries, and the Hudson's Bay Company, which was in fact the government, did not concern itself with religion at first. The various free traders were also uninterested in changing the religion of the northern people.

In 1823 after the uniting of the Hudson's Bay Company with the North West Company there was no more need for the use of liquor in trade, and the Company wanted peace everywhere to improve business. They passed a resolution urging that more religious teaching be provided at each post, and gradually the use of the fur brigade canoes for travel, together with other help, was given to both Protestant and Roman Catholic missionaries.

Although the official policy was in favour of aid to the churches, some traders were doubtful about the effects. The crusty and efficient Governor George Simpson of the Company wrote in June 1859 that he was afraid of the missionaries becoming involved in politics and of the effects of rivalry between the two faiths. However, he considered their presence "A necessary evil for the benefit of the Indian population".

Some traders resented the missionaries, who naturally tried to stop the free and easy frontier habits of wild drinking and temporary marriage between Indian women and European men. There were problems of loyalty, since most of the trading post staffs were English-speaking and Protestant, while most of the canoe brigade men were French-speaking and Catholic. On the whole, however, the Company and its field staff did their best to help both Protestant and Catholic clergy.

The main conflicts between traders and missionaries were economic in nature. The missionaries needed meat and fish to eat, and so became another drain on the resources around each post. They employed Indians who should (in the traders' opinion) have been out trapping, and one or two of them paid for their meat and skins with ribbons and other fancy goods. The Church ban on Sunday work and travel interfered with trapping routine and the movement of the fur brigades during a critically short season. The missions sometimes gathered Indians for baptisms and services at times which interfered with trapping and with hunting for winter supplies.

The root of the trouble lay in the wish of the missionaries for a settled congregation like those of European farm villages, and the need of the fur traders to have a scattered population of hardworking trappers. Little by little the missions became independent of the traders, particularly the Oblates, who had their own steamboat, the *Saint Alphonse*, on the Mackenzie in 1895, and their own airplanes in both the eastern and western Arctic by 1938.

Signing up souls

Just as the Mackenzie had been the scene of competition between fur companies with the Indians and Inuit as the prize, the Catholic and Protestant missionaries moved down the valley in a race for converts which continued — at a lesser pace — into the whole Arctic. In 1858 Archdeacon Hunter went down the Mackenzie River with the annual fur brigade. Father Peter Henry Grollier joined the brigade, and the two missionaries travelled together, each trying to win over the Indians to their cause.

The Oblate fathers were the most successful among the Mackenzie tribes, assisted by the Grey Nuns who entered the Northwest Territories in 1866 and founded several convents. Their presence, their hospitals, schools, and orphanages had special effect among the Indian women. The wife of Hudson's Bay trader Gaudet, one of the few Catholic Company wives, helped the Oblates in their work and taught Cecilia, the woman leader of the Arctic Red River Loucheux. Cecilia taught Father Seguin the Loucheux dialect and persuaded her followers to become Catholic. She died in 1942.

François II Beaulieu was a rough, tough Métis leader, but in 1848 at the age of 71 he was baptized a Catholic and gave up seven of his nine wives. He began to act as priest when the Oblate father was out of the country. Madame Houle, the fiery Métis freightboat boss, also became Catholic and made converts by the strength of her arm.

In 1864 one of the first Hare Indians, Tatekoye, was baptized by
Father Petitot, as the frontier of Christianity moved on into the
Yukon mountains and the country of the Mackenzie Delta Inuit.

Not all the Mackenzie people took to the Roman Catholic faith,
and in 1893 the Anglican Rev. T. J. Marsh went to Hay River in
answer to a request by the Slaveys there.

The Reverend Kirkby, who became bishop, was in 1852 the first
Anglican to visit the Loucheux or Kutchin of Fort Yukon. The
Oblate missions were never successful there, and Kirkby was succeeded by the Rev. Robert McDonald, an Ojibway-Scots Métis
from Red River. McDonald translated the Bible, prayers, and
hymns into Tukudh Loucheux, and married a Loucheux girl. In
1875 he became Archdeacon of the Peel River. Bishop Bompas of
the Anglican Church began his northern service in the Mackenzie
Valley, and was helped by Christian Kaia of Great Bear Lake, who
fed, housed, and taught the minister. The Indians of the southern
Yukon were badly disorganized by the Gold Rush, and Bompas
spent many years among them. The school at Carcross was
founded toward the end of his life.

Eventually the Yukon and Mackenzie regions were occupied by
both Anglican and Oblate missions, each with schools, hospitals,
orphanages, and homes for the aged. Each of the two religions had
its particular appeal to Indian or Inuit people. The wives of Anglican ministers were influential, as were the wives of many Hudson's Bay Company men, in spreading their faith and customs. On
the Catholic side the Grey Nuns were able to train children in
institutions, and the priests, being unmarried, often had greater
freedom to travel and hunt with the people. They were also more
likely to remain at one post for a long time — over 40 years in
some cases — becoming a real part of the community.

One advantage of the Anglican system has been the greater use
of native clergymen as clergy, catechists, and lay readers. The
Rev. Edward Sittichinli, a Loucheux, was the first native priest,
ordained in 1903 after 35 years as a catechist. The Rev. John
Tssiettla was the first clergyman to be ordained within the Arctic
Circle, and other native priests of the early mission days were
Amos Nootl of the Porcupine River, John Martin of Ross River,
and Joseph Kunizzi of Peel River. Among the eastern tribes, Fred

Mark and Andrew Wesley, both Cree, were ordained at Moose Factory and Albany in 1925, and Sandy Clippings became the first Chipewyan Anglican minister at Duck Lake in 1947.

Among the western Inuit

Although the Mackenzie Inuit had met missionaries during their visits to Fort McPherson, the first one to visit them was Father Emile Petitot. In 1865 he went from the fort to the Anderson River village as a guest of the leader, Nulumaluk. Petitot was able to write about the way of life of the Inuit, and to write a dictionary of their language, but he made no converts. Later some of the Inuit blamed him for an epidemic of scarlet fever that almost destroyed the Anderson River band.

Shaputaituk, another leader, took the Anglican missionary Bompas from Fort McPherson to the coast in 1870. Bad ice conditions hampered their return journey, and some Inuit wanted to kill Bompas, whom they held responsible. Shaputaituk told his people that in a dream he had been warned not to attack the missionary for fear of revenge by Indians and foreigners. Bompas reached home safely, but the Inuit rejected Christianity for over 30 more years.

Father LeFebvre had no luck during his stay with the Mackenzie Inuit about 1890, but by then Alaskan Inuit, converted by the Moravians and other missionaries in Alaska, were moving east with the whaling fleet. They had learned to write and read, and taught these arts, as well as the new religion, to the Mackenzie Inuit.

The Reverend Whittaker of Fort McPherson produced many scriptures in the Inuit language, and in 1894 the Reverend Stringer moved to Herschel Island to preach among the whalers and Inuit there. Thomas Umaok of Herschel Island became one of the first Anglican catechists, and was ordained in 1926. Stringer, who became a bishop, was guided during his dog-team travel in the Delta by Takatshimak, a son of Shaputaituk. In 1908 the mission at Kittigazuit in the Delta was built.

The Oblates, unsuccessful among the Delta Inuit, turned farther eastward. One family of Inuit — Natsil, Kuneak, and their son,

Katuktuk — visited Fort Resolution, deep in Indian territory, to teach their language to Oblates there. In 1912 Father Rouvière, who had been with the Hare Indians, visited the Copper Inuit together with Father LeRoux. The two priests were not welcomed by all the Inuit and were asked to give away one of their rifles. Finally they were murdered near Bloody Falls by Sinniksiak and Uluksak. This tragedy slowed down the Oblate movement.

In 1916 an Anglican mission was built at Bernard Harbour, and in the following year the Oblates built one farther west at Letty Harbour near Cape Parry. In 1929 both churches built missions at Coppermine, and another period of rivalry was underway. The Oblates, under Bishop Breynat, bought their own supply schooner, the *Nakotak*, and with it and similar vessels opened several missions in the region of Victoria Island. Both groups of missionaries produced religious texts in the western dialect, and the Christian movement, using Roman letters for its prayer books, moved eastward until it met the westward wave of missionary work based on the syllabic alphabet.

The Bible in the eastern Arctic

Some of the Inuit living in or trading at Churchill were converted to Christianity by about 1800 or earlier. One man, called John Easter in English, went to the Red River Colony in 1931 as an assistant to the Reverend Cockran. There he wrestled with and defeated a medicine man of the Peguis Indians.

In 1853 the Inuit of Fort George in James Bay were visited by the Reverend Watkins, and the Anglican movement spread northward. One of the first Inuit to be baptized was Thomas Fleming, who took the name of the missionary Fleming, who later became a bishop, called Inuktakaub by the Inuit of Baffin Island.

A Moravian missionary in Labrador had translated the New Testament from German into the Labrador Inuit dialect, using Roman letters. The Reverend Peck, who founded the mission at Little Whale River in 1876, converted the Testament to syllabics. This and other writings spread along the coast well ahead of the missions.

Peck was helped by Nero Anorak, whom he adopted, by Adam Lucy of Labrador, and by John Miluktok, who was baptized by

Bishop Horden in 1877. Miluktok preached to Inuit along the coast, and at times there were great gatherings at Great Whale River. People neglected their hunting and were almost caught by the winter ice. Another convert, Uyuviniltuuti, carried the gospel north to Hudson Strait.

At one time the trading power of the Moravians in Labrador had worried the Hudson's Bay Company. In 1872 they invited the Oblate Father Charles Arnaud to visit Fort Chimo in the hope that he could establish a mission there and head off the Moravians. Father Arnaud was not successful, nor was Father LaCasse in 1876, but an old woman, Augiak, brought the Protestant message from Labrador a few years later.

The Anglicans and Moravians agreed to divide their territory at Port Burwell, and in 1884 the Rev. Sam Stewart began the mission at Fort Chimo. Unofficially Augiak and Joshua had already begun it.

The Reverend Peck helped Stewart, then moved to Baffin Island, to which Inuit had also taken the Anglican message. Peck, called Ohamak by the Inuit, began his mission at Omanakjuak, Blacklead Island in Cumberland Sound. Peter Tulugakjuak was the first catechist there, and Padlo, a woman, spread the message to Kivitoo, farther north. In 1902 a one-room hospital was built there, but closed a few years later when the whaling station moved away. From 1907 to 1908 the Inuit preserved the missionary Greenshield's food supply while he was in England, despite severe famine. In 1930 a new hospital was opened at Pangnirtung to be operated with government help. In 1940 an old folks' home was added.

Gaston Herodier, a Catholic trader, took Peck's syllabic Bibles to Pond Inlet in 1921, and one man, Umik, began to preach his own version of Christianity. He took his message to Igloolik, and flew a special flag on his tent. Several Inuit were baptized by him as Protestants. Father Bazin of the Oblates moved from Pond Inlet to Igloolik in 1931 and baptized the leading couple, Itukshardjuak and his wife Atavgutarluk.

From Churchill the Oblates moved up the west coast of Hudson Bay. In 1901 Father Turqetil (later Bishop) visited the Keewatin coast, and in 1912 he began the mission at Chesterfield Inlet. In 1931 the Grey Nuns' hospital was built, and an old folks' home added in 1938. A boarding school followed in 1955, and children were brought to it from Catholic communities such as Igloolik.

The Oblates had their own supply boat operating out of Churchill, and during the summers of 1938 and 1939 Father Schulte piloted a mission plane as far north as Arctic Bay. Among those whom he took to the Chesterfield hospital on mercy flights was Okamarluk of Igloolik, who was accidentally shot.

A number of Inuit helped to begin the Anglican missions along the Keewatin coast. Joseph Varley aided Bishop Marsh to open the Eskimo Point mission. Luke Kidlapik began the Southampton Island mission in 1924, and in 1961 Moses Aligak opened the church at Whale Cove. In that year Armand Tagoonak became the first of the ordained Inuit ministers in the eastern Arctic. Most of the Anglican missions now have Inuit priests.

Church and change

The Indian and Inuit people did not welcome the first missionaries as they had welcomed the first traders. The value of guns and metal pots was obvious, the value of new religious beliefs was not. Often the missionaries who first preached were opposed — usually by the shaman, the medicine men such as the powerful Sappa of the Ungava Inuit. They were blamed for sickness and hunger, ill-treated, and insulted. Often they were threatened, and a few were killed.

Considering, however, the changes demanded by Christianity, and that at first the missionaries had to be assisted but could give little in return, the northern tribes in general accepted the new religion quickly. Apart from the advantages of more peaceful behaviour, the new religion was a hope when foreign intrusion had upset the balance of native life, and people had lost their spirit. At first the new religion was thought of as a new set of taboos, something to use against sickness or enemies, to call caribou or bring good weather.

Although the missionaries were sure that they were doing the right thing, their actions sometimes brought confusion and sorrow. Those who stopped the drum dancing, forbade the Coppermine Inuit to wear lip ornaments, and christened children with foreign names were little by little helping to destroy independence and pride. Some of the missionary ideas about hygiene, sex, and God were fine in Europe where they were part of a whole way of life. Trying to fit them into native ways caused many problems, and people became mixed up as to what was right and wrong, true or false.

When men were asked to stop having several wives, the wives who were "dropped" often had a very hard time. Some were left on the missionary's doorstep because it was his idea. One of the Labrador Inuit gave up some wives, but asked for them back to help row the umiak south for trading. There were other strange incidents too, as when three Cree men, about to be baptized by the Reverend Walton, asked for a week's delay so that they could go north to kill a few last Inuit.

One other sad side of missionary work was the way in which native children were brought from far-away home camps to the church residential schools of the Mackenzie. Some were taken very young and some did not see their families again for several years. The value of the education was outweighed by the way children were cut off from their parents, language, and customs.

The greatest fault of the missionaries, however, was, and still is in places, their private "war" for power. (Anglican and Catholic formerly, now Bahai, Pentecostal, and other faiths.) The struggle between Anglican and Roman Catholics divided tribes, families, and school children against each other, wasted lives and money, and betrayed the whole idea of the missions. Someone summed it up once by saying "Rival missionaries eager to convert the same cannibal are apt to behave like rival cannibals stalking the same missionary."

Along with police, Company officials, and the general trend of foreign feeling, the missionaries helped to cut down the abuse of alcohol which had been a disaster of the whaling and fur-trade competition period. Fighting and murder were reduced, and so were infanticide and the neglect of orphans.

Native women benefited from the presence of the missionaries. In 1850 Ethikkan, "Big Head", a Chipewyan girl, refused to be married by Father Faraud to Toqueiyazi, "Little Hay", because she had been taken by force, against the priest's teachings. Such customs as the Slavey one of cutting off the noses of unfaithful wives ended (nothing happened to unfaithful husbands). The hostel of the Grey Nuns filled with Indian girl children who would otherwise have died due to abandonment or hardship.

Most missionaries gave all the medical help they could. Bishop Bompas inoculated over 500 people during the Mackenzie epidemics. The first hospitals and old folks homes were built by the Oblate and Anglican missions. Oblate fathers and the wives of Anglican missionaries worked as lay dispensers until a few years ago, the only medical workers in many small communities.

One of the most important things the missionaries did was to study and record the native languages, to invent ways of writing them. Some of the northern tribes were able to read and write at a time when most foreign people could not. A great deal of knowledge, perhaps the survival of northern native languages, is the result of missionary work.

Prophet movements

In many parts of the world hunting peoples have had their ways of life turned upside down by European soldiers, traders, diseases, and religion. As they become Christians the mixture of old and new beliefs and the feeling of powerlessness result in certain actions. These actions are called revival, nativistic, messianic, or millennial movements.

One kind of movement is based on the idea of the second coming of Christ to the earth. In 1922 at Home Bay on Baffin Island, and in 1941 on the Belcher Islands, some Inuit read the Bible and became very confused. People claimed to be Christ or God, and at both places those who did not believe were murdered.

Once at Port Harrison some people waited so long for the second coming of Christ that they almost starved. Several Inuit, soon after hearing about Christianity, set up their own missions, including Kakaluki at Leaf Bay, Ungava, during the 1850s, "Eskimo Miller" at Fort Chimo in the late 1920s, and Umik at Igloolik early in the 1920s.

In another version of the revival movement, well known among the tribes of the South Pacific, people believe that Europeans, who are bad, must go away, but that their trade goods, which are good, should continue to come. About 1812 such a movement was begun by an Indian prophet near Fort Chipewyan.

Prophet movements are a way of fighting back against the weight of European power. Gu Sais led a revival movement among the Indians of the Pelly and Ross rivers in the Yukon Territory. In recent years a strong movement has spread to the Mackenzie tribes from Alberta. Its leaders are against alcohol, and mix ancient Indian beliefs with Christian ones. Naidzoh of Fort Franklin, son of Big Wolverine, is one of its teachers. Ernest Tootoosis, a Saskatchewan Cree, is a co-founder of the Indian Ecumenical Movement, which is also against alcohol and smoking, and wants a return to nature, spiritual things, and the Great Spirit.

In 1969 a young Chipewyan man of Fond du Lac began to work as a healer, mixing Christianity with older beliefs. In the same year the Rev. Armand Togoonak left the Anglican church to begin his own church, very similar but governed only by Inuit.

Summary

A complete and long book would be needed to tell the full story of the coming of Christianity to the northern tribes. The foregoing pages show only glimpses of the human struggle involved, and the deep changes which swept through the lives of Indians and Inuit.

The advance of Christianity accompanied or closely followed other events such as trade, whaling, and great epidemics of disease. The effects of missionary work, both good and bad, have to be considered in the light of these other currents of history.

During the absence of Canadian government the missions tried to give education and medical help over a vast country, working with few people and limited money. Although the missionaries did their part in destroying the original native way of life, they have become, in these days of new invasions of the north, defenders of native language and custom.

To many of the older generation of Indians and Inuit the churches are part of their heritage, something solid and communal in a bewildering world of changes.

CAUGHT

IN A NET

By 1900 radio, telephone, and gasoline engines had been invented, and men were building the first airplanes. Southern Canada was linked by railway from coast to coast, and most of the farmland was occupied by settlers. The government of Canada, just over 30 years old, found time and reason to look toward the vast north.

Slowly at first, then faster and faster up to the present, Inuit, Indian, and Métis people became surrounded by new boundaries, laws, machines, and people. The north and its native people became part of a complicated industrial Canada and a speeded-up world. There are people today who have watched films of men walking on the moon, but who remember striking fire with stones.

Government spreads its wings, 1900 to 1939

Up to the outbreak of World War II very few Canadians or the men they elected to govern them had knowledge of the north and its people. Three main reasons forced the government to take more interest in northern affairs, and those reasons are still in effect.

The first reason was the need to show that Canada owned its huge northern lands. In 1900 Americans were challenging Cana-

da's right to govern the Yukon and the many islands of the Arctic.
Norwegian explorers and Danish officials in Greenland disputed
Canada's claim, made in 1880, to the Queen Elizabeth Islands.
None of these nations, of course, considered the right of the native
people of the north *not* to "belong" to the U.S., Canada, Norway,
or Denmark.

To show the world its ownership, its *sovereignty*, the government of Canada set up police posts in various parts of the north,
and began yearly patrols by ship in the eastern Arctic.

A second reason for southern Canadians to take an interest in
the north was the discovery of *mineral wealth*. The Yukon gold,
then oil at Norman Wells, and later radium at the eastern end of
Great Bear Lake, each brought a rush of prospectors and other
"outsiders" into the north. These people had to be governed,
taxed, and protected according to southern Canadian laws.

Third in the list of reasons for action by the government in the
north was concern for *native welfare*. Although a few regions still
had enough wildlife to support hunters, and there were some
"boom" periods for trappers, on the whole the condition of northern Métis, Indian, and Inuit people continued to decline after 1900.
With their territories encircled and overrun by "outsiders", with
wildlife badly thinned out, and weakened by epidemics, the northern native people had lost control of their world.

Throughout the early 1900s the government slowly increased its
wildlife preservation measures, its education, medical, and welfare
services. The approach, however, was that of "Father knows
best." No real effort was made to give the northern natives control of their lives, and almost all programs were in the hands of
the "Big Three" — missions, Hudson's Bay Company and RCMP,
each of whom had its own separate purpose for being in the north.

This land is your land, this land is my land

When outsiders take over a whole country (something very common in the history of the world), there is the question of who owns
the land, and how much of it. The ownership of lands and waters
by the first inhabitants is called "aboriginal rights".

The new people can ignore the rights of the first people simply
because they are stronger — this has been the case during most of

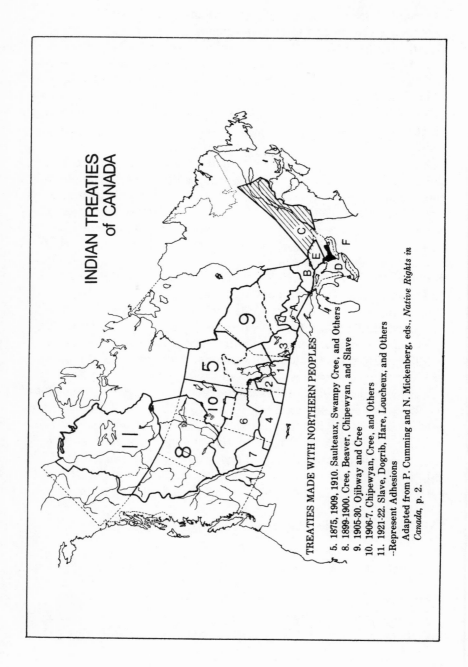

INDIAN TREATIES
of CANADA

TREATIES MADE WITH NORTHERN PEOPLES

5. 1875, 1909, 1910. Saulteaux, Swampy Cree, and Others
8. 1899-1900. Cree, Beaver, Chipewyan, and Slave
9. 1905-30. Ojibway and Cree
10. 1906-7. Chipewyan, Cree, and Others
11. 1921-22. Slave, Dogrib, Hare, Loucheux, and Others
--Represent Adhesions

Adapted from P. Cumming and N. Mickenberg, eds., *Native Rights in Canada*, p. 2.

world history. In Newfoundland and Quebec this was so. The
Beothuk Indians and the southern Labrador Inuit were destroyed.
Some Labrador Inuit signed a peace treaty with the British
Governor Palliser in 1764, but it gave them no land rights, and for-
bade them to visit their old territories along the shores of Belle Isle
Strait. All that remains of that treaty is the name Palliser, which
was adopted by the Inuit and still used.

In the American colonies the British government believed that
Indian rights to the land should be *extinguished*, that is, given up
to the queen or king through friendly agreement. Such agreements were called *treaties*, and payment was usually made for the
land rights. The idea of native land rights was brought to Canada,
and an Indian Superintendent was appointed in 1755. When Britain
took over Quebec from France in 1763, native rights were mentioned in the Royal Proclamation. The government of Quebec was
given the right to make treaties and payments for Indian lands, but
this has not yet been done.

The first treaty in Canada involving land was made between
Indians and Scottish settlers at Red River in 1817. Beginning in
1850 several treaties were made with the tribes living along the
north shores of the Great Lakes. Later 11 treaties were made with
the tribes of the Plains, the Mackenzie, and the rivers flowing into
southwest Hudson Bay.

The treaties which affected northern Indians were numbers 5, 8,
9, 10, and 11. Treaties 8 and 11 in particular were put through because of the Yukon Gold Rush and the Norman Wells oil discovery. Some Indian groups, tired of having their hunting grounds
invaded by outsiders who took much more than they gave, began
to fight back. Newspaper reporters wrote dramatically about new
"Indian Wars", and the government became anxious to make
peace for what it called the "opening" of the north.

Booklets published by the federal government, one for each
treaty, describe how the treaties were made and what each one
contains. In each case a small group of officials called "commissioners" travelled the treaty region, usually by canoe, meeting
Indian bands. With the help of interpreters — usually Métis northerners, missionaries, or traders — the commissioners explained

the proposals of the government. In exchange for land which was needed for farming, mining, lumbering, and other uses, the Indians would be paid certain sums of money and receive other forms of payment.

All the treaties were similar, though the details varied. Some bands signed the treaties years later than others, but the agreements were the same. This summary, taken from the booklet *The Canadian Indian*, published by the Department of Indian Affairs and Northern Development in 1966, shows the main points of Treaty Number 11:

Treaty No. 11	— June 27, 1921 — Slave, Dogrib, Loucheux, Hare and other Indians. The Northwest Territories north of Great Slave Lake. Area ceded, 372,000 square miles.
Government Obligations	— Reserves 1 square mile for each family of five, subject to Government's right to deal with settlers on reserve lands; right to sell or lease reserve lands with consent of Indians and to appropriate reserve lands for Federal public purposes subject to compensation for improvements and lands; right to hunt, trap and fish in ceded area subject to Government regulations; salaries of teachers.
Treaty Presents	— Medals and flags and copy of treaty for each chief, fishing, hunting and trapping equipment to value of $50.00 for each family of band; miscellaneous equipment.
Annuities	— Indians $5.00, chiefs $25.00, headmen $15.00; triennial suit of clothes to chiefs and headmen; annual distribution of twine, ammunition, etc.

All the Indians who discussed the treaties with the commissioners were concerned most of all about keeping their rights to hunt, trap, and fish. They had little or no understanding of how the Canadian government worked, but thought in terms of the king or queen as sort of super-chief whose spokesmen were the treaty commissioners. This extract from the James Bay Treaty booklet gives some idea of the way the talks went:

A more general conversation in explanation of the terms of the treaty followed than had occurred at Osnaburg. Moonias, one of the most influential chiefs, asked a number of questions. He said that ever since he was able to earn anything, and that was from the time he was very young, he had never been given something for nothing; that he always had to pay for everything that he got, even if it was only a paper of pins. "Now," he said "you gentlemen come to us from the King offering to give us benefits for which we can make no return. How is this?" Father Fafard thereupon explained to him the nature of the treaty, and that by it the Indians were giving their faith and allegiance to the King, and for giving up their title to a large area of land of which they could make no use, they received benefits that served to balance anything that they were giving.

The treaties gave the government of Canada a very good bargain. In exchange for about half the area of Canada the Indians were paid small amounts, and the yearly payments have become almost nothing in modern terms. The right to hunt, fish, and trap was guaranteed, but subject to such changes as the government might make. Gradually the *opportunity* to hunt, fish, and trap has been reduced in many parts of the north. Buildings, people, machines, roads, railways and airports, pollution, and game laws have all changed the environment.

Neither the officials nor the Indians at the time could have foreseen the speed of change which was to sweep the north. Although medical, police, welfare, and education services have since been provided by the government *outside* the treaty agreements, the treaties (except one) made no mention of police or medical help. It seems that some things said by the officials were taken by the Indians as promises, even though the words were not written into the treaties. Chief Pierre Squirrel signed Treaty No. 8 in 1899 at Smiths Landing, but later, after the great measles epidemic of 1903, he said: "You see how unhappy we are, how miserable and sick. When I made this treaty with your government, I stipulated that we should have here a policeman and a doctor; instead of that you have sent nothing but missionaries."

Another drawback of the treaty arrangements was that the idea of electing a chief and councillors every few years did not fit the tribal way of choosing leaders. Sometimes the elected chief was a nobody, chosen to keep the government happy while the Indians looked to someone else for leadership.

Despite the drawbacks of the treaty arrangements, Treaty Day during the early 1900s became a festival time, when trappers and their families gathered to receive their payments, dance, hold athletic competitions, trade, and gamble. Nowadays it is less important, but still an event, when chiefs wear their uniforms with pride.

Some of the northern Indians have not yet claimed the reserve land to which they are entitled under the treaties. Indian associations are now arguing that the treaties were not fully understood by those who signed, and were forced upon the Indians who had no choice. The government, on the other hand, has announced that the treaties cannot be re-negotiated or re-arranged.

The question of *land rights* apart from treaties is still unsettled, and will be discussed in the following chapter.

Labels and numbers

One of the changes brought to northern Indians and Inuit by Europeans has been the gradual replacement of native names by European ones. The traditional ways of naming people varied among Inuit, Athapaskans, and Algonkians, and even among tribes. Each way of naming people had certain rules and sometimes a religious meaning.

Europeans who dealt with native people could rarely pronounce or remember the Indian and Inuit names, and gave the people European names. Many northern native people adopted the names of Europeans whom they liked, or who in some cases were their fathers. The Métis almost all used European names.

Missionaries christened their converts by French, British, or Biblical names. The clerks who wrote down the names of those Indians who signed treaties often changed the Indian names to European ones. In this way the Dogrib "Monphiou" became the Irish "Murphy", and many people were called Elk, Beaver, or some other translation of their Indian name.

In recent years the Inuit of the Northwest Territories have been asked to choose surnames so that they will fit more smoothly into the general Canadian way. Many Indians and Inuit still use two sets of names — a European one at school or at work, and a native one at home.

Native names for rivers and other parts of the landscape are used on maps, but are often used or spelled wrongly. *Tasik* means *lake* in the Inuit language, and many lakes are called in English Tasik Lake, which is silly. In northern Quebec native people must know their own names for places, the English names which were used for many years, and the French names which have replaced them.

The federal, provincial, and territorial governments each have special dealings with Indians, Métis, and Inuit people, but the matter of deciding who is who and who gets what from which government is complicated. Here are the main labels used to classify northern native people:

Registered or Status Indians   Under the Indian Act of 1876, revised in 1951, most Canadian Indians belong to registered bands and have a band number. Some, but not all, live on reserve land. There are no reserves in the Yukon, though certain settlements and woodlots have been set aside for Indian use by the Commissioner. The Northwest Territories, northern Quebec, and Labrador have no reserves, but each of the five provinces to the west has a few reserves in its northern part.

Treaty Indians   All members of Indian bands which signed treaties are known as treaty Indians, and receive treaty payments each year. All treaty Indians are Status Indians.

Non-Status Indians and Métis   At the time of the northern treaty agreements some Métis people were given a choice of signing the treaties and thus becoming "official Indians", or of taking a payment for their land rights, after which they would be treated as European Canadians. Treaty 11, for example, refers to "fifteen half-breed families who would be dealt with separately, and seventy-five families who would become treaty Indians".

Of the Métis who took the payment, many did not follow a European way of life, but an Indian one. They and some Indians who were not registered or treatied with were ignored by the government for years, until it became obvious that here were people who lived outside the Canadian system and in some cases had more Indian blood than the Status Indians.

In 1934 the government of Alberta began to study the situation, and in 1938 passed the Métis Population Betterment Act. Eight reserves, called "colonies", were set up for northern Métis. Manitoba and Saskatchewan began similar programs and today the federal government deals with Métis and Non-Status Indian associations.

Eskimos   For a long time neither the federal nor provincial governments worried about fitting Inuit into the official system. They were far away from cities and farmland, and at that time no one thought of the oil, gas, and minerals in Inuit country.

Treaty 11 included some of the Mackenzie Inuit territory, but their leader, Mangelarluk, refused to sign the Treaty. Gradually, however, the Inuit everywhere were drawn more and more into the southern economy and into a web of government supervision. Although it became obvious that health, education, and welfare services were needed, the responsibility for Inuit affairs was passed around during the early 1900s among different levels and departments of government.

In 1912 the Government of Canada transferred to the Province of Quebec a portion of the Northwest Territories which was inhabited by the Inuit. The name given to that portion was New Quebec, and the federal government interpreted the transfer as meaning that, in matters of provincial jurisdiction like education, health, municipal development, the Quebec government was responsible for its Inuit inhabitants. This interpretation was challenged by the government of Quebec which claimed that the Eskimos were Indians and consequently the responsibility of the federal government in all parts of Canada. The case was brought to the Supreme Court of Canada in the 1930s and Quebec won its point. The exact Court decision was:

Re ESKIMOS.   Can.
Supreme Court of Canada, Sir Lyman P. Duff, C.J.C., Cannon,   S.C.
Crocket, Davis, Kerwin and Hudson, JJ April 5, 1939.

1939

Constitutional Law II — B.N.A. Act, ss. 91 (24), 146 — Whether Eskimos are "Indians".

The exclusive legislative jurisdiction of the Dominion Parliament under s. 91 (24) of the B.N.A. Act over Indians extends to Eskimos, who, by well-

established usage at the time the B.N.A. Act was enacted, were regarded
as Indians throughout British North America, and it is immaterial that
there were no Eskimos within the original confederating Provinces, for
the B.N.A. Act (s. 146) provided for the inclusion of the Hudson's Bay Co.
lands, where the Eskimos then resided.
27 -- (1939) 2 D.L.R.

As a result of the Supreme Court decision the government of
Quebec refrained from exercising any jurisdiction toward the Inuit,
and the federal government administered Inuit affairs in Quebec
in much the same way as in the N.W.T. until 1963. But, in spite of
the judgement of the Supreme Court which recognized its legislative
power over all Inuit matters, the federal Parliament has not passed
a special Act to appropriate the provincial jurisdictions, as it did
for the Indians (Indian Act). Consequently, while it is clear that
the federal government has the power to legislate, it is not clear
that Quebec has lost its actual jurisdiction over the Inuit of its
territory in matters of normal provincial jurisdiction.

For over 30 years all Inuit except those of Labrador were registered, usually by the RCMP on "disc lists", so-called because at
birth each person was given an identity disc with a number and a
regional code letter. This system has now been replaced by the
adoption (in most cases) of surnames, and the use of birth certifi-
cates and social security numbers.

People in boxes

In place of the old arrangement of leadership and hunting territories, the twentieth century brought many ways of dividing up
the north. Layer on layer of laws and levels of government grew
around, among, and over the native people, who had little or
nothing to say about this organizing and slicing up of their homeland.

In 1895 the Northwest Territories were subdivided into the
three districts of Mackenzie, Keewatin, and Franklin. The present
Yukon boundary was set in 1898. Alberta, Saskatchewan, and
Manitoba emerged in their present form in 1905. In 1912 the land
and people of Ungava were included with the province of Quebec.
In 1949 Labrador and Newfoundland became part of Canada.

The five northern treaty boundaries were arranged between

1897 and 1921, sprawling across provincial lines. Smaller divisions
were also made — wildlife sanctuaries, beaver conservation areas,
fur conservation blocks, registered trapline areas, and provincial
and national parks. In the northern parts of the five western provinces Indian reserves or Métis colonies added to the network of
boundaries.

Each division of land brought new regulations. A man might
hunt ducks in one province on a certain day, but not in another
province over the hill. He might sell a beaver skin but not a caribou skin. To travel and hunt legally all the way from Yukon to
James Bay today one would need many maps, licences, and copies
of regulations. Sometimes the laws and boundaries work to peoples'
advantage, and some Inuit who live at the meeting of two provincial boundaries and one territorial have profited from a bounty
paid by one province for ranger seals.

We stand on guard for thee

For centuries the northern Indians and Inuit had lived according
to their own ideas of law and justice. The competing fur traders,
the gold-rushers, and the whalers often behaved badly, ignoring
the native rules and those of their own cultures.

During the mixed-up days around the turn of the century some
men such as the Reverend Stringer on Herschel Island, George
Mitchell on the Peel River, and John Firth at Fort McPherson
tried to keep law and order with their fists and strength of character. Firth, the strong-armed trader, was made the first government law officer from 1894 to 1903.

The Royal North West Mounted Police had gone west at the
time of the Riel Rebellion and by 1900 their posts dotted the north
of all five western provinces. They moved to the Yukon to keep
order in the raw new mining towns, and in 1903 the first posts were
built on the arctic coast. The main reason for the posts was to show
Canada's ownership, and to enforce Canadian laws. The posts were
at Fort McPherson, Fullerton, and Herschel Island, and the policemen had orders to confiscate all liquor in order to protect the Inuit.

For the next 30 years new police posts were established on the
arctic coast, until 12 of them showed the presence of the Canadian

government. The most northerly of them, on Ellesmere Island, was 400 miles north of the nearest group of Canadian Inuit.

The police force had been renamed the Royal Canadian Mounted Police in 1920. All through the early 1900s they were the main government influence in the north, with the exception of the Yukon and Labrador. Despite some sensational murders, crime was rare in the north, and the police performed as explorers, game officers, nurses, census-takers, tax-collectors, and many other things.

In northern Labrador Inuit village elders had kept order until hunger caused riots in 1933. The Labrador Constabulary was formed in 1934, then in 1935 the Newfoundland Rangers. Four out of ten Rangers were posted in the north, but they were young, untrained, and without direction. They issued relief during the terrible late 1930s, and continued until 1950, when the RCMP took over.

The police did their best, but they were not trained or equipped to be a whole administration. One well-known writer on the north, Dr. Diamond Jenness, pointed out in one of his books that in 1939 the Canadian government spent $17 on police in the north for every one of the Inuit; Denmark spent nothing, for there were no police in Greenland; and only 41 cents was spent in Alaska. At the same time Canada spent only $12 a head on education, health, and welfare of Inuit compared to $13 in Alaska and $44 in Greenland. Of Canada's $12, five was paid by Inuit from taxes on the furs they sold.

The application of Canadian laws to Indian and Inuit people was and still is a problem. The laws themselves varied according to boundaries like those between Labrador and Quebec, or Alberta and the Northwest Territories. Even the boundaries were strange to people who had no part in their making. Some game laws contradicted the treaties, and often contradicted the law of survival during times of starvation. For people accustomed to settling matters themselves or by a meeting of the elders, it seemed wrong and childish to refer everything to some outsider. They did not feel that the Canadian law and justice belonged to them, for no Indians or Inuit were policemen, justices of the peace, or magistrates. In 1930 the Indians of Rae complained to their agent, Cler-

mont Bourget, that they were continually being punished for breaking laws which they did not understand.

Most of the murders committed by Europeans and native people
in the north during the early 1900s have been written about elsewhere. There is no doubt that the presence of the police gradually
ended the custom of blood feuding and, to a lesser degree, infanticide, but on the other hand most of the murders famous in northern native history were the direct result of European influence.
Liquor was one cause, starvation due to lack of wildlife another,
misunderstanding of Christianity was a third, and fourth was the
fear generated when Europeans were isolated with native people
in cold barren places, unable to understand each other's languages
and habits.

Agents and go-betweens

As a result of the treaties and the general northward movement of
government, Indian agents were appointed to various parts of the
north. The Fort Smith and Fort Simpson offices opened in 1911,
Dawson City in 1914, Fort Resolution in 1926, and Fort Good Hope
in 1931. Some Indian agents were kept busy with a variety of
tasks. Clermont Bourget of Fort Simpson, for instance, was also
the regional medical doctor, coroner, justice of the peace, and
school inspector. Others were less occupied, and many treaty
Indians only saw their agents at the annual treaty payment.

The agents became "go-betweens", like the traders, missionaries, and policemen. For half a century in the north a curious situation prevailed in which the whole power and knowledge of the
Canadian government and people on one hand, and the whole
native society on the other, were in contact only through a handful
of people. Some of the go-betweens, particularly missionaries and
Hudson's Bay Company traders who came straight from Europe to
the north, knew very little about Canada and its government. It
was no wonder that to most Indian and Inuit people the control of
Canada seemed to be divided up between the missionaries, the
Hudson's Bay Company and the RCMP, under the eye of a king
and queen.

The new medicine men

In the year 1900 about half of the northern Indian people were within canoe range of half a dozen mission hospitals and government doctors. There were no doctors or hospitals in the territory of the Inuit.

Southern Canada itself was a new society, short of medical help, and the northern population was scattered and nomadic. If the Indian and Inuit people had kept their old standard of health, need for government help would not have been urgent. As it was, hunger and disease were destroying the health of the hunting tribes.

As in all things, the government moved cautiously and by way of the "Big Three". Medicines were issued to all missions, police posts, and most trading posts. All through the early 1900s and in some places much later, missionaries, police, traders, and other amateurs performed with varying skill as nurses and first-aiders.

Some of the treaty commissioners gave vaccinations or inoculations as they travelled among northern Indians. In 1900 a doctor began annual patrols down the Mackenzie to Fort McPherson and later to Herschel Island. From 1903 on, with a break during World War I, a doctor toured the eastern Arctic on the yearly patrol ship.

A small Anglican hospital had been built in 1902 at Blacklead Island in Cumberland Sound on Baffin Island, but it closed with the end of the whaling station there. In 1926 Doctor Livingston was posted to a new government medical station at Pangnirtung, and in 1928 an Anglican hospital was built there. The doctor and his successors toured the region by boat and dog team and gave advice by radio to people hundreds of miles away.

In 1926 and 1927 the Anglicans and Oblates each built hospitals at Aklavik. These were served by one doctor, who was given a boat in 1930 with which to patrol the coast eastward. In 1929 the Oblates built a hospital at Chesterfield Inlet. This was staffed by government doctors, and government funds, as with all the mission hospitals, paid some of the costs of operation.

In 1929 a government medical station was built at Coppermine, but it closed after two years because of lack of support. By 1939 there were four doctors and five registered nurses employed by the government at four mission hospitals on the arctic coast, and a few airplane mercy flights had been made. A dozen mission hospitals served the northern Indians from James Bay to the Yukon, and medical patrols by airplane, railway, canoe, and sled helped to carry medical help to remote camps.

Dr. Samuel Hutton built a hospital at Okak in Labrador in 1902 and travelled by dogteam, sailboat, and rowboat around the coast until his health broke down in 1908. In 1905 the Grenfell mission opened a larger hospital in St. Anthony, Newfoundland, serving people as far as Makkovik. In 1910 medical steamboat patrols began along the Labrador coast.

An increasing number of Inuit and Indians by 1939 were being sent to southern hospitals for tuberculosis and other treatment. Those who returned brought back new ideas and knowledge of industrial Canada.

Knowledge and power

According to the old Indian and Inuit way, children learned from their parents and other adults everything they needed to know in life. The missionaries were the first to change this custom when they built schools and gathered children for instruction in the European way. As early as 1873 the government paid the salaries of teachers at mission schools at Norway House and Nelson River. In 1884 several boarding schools were built by the two churches, and by 1887 in the northern prairie provinces there were 44 reserve day schools and 5 boarding schools.

In 1894 the government made its first grant to a school in the Northwest Territories, $200 for 31 students at the Anglican school in Fort Resolution. In 1896 a further $200 was given for 26 students at the Roman Catholic school in Fort Providence.

The number of mission schools and the amount of government financial help slowly increased, until by 1939 there were nine day schools and five boarding schools serving Inuit children, including those of Labrador which was then not a part of Canada. The northern Indians were equally served by mission schools at places like Fort George, Attawapiskat, Fond du Lac, Fort Chipewyan, Lower Post, and on into the Mackenzie and Yukon. Some Indian children went south to the boarding schools at places like Brandon and Sault Ste. Marie.

Despite the spread of schools through the north, education progressed very slowly. Some reasons were the size of the north, the seasonal movements of Indians and Inuit, and the uneven distribution of schools. There were two at Aklavik, two at Fort George, none at all (as with hospitals) in the whole of Ungava. In 1935 80 percent of the Métis people of school age in Alberta were not attending schools, and as late as 1944 over 80 percent of Inuit children were not being schooled.

The missions did their best, but many of their teachers were not trained, and they had few good texts and other classroom materials. The boarding-school system took children away from their homes and relatives for years at a time without holidays, sometimes without even letters exchanged. In some schools children were taught in their own language, in others they were forbidden to speak it. The mission schools tended to concentrate on religious teaching at the expense of science, mathematics, and other necessary knowledge. All too often they taught children to dislike and distrust the children who attended schools of the other faith.

The European settlers in the Yukon got public schools for their children, and in a few years after gold production began in 1934 at Yellowknife, the Europeans there and at Fort Smith demanded and received local government and public schools. Some Métis and Inuit of the Mackenzie Delta, who by way of Alaska and the whalers had learned a lot about the modern world, asked in 1928 for a public school, and offered to pay for the school and a teacher.

Mr. O. S. Finnie was the Director of the Northwest Territories Branch of the Department of the Interior from 1921 to 1931. He wanted to provide a public school in the Delta and in fact to set up a modern system all over the north of schools, adult education, and vocational training. He had the same dream for medical services and training, but the government did not support him. In 1931 a new government was elected and the economic depression began. Finnie and his senior staff were all laid off.

One serious fault in the education of northern native people was that it neglected the adults. Little or nothing was explained to them about the workings of the fur trade, the Indian Act, or the whole system of Canadian government. The only book printed for the education of adults was one made by the Hudson's Bay Company in

1931 for the Inuit of the eastern Arctic. It was printed in English and in the eastern Inuit language.

The Eskimo Book of Knowledge was written to improve the fur trade of the Hudson's Bay Company, but it also attempted to educate adult Inuit about health, saving, game preservation, laws, and the changes coming to the north. What the book says, and the fact that a business company found it necessary to print it, shows how little in 1931 the Canadian government was doing toward native adult education.

The Book of Knowledge is a token of friendship provided for you...and for your family by the Governor of the Company. He is a man of great understanding and wisdom who decides the difficult problems of the Company and directs the traders in their duties.

Being a good citizen, loyal to the King and to those who rule the British Empire for the King, he wishes that you and your children, who are also citizens of the British Empire, should learn more of this Empire to which you belong, so that you may fully share our pride in the King who lives in the Mother Country far beyond the seas; and he wishes that you should also share the King's pride and our pride in those parts of the British Empire called Canada and Labrador of which you inhabit the northern regions. Furthermore he wishes that by your good actions and by your mode of life you should add your share of honour to the British Empire.

Being also a happy man rejoicing in his children and in the love of his family, he shares with you the cares and the joys of your family; and by this Book of Knowledge he will surely diminish the cares of your family and add to your joys, if you are wise enough to pay heed to his advice.

In the first part of this book the Company will tell you and your children about the British Empire and about Canada and Labrador and how you are entitled to the privilege of regarding our King as your King.

In the second part of the book the Company, which has consulted with many Traders and the most learned Doctors and the Men of God, will explain to you the change which has come to your mode of living and will show you by what means you will bring better health and therefore greater happiness to your children and to yourselves.

In the third part of this Book of Knowledge will be shown to you the means whereby you may gain greater possessions in trade for the benefit of your children and yourselves.

Let those of you who can read, recite the book to those who cannot read. In your camps discuss the book; talk of it in your igloos at night when your pipes are lit. It is a good book and a true book — this Book of Knowledge.

The whalers came to your country; the Men of God came and the Traders of the Company came. They altered the conditions of your lives. The bows and arrows which your fathers used, you have discarded for rifles:

the kayak and umiak which your fathers used, many of you have discarded for the wooden boats with engines: the rich seal meat and the deer meat which were the life blood of all your people, some of you have discarded for White Man's flour.

When you first see a hunter very far away on the ice with his dogs, it is some time before you can tell for certain in which direction he is moving.

It was the same way with the officers of the Government and with the officers of the Company who could not tell at first whether your people derived good or evil from the use of the things which the White Men brought to your country.

In those days also White Men knew not of the things which are likely to happen when a people such as yourselves suddenly begins to use the things which White Men gradually learned to use over a great period of time.

Take heed to what is written here, all you men and women of the North. Your people have not derived good from the use which you have made of the White Men's things. The things which have been brought to you are good things in themselves, but you have misused some of these things, so that to-day you are a feebler people than in the old days when your fathers did not know the White Men. Your sons are less hardy, your wives bring forth fewer children. There is sickness among some of you.

Here you shall learn how you have brought this weakness about.
(From *The Eskimo Book of Knowledge*, Hudson's Bay Company, 1931.)

There were some exceptions to the general lack of adult education in the eastern Arctic. Around 1928 four men were taken from Chesterfield Inlet by ship to Montreal, where they worked for a year learning cooking, shipbuilding, and other trades. They were Putjuut (the oldest at 33), Athanasi Angotitak, Lionel Angutinguak, and Louis Tapati.

No place to hide

The inventions and science of the late nineteenth and early twentieth centuries speeded up the advance of Europeans into the north and ended the isolation of northern native groups.

By 1900 steamboats were clanking along the Yukon rivers and the Mackenzie system. A little later steamboats ploughed Lake Winnipeg and its rivers. Paddlewheel tugboats hauled scows from the railway to Fort Albany. Indian and Métis men changed from canoemen to deckhands, dockers, and woodcutters, and the forest was cut far back from the river sides to keep the steamboats in fuel.

About 1922 the first canvas-covered freight canoes were made in the Hudson's Bay Company factory at Rupert House. These canoes spread all over the north, replacing many of the bark canoes and heavy plank boats. Outboard motors appeared in the 1920s, making water travel easier and faster, but bringing a need for money to pay for gasoline and motors.

In the arctic waters Roald Amundsen, a Norwegian explorer, made the first complete passage by boat from east to west in 1903. In 1937 two Hudson's Bay Company ships, the *Aklavik* and the *Nascopie*, met from west and east in Bellot Strait, the first trading link by sea between the northern oceans. In addition to the wooden whaleboats and the Mackenzie schooners which had reached the Inuit by way of the whaling fleets, the Hudson's Bay Company in the 1920s and 1930s brought Scottish peterhead fishing boats to the Inuit of the eastern Arctic.

Government ship patrols, beginning at the turn of the century, visited most communities of the eastern Arctic every year with doctors, game officials, post officials, customs officers, police inspectors, and assorted tourists. The arrival of such patrol ships as the H. B. Co. *Nascopie*, 1912 to 1947, and the arrival of the scow brigades on northern rivers, was a busy, happy time when everyone helped to unload supplies. There were sad moments too, as when Europeans left after their time of northern service and Indians or Inuit sailed south to some southern hospital.

During the early 1920s the first airplane flights were made into the Canadian north. Two aircraft flying along the Mackenzie Valley had to land in rough conditions, and each had a smashed propeller. New propellers were made from local timber, using tools from a mission workshop. Government, missionary, and commercial pilots opened new routes into and across the Arctic.

Native people were usually on hand to help the early bush pilots. One of the pilots of those days, Jack Marr, said at a meeting in 1967:

> I would like to acknowledge the debt of the bush pilots to the native population in the North, especially the Eskimos. We probably could have gotten in and out of the country safely, but they made it a lot easier. They knew the country and how to live in it; we didn't. We could fly over the natural barriers which they found so difficult but once we landed it was man against the elements as it always has been and is today. The Eskimos

adopted the attitude, "here is another poor white man that we have to look after." It may have been hard on the ego but once you accepted the situation you could learn a lot about how to live in their country.

Mining development crept north in the Canadian Shield from Chibougamau to Noranda in Quebec, Kirkland Lake to Pickle Crow in Ontario, Flin Flon in Manitoba, and on to Lake Athabasca. Hydroelectricity dams, plants, and transmission lines followed, and logging operations helped to push back the trapping and hunting boundary of the Naskapi, Montagnais, Cree, and Chipewyan Indians. Apart from some labouring work for the men and a market for handicrafts sewn by the women, the march of industry into the north did little economically for the Indians, but it brought great social changes.

Radio communication developed with flying, and by 1931 four government stations were transmitting to the north. By 1937 the new Department of Transport had radio and weather stations at Coppermine, Frobisher Bay, in Hudson Strait, and on each shore of Hudson Bay. Similar stations operated by the Army Signal Corps were set up in the western Arctic, and all were linked by radio to telegraph stations such as the one at Churchill. In 1935 the Hudson's Bay Company began to equip all its northern posts with two-way radios, followed by the Oblate missions and the RCMP.

Welfare and wildlife

Early in this century the hunting tribes of the north were already suffering from severe shortages of wildlife for food, clothing, equipment, and dwellings. Some of the shortages were due to European demands on territory and wildlife. Fishermen, loggers, settlers, miners, and whalers encircled the north, nibbling even deeper toward its centre. European and native trappers had cleaned out whole regions, especially of beaver.

Some of the blame lay with those native hunters who wiped out the helpless musk-ox with rifles, and slaughtered migrating caribou by the thousands at mountain passes and river crossings. Many animals were killed for their tongues or livers alone, and hides and meat were left to rot.

Far-seeing people hastened to save the wildlife, hoping to save with it the independence of Indian and Inuit hunters and trappers.

Finnie's game officers travelled through the Northwest Territories counting the numbers of various species and recommending conservation to the hunters. Around Rupert House in James Bay the Hudson's Bay Company trader James Watt began his scheme for beaver preservation. Archie Belaney, an Englishman who pretended to be an Indian, Grey Owl, also began a beaver conservation scheme.

Beaver preserves, trapping regulations, trapline registration, native hunting preserves, and wildlife sanctuaries were set up throughout the north. Some of the measures created hardship at the time for native hunters and trappers. The many regulations bewildered people, but most of them were necessary to keep something for the future.

Although there were bright spots such as trapping booms, and although some regions were richer than others, in general the years from 1900 to 1939 were hard, sad ones for the northern native people. There had always been starvation in the north, but with abundance in between. Now even as radio and aircraft "opened up" the north, families died of hunger in Ungava, Keewatin, the Arctic Islands, and elsewhere. For those who did not starve, a steady diet of bannock and fish, the cold in wooden shacks or canvas tents, the flimsy covering of woollen clothing, and an endless round of epidemics weakened both body and spirit. The 1930s, when the price of fox fur collapsed but the price of flour and ammunition rose, were especially bad. Many people of the north can remember terrible experiences during those years.

The government took some long-range action through its game and trapping regulations. Caribou hides were sent from good hunting areas to poor areas. In one case green buffalo hides were shipped to the Arctic, but they were useless for clothing to the Inuit, and heavy even as bedding to be carried.

We have already seen in Chapter 6 how the Baffin Island and Mackenzie Delta reindeer experiments fared. In 1921 the government set aside Southampton, Coats and Mansel Islands as reindeer and musk-ox ranges, but these animals were never taken there.

Missionaries, Hudson's Bay Company, and government had all tried to find alternatives — farming, gardening, white-whaling, sawmilling, canoe-building, commercial fishing, fox farming, and similar projects. Some succeeded in a small way. Some failed because the native people had no experience and no heart for the work, or because the north was just too far from city markets. None of them could hope to solve the main problem of a dying way of life.

One of the saddest things about the pre-war years, and even after, was the business of relief rations. For cases of hardship the government provided, or paid traders to provide, food such as flour, lard, baking powder, and tea, and goods such as ammunition, canvas, and twine. In most cases the decision whether or not to give out relief was left to traders, though sometimes to missionaries, police, or Indian agents. Some native hunters relied too heavily on free rations and some traders withheld rations from hungry people in the belief that the natives should try harder to hunt and trap. Mostly both traders and trappers used the rations in good faith, but the whole system showed the loss of independence of the northern people.

People unprepared

Nothing is easier than to pick fault with things done in the past. The handling of northern native affairs by the government from 1900 to 1939 reflected the state of the whole country — young, thinly spread, without a strong philosophy to make government, business, and religion work toward the same goals.

Perhaps nothing better could have been done under the circumstances, but in 1939 Soviet Inuit were piloting aircraft, Alaskan natives were running businesses, and Greenlanders were electing their own people to their own councils. Canadian Indians, Métis, and Inuit of the north in that year were without a voice in economics, religion, education, laws, or politics. From proud people who rather pitied the clumsy foreigner they had become bewildered bystanders, an embarrassment to a government that did not know just what to do next.

Shock treatment

Even though aircraft and radio were helping to change the north, things went slowly until the outbreak of World War II. In the fall of 1939 a war began which was to involve most of the world. No fighting took place in North America and no bombs fell, but still the war brought great changes to the Canadian north.

In the northwest the Alaska Highway was built, mostly by the U.S. Army. Thousands of men and machines camped and clattered through northern British Columbia and southwestern Yukon. Branch roads and airfields were built, and over the Mackenzie Mountains to Norman Wells went a new road and oil pipelines. The effect upon the Indian people was like that of the Gold Rush twenty-odd years before.

In addition to the airfields and weather stations through the Yukon, a similar staging route was built along the Mackenzie, and a third in the eastern Arctic. At five points in Inuit territory the United States Air Force moved in by air and sea, creating instant towns on the tundra. At Fort Chimo, in the year when Naskapi and Inuit were living a hand-to-mouth existence, and a woman dragged her children 60 miles on a sealskin seeking food, a thousand soldiers and workers arrived, to stay for seven years.

To the new Fort Chimo, a few miles up river from the old trading post and missions, flocked Inuit, Naskapi, Montagnais and some Cree from all over Ungava. Some found work as carpenters, cooks' helpers, drivers, and labourers. Even children learned to dance and sing for coins and treats, entertaining the soldiers. Indian and Inuit workers were paid in cash for the first time in their lives, instead of in goods or credit at a store. Although the average wage was only $2.00 a day for native workers, as recommended by the Canadian government, the workers could make more in a year than their kinsmen who kept on trapping and hunting. Fur prices had risen once again since the depression, but trapping in Ungava was poor.

The new money income created problems and jealousies among the native people. The poor trapper, formerly looked down upon, might now drive a truck, live in an unused army building, and own a radio, beds with mattresses, and other belongings. People who got meat were by custom bound to share it. Those who got money or gifts from the Americans often did not share. Where one ship had come each year with supplies, there were now dozens. There were movies, poolrooms, laundries, and an unbelievable supply of goods of every kind in front of the eyes of people who had lived with hunger, and who had been grateful for a relief issue of a few cupsful of flour. Bins full of food were thrown away each day from the army cookhouses. Clothing, machines, furniture, magazines, and other things were dumped continuously. From 1949, when the Americans left, to 1962 when the supply ran out, the Inuit of Ungava operated their boat motors on free aviation gasoline left behind at Fort Chimo. Like those native people who lived near the other bases, their lives and their views of the world could never again be the same.

Away from the air bases and the new highways, the war brought smaller and slower changes. Some Indian and Métis men who lived closer to southern cities volunteered for the armed forces and fought overseas. They returned with a new understanding of the world beyond the north, and a feeling of discontent with the way their people lived. Inuit men trained as Rangers, but most were still remote from the war.

The Indians of Old Crow and the people of other northern communities sent money gifts to war orphans and to the Red Cross in Britain. On the arctic coast the Inuit were warned to watch for German submarines. One man of Igloolik, out sealing in a small boat with his wife and another couple, tells a funny story of their fright when they mistook a piece of ice, floating through the mist, for a submarine and rowed like mad for the shore.

During the war years Inspector Larsen of the RCMP took the ship *St. Roch* through the Northwest Passage from west to east, and back again from east to west. Pannikpakutchuk and his family, Inuit from Pond Inlet, travelled with Larsen as guides, hunters, and tailors, all the way to Herschel Island.

Throughout the war years the Canadian public and the various governments became more and more aware of the existence and problems of the northern native people. Reporters, military people, and others told of their experiences in the north, and most were shocked at the conditions of life they saw there. In 1944 Dr. Andrew Moore was asked by the Social Science Research Board to investigate the condition of native education in the north, and Dr. G. J. Wherrett was asked to do a similar report on health. Both men urged that the government increase its program greatly and immediately. Three-quarters of all native northerners were still without schooling, and the rates for infant deaths and epidemics were extremely high.

In 1942 the federal government had begun to send codliver oil and diet biscuits to mission schools in the north. In that year the Alberta government brought out a new Betterment Act for its Métis population and set up a new Northlands school division. In 1944 the government of Saskatchewan began its fur marketing and controlled trapping system in the province. Six government retail stores, co-operatively run, were opened. Although the fur-buying system was a good thing in the long run, many Métis resented the waiting time for government cheques, and the loss of instant credit at the Hudson's Bay Company and other stores.

The war had jolted parts of the north rudely out of the fur-trade days and the days of rule by the Big Three, police, trader, and missionary. By the war's end the federal and the prairie governments were committed to a new responsibility for the north and its original people.

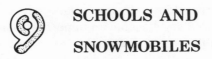# SCHOOLS AND
SNOWMOBILES

By the end of World War II the Canadian north and its people
were being drawn into the spider's web of modern life. Airlines,
dams, roads, mines, and oil-rigs were marching north. A time of
cold war between the two giants, the U.S.A. and the U.S.S.R.,
brought more radar sites and air bases to both timberland and
tundra.

At the same time the various governments of Canada stepped
up their programs to improve native health, education, and in-
comes. Things have moved so fast that it is difficult to say whether
the results are good, bad, or somewhere in between. North and
south, natives and newcomers are merging in this jet age.

A few main currents such as government, education, health,
construction, and life on the land can be seen in the broad and
churning river of recent northern history. We will try to follow
each one, gathering ideas along the way with which to end this
book.

X-Rays for all

Tuberculosis had become a great danger to northern native
people, and the government declared war on it. During 1956 one in

every seven of the Inuit spent time in a southern hospital, and almost every Indian family too watched someone go "outside" for months or years. Hospitals such as Charles Camsell and Brandon became little islands of northern native patients, linked to home by slow mail and regular radio broadcasts.

Each year medical teams came north, turning up at Treaty gatherings and with the annual supply ships or river barges. They visited far camps X-raying and inoculating, and a stream of patients were sent south in their wake.

The government patrol ship *C. D. Howe* sailed the eastern arctic seas from 1950 to 1968 and became an important part of life for the Inuit there. When it arrived at a settlement, there was a rush of X-raying, inoculation, doctoring, dentistry, social work and so on. George Tayarak of Sugluk described it in his song which begins "*C. D. Howe* tikitsimayuk, maktavigivaktavut... the *C. D. Howe* has arrived, time to undress again."

The going away of children and parents to southern hospitals was a sad business and upset many families. Some T.B. patients came home with lungs or bones missing, and could no longer hunt or trap. Some patients were "lost" for years because of official mistakes, and children who forgot their languages came home unable to speak with their people. Years in over-heated hospitals with little exercise, constant cleanliness, and prepared foods made it difficult for ex-patients to fit back into northern life.

Government hospitals were built in various places such as Moose Factory 1948-50 and Frobisher Bay 1958, and one was placed at North West River 1954-55 by the Grenfell Association with government help. The medical staff of the DEW and Mid Canada stations treated native patients. In northern Saskatchewan, Newfoundland, and elsewhere air ambulance services began.

In 1965 the government of Quebec, at the request of the Inuit, built a hospital at Fort Chimo, replacing the former nursing station. It is operated by an administrative board elected from the community. The Oblate hospital built at Fort George during the early 1950s was transferred in 1964 to an Indian operating corporation. In 1972 the Anglican hospital at Pangnirtung, which had been such a part of the region's history, was closed, and a nursing station built in its place.

Nursing stations staffed by one or two nurses began to appear after the war, and now almost every village has one. At first nurses were sometimes blamed for deaths just as the missionaries had been, and men sometimes preferred to be treated by a man amateur or "lay dispenser" than by a trained woman nurse. On the whole, however, the daily care and health teaching given by nurses has made a great difference, especially in reducing the rate of infant deaths.

Along with and at times instead of the government services, native medicine — sweat baths, charms, and herbal remedies — are still used. In faraway places or during a long spell of bad flying weather some nervous volunteer with one eye on a handbook may still pull an aching tooth.

Going to hospitals in the south can still be a very strange and lonely experience for native people who speak no French or English. Sisters have come south on the same aircraft and with the same medical trouble, only to be placed in separate hospital rooms, each unable to speak to her non-native roommates and not knowing where her sister was. Some emergency operations have had to be done without the consent of patient or family, and one old Inuit man went for years unable to speak to anyone at all, because no one who knew his language ever came to that hospital. There are interpreters in some southern hospitals, but not everywhere and not all the time.

There are registered nurses aides and community health workers among the northern native people, but only a few fully qualified nurses and one doctor. Although health services have been greatly improved, they are still something provided for or done to Indians and Inuit.

During the early days of the nursing stations all over the north there were native men and women who were most important as nursing assistants, guides, and interpreters, often all three. One of the most capable and hard-working of these was Mrs. Daisy Watt of Fort Chimo, who has done more for the health of the Inuit of northern Quebec than any other person, and who learned her nursing skills through long experience rather than by formal training.

As the dangers of tuberculosis, smallpox, and the old diseases are reduced, other problems arise. Venereal disease is now a great menace. The strain of modern life makes people turn to drugs and alcohol. Lack of home care or understanding makes children's ear infections a constant task for nurses.

Native people now eat less meat, eat and drink more sugary things, and get less exercise. As a result many children are taller than their parents and grandparents, but not as strong and enduring. Bad teeth, acne, overweight, diabetes, liver, heart, and gall-bladder troubles are all fairly new.

The military wave

In 1945 startled hunters near Eskimo Point saw a spinning and clanking cavalcade of Canadian army tracked vehicles. This was Exercise Lemming, from Churchill to Padlei and back over the snows of the treeline. Next year more musk-ox, caribou, and people in lonely places saw a bigger show as Exercise Musk-ox clattered and skied from Churchill to Cambridge Bay, and from there to the Alaska Highway at Fort Nelson. In 1950 and 1951 the Inuit of Keewatin and Ungava saw the paratroops of Operation Sun-Dog dropping from the skies like giant ptarmigan.

Although Russia had fought on the same side as the U.S.A. and Canada during World War II, a "Cold War" began, mostly between the U.S.S.R. and U.S.A.   Each side tried to keep ahead of the other in military strength, including atomic bombs. The homeland of Canada's northern Indians and Inuit lay under possible air routes from Russia to America, and so defences were built there.

Canada and the U.S.A. joined in building weather stations, signal stations, and air-defence posts in the north from 1946 to 1956. Some, like the stations of the Queen Elizabeth Islands, were built far to the north of native settlement. Others, such as those at Cambridge Bay and Hopedale, attracted hunters and their families who hoped to find work, salvage "goodies", and taste excitement. The tiny army signals post at Ennadai in the Keewatin operated from 1949 to 1954, and was a refuge for the very poor and often hungry Inuit families who lived nearby.

In 1955 work began on three great lines of east to west radar stations intended to warn southern cities of enemy planes or missiles coming from the north. The DEW or Distant Early Warning Line girdled the arctic coast with small and large airstrips, "space-age" domes and scanners, bunkhouses, and recreation halls. At Tutoyaktuk, Cambridge Bay, Hall Beach, and other points workmen, soldiers, airmen, bulldozers, trucks, planes, barges, and ships swarmed and bustled into the quiet arctic scene. Farther south the Mid Canada Line passed through Great Whale River, affecting both Inuit and Cree. From there it curved east and west through the northern bush country of Algonkian and Métis trappers.

As had happened with the air bases, many Indians and Inuit moved to the radar sites. Some men found employment and moved along the Mid Canada or DEW Lines into strange regions. Some eastern Inuit adapted the round-hooded, fur-trimmed, and fringed parka of Mackenzie migrants, and marriages were made across the old boundaries of dialect and kinship.

Eventually the Cold War died down and the fantastically expensive warning system became out of date. The self-contained "ants' nests" of barracks, bars, bowling-alleys, and corridors were abandoned or put to other uses. The overfed and womanless "armies" returned south. The north, however, had been "opened up" still further, and the native people pushed another long step along the way of change.

Recently the Canadian armed forces have increased their northern activities, doing construction, medical research, and rescue work, and recruiting native people. The first group of young Inuit men recruited as full-time soldiers scored better all round in their training than their southern companions.

Taking the rocks

Most people know the story of the old Indian who watched a mine working and said "First, white men come and take all the beaver, then come back and take all the trees. This time they're even back for the rocks!"

The mining industry continued its northward movement around the edge of the Canadian Shield. On the Quebec-Labrador border, Schefferville and Wabush sprang up in the heart of Naskapi-Montagnais travelling country. A railway was built south to the coast at Seven Islands. Huge tractor trains crossed frozen muskeg and lakes and battered down the skinny tamaracks on their way to mines, dams, and bridge-sites. Chibougamau, Lynn Lake, Pine Point, Cassiar, and points farther north began to send their ores south by road, rail, and ship from former wilderness.

In the country of the Inuit the Rankin Inlet Mine was worked with government help and Inuit men learned a new trade underground from 1953 to 1962, when the mine closed. On the south coast of Hudson Strait asbestos and nickel mines have been developing for ten years, employing Inuit, and on northern Baffin Island iron and zinc mines may soon change the lives of all the native people around.

During the 1960s the oil and gas industry began a surge of expansion into the north. From Alberta to the Mackenzie Delta, west over Yukon and Alaska, east and north to the arctic islands, go the exploration trails and plastic streamers. Drilling goes on at sea and on land, and Canada is abuzz with plans for pipelines (or railways) down the Mackenzie Valley and the coasts of Hudson Bay.

Inuvik is filled with bustling strangers. Resolute Bay and far-thest-north Eureka are busy airports. The great U.S.A. tanker *Manhattan* with Canadian ice-breakers has broken the trail of ice for future movement by sea of oil and metal ores.

While pipelines take up the news, new roads creep north. The Dempster Highway will soon reach Inuvik from the Yukon, and the Mackenzie Highway will join it, leading to Tuktoyaktuk and the Arctic Ocean. The camper vans, the Texas trailers, the motels, picnic sites, and salesmen will soon arrive where 50 years ago there was not even radio.

All this and much more. Mrs. Blackduck or Mrs. Pitseolak who only 15 years ago lived in tents three days' journey from the nearest store can now gossip by telephone from their oil-heated houses on stormy days. Their children can telephone home from southern schools or hospitals a thousand, perhaps two thousand, miles away. At Churchill and Inuvik for several years people have watched taped television broadcasts a week old. The artificial satellite Anik, to which someone gave its Inuit name "sister's brother" because it sounded "cute", now transmits instant television and radio broadcasts all over the north.

Hydro development at Ashuanipi and Grand Falls, Labrador,

together with mining, has changed the country of the Naskapi. Now one more tremendous change is under way in northern Quebec. From James Bay to Mistassini Lake and north almost to Fort Chimo the provincial government is preparing to build great power dams and other industrial developments. Large areas will be flooded and affected.

All of this industrial activity in the north has brought very great changes to the native people. For some, it has meant new employment, for others yet another invasion of their land and customs. Many are afraid that the whole meaning of their lives, of their roots in nature, is at stake. In the next chapter we will look more closely at native reaction to industry.

Empty traps, empty pockets

For the northern native people hunting, trapping, and fishing are not just a way of making a living like working in a garage or an office. They are things that were for centuries the whole centre of life. Everything important was based on wildlife and the land — customs of birth, marriage and death, growing up, and deciding what was good or bad.

Since the war, however, the actual amount of hunting and trapping done by the original people of the north has grown steadily smaller. In some places animals are scarcer, there is more noise, and there are more people. The price of furs sold cannot keep up with the price of all the things that people need to live in the modern way.

As families move into towns, hunters and trappers have to travel far beyond the town to find wildlife. Their wives and children stay at home and the trapper doesn't want to stay away long. Many young men and women are not trained to travel and trap, to chop ice and wood, to skin, clean, and stretch pelts. Some people do not like the cold and the messy work and have the false idea that hunting and trapping are for "uneducated" or "unskilled" people.

In a few areas people still live mainly by hunting, trapping, and fishing. The white fox is the mainstay of the proud people of Sachs Harbour. At Colville Lake, Jean-Marie River, Nemiscau, and Grise

Old-time Hudson's Bay Company trading post at Fort Resolution.

Cree trappers in Hudson's Bay Company store at Norway House.

Fiord the trap, the rifle, and the fish-net are still the vital tools of life. Everywhere else in the north the call of the land, at least part-time, is still strong. An Indian school janitor or an Inuk power plant operator will keep his canoe and motor or his snowmobile ready for spare-time trips. The moose, goose, fish, seal, and caribou they get have a much deeper meaning than the pay cheque.

The end of construction or the closing down of wartime and cold war bases threw many native people back into reliance on the land. In many cases the land could no longer support them, or they had lost the will, skill, and equipment of former years. As late as 1960 families all over the north lived in poverty, wearing old clothing sent from the south by southern churches, living in tents patched with flour sacks, eating an endless diet of tea, bannock, and fish.

There was help from the governments; family allowances, old age pensions, old age assistance, blind persons' allowance, needy mothers' allowance, and relief. Until the 1960s, however, all such help was measured out (in many areas) by officials according to a list of "sensible" goods to be bought from the store. The relief ration was as much a part of life as the snow — flour, lard, baking powder, molasses, ammunition, and the canned tomatoes that were often dumped off the sled outside the settlement. The allowances and relief saved lives, but what happens to the pride of a man whose mother's tiny pension is more than his earnings?

Starvation, always a part of the ancient way of life, continued to kill scores of northern native people until the late 1950s. The famine of Keewatin was written about by the author Farley Mowat. His account of the plight of both Chipewyan and Inuit shocked many people in southern Canada. As one result the six-year-old federal Department of Northern Affairs was given more money and staff to improve conditions in the north.

New migrations

One answer by government was to move people to better hunting grounds or to places of employment, perhaps to both. In 1955 Inuit families from Port Harrison in Quebec and Pond Inlet on Baffin Island were moved north to the new communities at Resolute Bay and Grise Fiord. Wildlife was more plentiful at both places than farther south, and there were a few jobs to be had at the Resolute air base. The people, however, had to learn how to adapt to the new land with its longer winters and ice cover. It took years for the two dialect groups to mingle closely. Today Grise Fiord is one of the happiest of northern communities, but it cannot pay its way, for meat and furs do not support houses, furnaces, snowmobiles, and schools.

In 1955 some Inuit families were moved from Fort Chimo to Churchill for work at the military and scientific bases. Some returned to Ungava, but others stayed to mingle with Keewatin Inuit, Europeans, Cree, and Chipewyan as time went by. A year later the Fort Chimo band of Naskapi Indians moved to Schefferville by both air-lift, which took mostly women and children, and canoe-brigade for men and dogs. In Schefferville they live with other Naskapi and Montagnais in an uneasy halfway stage between the iron-mine and its town and their ancient wilderness home.

The government of Newfoundland has closed many poor fishing villages in order to move their European populations to bigger centres. The same thing was decided for the Inuit of northern Labrador. In 1956 the people of Nutak, short of seals, fish and firewood, moved on their own to Nain, Makkovik, and Northwest River. In 1959 it was the turn of Hebron. Although the government was not ready, about 20 families "jumped the gun" and burned down their old houses. They waited in tents for the government to take them south. After some fast house-building and other preparations the provincial government, assisted by the U.S. Air Force, moved all 50 families to more southerly towns, leaving over 300 miles of coast without people.

Inuit from Quebec and Keewatin had migrated to Rankin after 1953 to work in the mine there. After 1957 the starving people of Garry Lake and other hunting camps were brought to Rankin Inlet, Baker Lake, Eskimo Point, and a new community built at Whale Cove. Hunters learned to be miners. When the mine closed in 1962 they learned to be carvers and pottery workers. Men who had not seen the sea before learned to hunt seals, and women began to work in a government cannery.

Around 1959 the federal government began a new town and airfield on the east side of the Mackenzie Delta. The new place was called Inuvik, and was intended partly to be a transportation centre for the northwest coast, partly to replace Aklavik, which was being cut away by the river. The government intended that the town of Aklavik should close down, and all its people move to Inuvik, but the matter was poorly handled — the first word the Aklavik people received was by way of the radio station in Fairbanks, Alaska. In any case the people did not want to leave their pleasant home, despite problems with river erosion. They had a song in which Inuvik was called "Toytown", and the school motto was "Aklavik, never say die!" Today Aklavik is still a close-knit community. Many Inuit, Indian, and Métis people moved to Inuvik, however, some from Aklavik, some from other Delta villages.

After the Rankin Inlet Mine closed, Inuit miners and their families moved to mining towns such as Yellowknife and Lynn Lake. Other Inuit, together with Indian families, moved south to work on the Northern Alberta Railway. In Labrador, Goose Bay and Happy Valley have drawn many Inuit southwards.

In 1947, because of poor fur returns, the Hudson's Bay Company closed its store at Fort Ross, and the Inuit there, already migrants from far away, had to move to the Netsilingmiut community of Spence Bay. For similar reasons the Cape Smith Inuit of Quebec had to move to Povungnituk. The Duck Lake Chipewyan and the York Factory Cree in Manitoba had to go to other centres when their stores closed.

The federal government in 1962 encouraged families around Ungava Bay to move to Port Burwell, where hunting was good. In 1964 the Quebec government began to build up Leaf Bay as a community at the request of local Inuit. The small Inuit community of Padloping on Baffin Island was closed down in favour of Broughton Island.

The Indians of Mayo village who had lived by the river were moved from there to the mining town in 1955. Sekani people of the Finlay Valley in British Columbia were moved to a useless new location when the Bennett Dam flooded their homeland.

These are just some of the many movements brought about by changes in the fur, mining, fishing, and other industries. It is true that the northern native people were nomadic in the old days, but usually within their own fixed territory. Even the great move-

ments of the fur-trade days left most tribes in one region and
apart from foreign society.

For people anywhere it is difficult to move among strangers of
different speech and custom. It takes generations for Netsilik and
Kingnait Inuit to mingle easily, or for Cree and Chipewyan Indians. It is much more difficult for northern native people to move
to modern mining or transport towns. Most immigrants to Canada
are used to the idea of changing, used to farms, banks, social
clubs, factory whistles, lunch buckets, and tax forms. It is not so
for native people. In any case most northern towns are ugly, queer
places with too many drifters and men without women, places
without roots in the land. The real nomads of the modern north
are the outsiders, the foreigners, not the native people.

On the whole the movement of native people to towns run by
"white people", foreigners, has not been a happy experience. Very
often the officials who planned the moves thought that a pay cheque
was the answer to everything and had no idea of the many other
things involved.

One of the greatest blunders and saddest examples was the
movement of the Chipewyan Duck Lake band to Churchill in 1957.
After years of despair, drinking, and violence the people with the
help of an Indian community development worker in 1971 have
made their way back to Tadoule Lake near their old home and
are regaining peace and dignity. The Chipewyan group is not the
first to retreat from the destructive influence of town life to a life
they understand. Simoni of Frobisher Bay tried it during the
1960s for similar reasons, and Chief Smallboy's return to the hills
of Alberta (to escape the social problems of the reserve near town)
is well known.

New looks at an old land

During the time that some native people were moving, or being
moved, to wage work in centres of government or industry,
another kind of change was going on. The government in Ottawa
and those in the provinces began to look for ways to improve fishing, hunting, and trapping, to try to make it possible for people to
earn money by using their native skill and experience.

Musk-ox round-ups and canned whale   In 1949 the Commissioner of the N.W.T. asked an ex-fur-trader called James Cantley to tour the north and prepare a report on ways to improve the living of the native people. About the same time the first of several Area Economic Surveys began in northern Quebec, with the same aim. Many of the things suggested have been tried, and the story of all the economic projects of the last 20 years is colourful.

Wherever conditions permitted, traders and missionaries began farms or gardens in the north. Indians near Great Slave Lake owned horses before the turn of the century, and in 1949 the Inuit of Aklavik saw their first cattle when the government doctor, Livingston, began a small dairy herd there. Today many Indian and Métis people in the northwest have vegetable gardens for their own use, but there are no real farmers. Fur-farming has been tried as far north as Pangnirtung on Baffin Island, but it has not prospered in the north. For several years the federal government rented a Tibetan yak, hoping to cross-breed it with other cattle and produce a hardy animal that could be herded by Inuit on the tundra. This idea did not work out.

The experiments with pigs at Great Whale River, chickens and sheep at Fort Chimo, caused headaches for the government officials and laughter for the native people, but the main benefits went to hungry sledge-dogs that ate the livestock. One project officer hoped to start a spinning and knitting or weaving industry, using the hair of husky-dogs. Others have hoped to use the fine under-hair of the musk-ox for spinning and knitting into high-priced scarves or sweaters. A small herd of musk-ox have been brought from the high arctic islands to Fort Chimo in northern Quebec for this purpose. The project is still at the experimental stage. In 1972 in the Mackenzie District a man was paid $5,000 to walk around pulling the musk-ox wool from bushes, but he did not get enough to knit a sock.

In a few places blueberries have been picked for sale to the south, and in several coastal communities the down of the eider duck is collected from nesting sites to be cleaned and sewn into arctic clothing. Because all animal skins have to be sent out of the north for tanning, even skins that are used in the north for handicrafts, there has been much talk of building a tannery in the north.

Only one has been tried, at Aklavik, but it shut down after one year.

The government has experimented with canneries on the Keewatin coast, producing canned seal meat, whale meat, and fish. The canned whale and seal meat were not popular in the south or north, and now the cannery at Rankin Inlet, staffed by Inuit, produces only processed fish. For a while pigs were fed on the cannery waste, but the pork got a very fishy or seal-oily taste.

Until 1963 the Hudson's Bay Company continued to employ Inuit in a white whale fishery at Pangnirtung. The hides were sold for leather, and the fat boiled into oil for margarine, cosmetics, and other uses. A similar whale fishery has been operated at intervals by the government at Churchill. Indian and Métis hunters have killed an average of 450 white whales a year there. At Whale Cove and Rankin Inlet whales have been netted for use in the cannery.

In many northern native communities, small handicraft shops have been organized by co-operative or government officers. Handwork and machine work are combined in the making of clothing such as the beautiful fur parkas of Aklavik, or novelties such as the Fort Chimo "Ookpiks". Other cottage industries include the weaving shop at Pangnirtung and a small knitting factory at Frobisher Bay, employing Inuit women.

Until the late 1960s Inuit of Lake Harbour built fine wooden whale-boats for sale by the Hudson's Bay Company. A few wooden dories were built from local lumber by the Inuit of George River in Quebec, but at present the only successful boat-building operations are the small canoe factories. One at Great Whale River is operated by Inuit. At Rupert House, Nelson House, and Norway House Indian craftsmen build canoes for sale.

As the tourist industry grows, more and more northern native people have turned to outfitting and guiding for a living. Band councils, co-operatives, and individuals are involved in looking after visiting fishermen, hunters, and other tourists. Polar-bear hunting in the N.W.T. has been opened to tourists on a carefully limited basis, and only Inuit can act as guides or outfitters. In the Mackenzie region a new kind of experience has been arranged for tourists. They can pay to spend a while with a trapper in his cabin

and on the trapline, to taste a little of his way of life. Frank La-
violette of Fort Smith, with fellow Indian guides, operates a buf-
falo-hunting camp. Willie Emudlik of George River, Quebec, and
his relatives operate a tourist fishing-lodge.

One of the most important economic alternatives for northern
native people has been commercial fishing. The Inuit of Labrador
have sold cod and salmon for over a hundred years, and the Yukon
Indians began to sell fish to miners during the Gold Rush. With
government assistance since 1945 fisheries have been started
throughout the north. Fresh or frozen fish has been sold locally in
the north or — by far the greater part — taken to city markets in
the south.

Northern co-operatives Co-operating means working together for
the same purpose. Co-operative societies are formed so that people can use their labour, ideas, and money to improve their lives.
In such societies, usually known as "co-ops", every member votes
on important decisions and shares the benefits of the organization according to his efforts.

Co-ops are an important part of northern native society and of
recent northern history. The idea of sharing, of local groups dealing with fishing, native handicrafts, hunting or house-building, is
close to the old native way of doing things. Unlike other businesses, the whole aim of the co-ops is to help the members, their families, and their communities, and the results of co-op effort are
open for all to see.

Because of the link with the old ways and the old economy, because of the small scale and local control, co-ops have offered northern native people a chance to deal with modern business matters in a partly native style, using their own language. Many of
the present community leaders and other prominent native people, particularly among the Inuit, received valuable experience
during the early days of co-op development.

The beginning and support of northern native co-operatives has
several sources. Fishing co-ops were begun among the Métis of
northern Saskatchewan by the provincial government in 1955.
Other provinces have also developed northern co-operatives.
In northern Quebec and the Northwest Territories, starting in
1959, the federal government began the native co-operatives, now

about forty in number, which today receive support from the territorial and provincial departments of development.

Southern co-operative organizations, such as the Co-operative Union of Canada and the Caisse Populaire of Quebec, have helped the northern co-ops. Several Oblate priests have played an important part in co-op growth, and other non-native people, both in and out of government, have worked hard to help the co-op movement. To such people the co-ops are not just a job, but something to believe in, an answer to the problems of native people in an industrial world.

The real heroes of the northern co-ops, however, are the hunters and trappers who, with little or no education or knowledge of the southern world, have taken on the task of learning accounting, management, federation, pricing, and all the things involved in co-op business. Younger native people have now received formal training for various kinds of co-op work, but every co-op owes much to men like the late Charlie Smith of Inuvik and Pootooguk Ohituk of Sugluk.

The northern co-operatives operate a wide variety of projects. The Churchill tourist camp and whaling plant, the building of a new school at Povungnituk, the Pelly Bay DC-4 Air Service, the Cape Dorset stone-cut prints, the Trout Lake tourist lodge, the Old Crow hotel, and the Port Burwell retail store are all examples. Fishing, fur-marketing, sawmilling, house-building, handicrafts, water and garbage contracts, and oil supply are other co-op activities. Most co-ops have several operations, and the Pelly Bay Co-op is involved in almost all aspects of community life. It is a good example of what can be done when native people are allowed to control their own change-over to modern ways.

Beginning in April 1966 there has been a steady growth of federations in which all the co-ops of each region band together. The northern Quebec Federation, formed in 1967, has its own marketing service in the south, and in June 1973 the N.W.T. Federation decided to take over Canadian Arctic Producers Ltd., a non-profit marketing company based in Ottawa and sponsored since 1965 by the federal government. With the federations working together there is a total native co-operative membership of several thousand people generating and handling several million dollars each year.

Artists and craftsmen   Generations of life close to nature, without books, buildings, and machines have given northern native people a great power to see, an ability to express their thoughts and what they see in drawings or carvings, in songs and dancing. Added to this is the skill in working by hand which comes from centuries of making all possessions for themselves.

The growth of Inuit art is one of the historic high-points of the post-war period. There are so many first-class carvers and print-makers, both men and women, that the names quoted here are representative rather than selective.

Although this book is about native people, the name of James Houston deserves special mention. Saunmik, "Left-Handed", as he is called by Inuit, went to Port Harrison in 1950 with the help of the Canadian Handicrafts Guild and the federal government. There he persuaded the people to try soapstone as well as ivory for carvings. Later at Cape Dorset he introduced the idea of making prints on paper from carved stone blocks or engraved copper sheets. He visited Japan to learn the Japanese methods and taught these to the Cape Dorset artists.

An exhibition in England in 1953 helped to put Inuit sculpture on the map. In 1959 the prints began, and soon were a success in world art circles. Almost every Inuit community now has a co-op or government craft shop producing clothing, woven goods, ceramics, batiks, paintings, prints, or sculpture. The Eskimo Arts Council has worked with government officers, the co-operatives, and Canadian Arctic Producers Ltd. to keep the quality of work high and to resist imitations.

Carvings and prints have become a favourite gift by Canadians to foreign visitors. At Expo 1967 in Montreal, two sculptors from Cape Dorset carved in public for weeks. At Expo 1970 in Japan this tradition was continued when the work of Elijah Pootoogook and his four companions was presented to presidents, kings, and queens from many countries. In 1972 and 1973 an exhibition of Inuit art masterworks toured Europe, and artists accompanied their work to Russia, England, and elsewhere.

The mace used in the Council of the N.W.T. is an outstanding example of artwork by several people. Tiktak, Lucy Tasseor, Osowetuk, Oonark, Pitseolak, Kalvak, and Johnny Inukpak have all been appointed to the Royal Canadian Academy. Makituk Ping-uartok of Cape Dorset won a prize for ceramics at an international festival in Italy. Kenoakjuak has been awarded the Order of Canada for her artistic achievements.

In 1961 Jeannie Snowball of Fort Chimo sewed a little imitation owl from sealskin, along with other bird and animal toys. The owl became popular at a 1963 Philadelphia trade fair, and since then many thousands of "Ookpiks" have been sold in Canada and abroad. Among the many Inuit painters Mona Thrasher, Mary Paneegoosilk, Germaine Arnaktauyak, and Henry Ivaluakjuk are well known.

The Indian people of the north have been selling arts and crafts for many years, and their work has not had the recent popularity, publicity, and novelty of the Inuit art. Poorly made handicrafts and factory-made imitations have spoiled the image of Indian work. Much has been done to overcome this, and there is an important production of birchbark art, hide-painting, beaded hide clothing, and other items.

Among the new wave of Indian painters and other artists of the north are Patricia Ningawanee of Ontario. Moses Bignell of Manitoba, Myles Charles of Saskatchewan, Alex Janvier of Alberta, William Atkinson of the Yukon, and Bob Abraham of the N.W.T. Tim Sikyea of Fort Rae opened in 1973 a fashion boutique in downtown Toronto featuring his own designs and the work of other Indian people.

Most of the present arts and crafts of northern native people depend on an understanding of nature and on skills which come from a hunting way of life. These may decline as people become more and more caught up in an industrial society. In the meantime the art and craft industry is very important — it is a way in which the land and its native people can produce, a way to make a living and to give the world things that no one else can make.

Changes at "The Bay"   The fur-trading store of the Hudson's Bay Company, usually called The Bay or The Company for short, has been part of northern native history for over 300 years. Although there are now co-operative and other stores in the north, the Company still does most of the business with northern Indians, Inuit, and Métis.

From 1900 to about 1950 the trading posts were usually small places with no heat even in winter, so that the trader had to write with freezing fingers in a cloud of his own cold breath. The goods sold were the simple long-keeping kind needed by families living in tents, snowhouses, and cabins and trading only a few times a year. Almost everything sold was paid for in furs, and in that sense the north paid its way; exports paid for imports.

With the gradual increase in pensions, wages, money from handi-crafts, and welfare the Company had to change its operations in the north. Modern heated stores with shopping carts and music replaced the old ones. Real money replaced the former Company metal tokens; in some places Inuit were just getting used to mo-ney in 1964. Fur has become less important to most stores than other income, and school-trained native men and women operate the cash registers and check-out counters.

Mechanical dogs   No history of the northern native people would be complete without mention of the small oversnow vehicles which are called motor-toboggans, snowmobiles, or (after the brandname of the first really successful model) skidoos. These machines have, of course, affected most of Canada, but in the north, especially among the Inuit, they have become an important part of native life. They have almost replaced sled-dogs, and a whole body of special skills and words has grown around their use in the hunt or on the traplines.

Before World War II Indian winter fishermen on the lakes of Manitoba used tractor-sleighs, and about 1958 small tracked machines with steering skis, called autoboggans, were being used in the north, mainly by prospectors. Despite mechanical diffi-culties they became popular, and in 1962 Jean-Luc Bombardier of Quebec produced a stronger, lighter model which he called a "Skidoo". Since then many similar machines have been made by other manufacturers in Canada, U.S.A., Japan, and elsewhere.

As with all things which show an obvious advantage, the Inuit and other northern native people quickly made the snowmobiles their own. Despite problems of breakdown and noise the machines enable people to travel almost anywhere that dogs could go at much greater speed. At first there were deaths when young men

Mechanical dog.

— travelling far without warm clothing, food, stoves, or snow-knives — were caught by storms or breakdowns. Some trappers, not trusting the machines, would carry two or three dogs on their sleds just in case.

Now the noise of the machines has replaced the howling of dogs as a fact of northern life. Girls and boys learn early to drive them, and they are used to visit church, store, or bingo game; to visit settlements hundreds of miles away; to haul freight and chase bears. They do not have to be fed and tied as the dogs did, but gasoline and repairs take money and accidents are frequent. The cost of the snow machines is really more than trapping, handicrafts, and other living based on the land can really bear, and some hunters are talking of going back to dog-team travel.

One-way education

At the end of World War II the federal and provincial governments began to increase the number of day schools for native children. In 1947 a school was built at Tuktoyaktuk, N.W.T. In 1948 the day school at Port Harrison (Inukjuak) opened. The government of Newfoundland took over the Moravian schools and built new ones.

Many day schools were built near trading posts and missions at a time when the people lived away in fishing or hunting camps or on traplines. Some children from the camps lived with relatives to attend school or stayed in small hostels. During the summer months some teachers lived at the camps, teaching in tents. Year by year, however, more and more families moved from the camps to be near school, nursing station, store, church, and so on. Very few small hostels are used now, though boarding schools for the higher grades continue at Inuvik, Yellowknife, Frobisher Bay, Great Whale River, and other centres. In some cases the hostels are operated by the Anglican or Roman Catholic missions.

There have been several main reasons for the provision of education by governments to the northern native children. One aim has been for the children to learn enough English, mathematics, and other things for them to fit into general Canadian life and to improve their chances of making a living. Another idea, common among administrators just after the war, was to train people for migration south, because there seemed to be no future in the north. More recently planners have looked at the schools as a way of preparing native people for work in mining, oil, gas, and other industrial development in the north.

Whatever the wisdom of these and other arguments for formal education, and though no one can deny the need for some preparation for survival in the modern world, the educational systems on the whole have been one-sided, designed according to southern ideas, and not adapted to northern native cultures and customs.

A foreign system   Those well-meaning people who designed the schools, set the studies, and hired the teachers did not think enough about the native way of life, the native way of education, the importance of language, and similar ideas. They did not ask the advice of native parents and did not consider explaining things first to parents so that they could then advise and control their own children.

At most schools almost all teachers spoke only English or French. Their ideas about food, games, manners, and time were different from those of the native people. Schools were far larger, better lit, and better heated than most native homes. The books

used in school were all about cities, farms, offices, and other
things the children and their parents never saw. The teachers
usually stayed only a year or two and the students were always
getting used to strangers.

Quiet native children were always being told to "speak up", and
encouraged to compete with each other. Native habits like the
silent facial yes and no of the Inuit were stopped in class. Altogether school was another world compared to the native homes
and life around them.

In the residential schools the young people were still further
away from native life and even "real" southern life. The modern
schools did not have that need for wood chopping, fishing, and
other chores that kept the mission residential schools in touch
with the land. Young Indian and Inuit people adopted the foreign
teenage culture with its pinup pictures, records, and changing
styles of hair or clothes.

The results were only fair educationally and terrible socially.
Parents and grandparents did not understand what the children
had gone through, and did not feel responsible or able to control
what the "white man's schools" were doing. They gave up trying
to teach their children at nights, weekends, or holidays in native
ways. When the children spoke English or French, they could not
understand.

The children often felt ashamed because they could not hunt,
clean skins or make things, travel, and stand the cold as the old
folks could. On the other hand they considered the older people
rather ignorant and old-fashioned. The old closeness between all
ages had been broken.

Young native people were trained as air-stewardesses, hair-
dressers, bulldozer operators, and so on, but when it came to working in the foreign world they often came to grief through not knowing or having different customs about sex, money, pastimes, prop-
erty, mealtimes, and a whole way of life.

Most young native people who went to school between 1950 and
1970 have suffered from the "in-between" feeling, not able to fit
into native life or life in the south. Either there are not enough
wage jobs in the north or the young people are not trained or settled enough to do them. In the small community of Baker Lake in
1971, 122 teenagers were unemployed.

This year's goose does not lead the flock   No people can remain
strong and happy if the adults, who must make a living and make
decisions, do not fully understand the world around them. One of
the most unfortunate things about the foreign takeover of the
north is that Indian and Inuit men and women have felt pushed
aside by strange laws, language, money, and education.

The Moravians in Labrador included both adults and children in
their community education schemes. A few traders, missionaries,
and others all through history took an interest in adult education,
but nothing much was done by governments until after World
War II. Manitoba and Saskatchewan began adult teaching just
after the war, and an early start was made in some of the sana-
toriums with northern native patients.

In 1950 the federal government put out a booklet for teaching
elementary English and budgeting to Inuit. Other booklets were
printed in English and the Inuit language about game laws and
handicrafts, but not much else was done until 1959. In that year
the northern co-operatives began bringing new learning to Inuit
and Indian men and women. In 1964 the "Q-book" of knowledge
was published in English and Eskimo. This book explained many
things about government, health, education, and so on.

The "break through" in adult education in the Northwest Territories and northern Quebec came with the beginning of a big
low-cost housing program. Money was provided to explain the
scheme to Inuit and later to Indian adults. Other kinds of adult
education followed — visits to the south, conferences in the north,
adult learning centres, and night schools. Films, tape-recordings,
videotape and newspapers are all used in adult education.

Unfortunately the adult education *most* needed was not and
maybe cannot be done — *the job of teaching foreign people* to
understand and respect native ways enough to "ease up" northern
change to a speed that native individuals and society can take in.

The brighter side   Despite the upset caused by poor educational
planning and by the general bulldozing of northern native life,
there are hopeful signs.

The schools and vocational training programs have, with all
their faults, turned out many native people who do not have to

rely so much on interpreters and officials to cope with the modern world. Some of them are now able to see what is happening to themselves and their people, to take pride in being Indian or Inuit, and to demand that foreign society make its share of changes. Travel, radio, and films have helped to educate each side, native and non-native, about the other.

Meanwhile the whole industrial world has been shaken up by new ideas about the environment, employment, government, and education. Things are changing fast in southern Canada, and government programs in the north have been affected. Within government departments, in citizens' organizations, in universities, radio, television and newspapers, in native organizations and local councils, people have worked hard to bring about a "new look" in education affecting northern native people.

Beginning in the provincial schools of northern Quebec, and now in some other provinces and the N.W. T., children in the early grades are now taught in their native languages. Several schemes are underway to put native teachers into classrooms, recognizing that the ability to speak Dogrib or Cree to children is as useful as a diploma in home economics or music.

More and more books are being written for and by native people about their history, land, and life. Older native people are teaching in classrooms and on the land as part of school time. Young Inuit at Frobisher Bay have begun their own Eskimo University to preserve the best of their culture. There are many native cultural centres, some supported by governments, which are part of a new revival of spirit. Several new schools in the N.W.T. have been named after native leaders, and more high schools are being built within northern regions.

The old divisions between technical, child, and adult education are being broken down, and at Rae the Dogrib people have their own community school. They choose the teaching staff and help decide what is taught.

Some southern universities such as Saskatchewan and Trent have specialized in native studies and the problems of education for and by native people in Canada. George Miller, an Iroquois, is the director of the Native North American Studies Institute, which in 1973 opened a college, mostly for native students and directed by

native people. David Masty, a Cree of Great Whale River, and
Evie Ekidluak of the Povungnituk Inuit were members of the original planning group.

Several associations representing northern native people have
submitted briefs to the governments calling for control of education by the parents concerned, and for changes in the whole educational system to fulfil a need for the continuity of native culture
and identity.

If non-native people raised the problem, some have tried hard to
find solutions and deserve mention in this history. There have been
many good teachers, both official and volunteer, too many to choose
from. Father André Renaud of the University of Saskatchewan
and Paul Robinson of the N.W.T. government have done important
work in curriculum development and teacher training. The former
Indian-Eskimo Association, now called the Canadian Association
in Support of Native People, has helped to bring about the new
day in northern education.

Government, friend and foe?

Because of the complication of modern life governments at all
levels — city, province, territory, and nation — have grown in size
and importance. Compared to 50 years ago government action
affects many more people in more ways.

The people who vote for government spokesmen cannot keep an
eye on everything that governments do through their huge organizations. Some actions please one group of voters and upset others.
The northern native people who are still adjusting to an industrial
society are especially affected by what governments do or don't
do. Here are some of the changes in government since World
War II.

Gradually all northern native people have received the right to
vote for various types of government. In 1952 the Yukon and
N.W.T. Mackenzie District, formerly one federal electoral riding,
was divided into two, and in 1962 the Inuit of the eastern Arctic
voted for the first time. In 1953 registered Indians received the
federal vote, and in 1972 Wally Firth became the first native member for the N.W.T. in parliament at Ottawa.

There are still many problems arising from the definitions of *status*. In 1969 the federal government produced a white paper proposing to cancel the Indian Act and end the Indian reserves. This move was rejected by Indian leaders who were afraid of losing their identity and treaty rights.

Even within the act there are unsolved problems. Indian status can only be passed on through the father. If a woman marries a non-Indian man she and her children are not officially Indian any more. Mrs. Jeanette Corbière-Lavell, an Ojibway woman, is trying to change this law, and Indian people have taken opposite sides in the argument.

Under the present laws it is possible for children of the same mother to be officially classed as Indian, Eskimo, or Non-Native. Related people of the same village may have to ride different school buses and look to different governments for housing or other help.

In 1966 the federal programs for Inuit and Indians were brought together in the Department of Indian Affairs and Northern Development. Since then, however, there has been a gradual move to reduce the special status of native people and to let them share the same government services as other Canadians.

Financial help has been given to various native organizations which aim to improve education, law, and economic affairs affecting their people. Other federal departments such as Secretary of State, Labour, Manpower, Health and Welfare, Public Service Commission, Regional Economic Expansion, and Communications have special services for and interest in native people, including northerners.

Early stages in Inuit affairs   It was not until 1953 that Inuit affairs were brought under one department of federal government. The Department of Northern Affairs and Natural Resources was formed, with an Arctic Division concerned only with Inuit.

Beginning in 1956, Northern Service Officers were appointed to work with Inuit in positions similar to Indian Agency Superintendents but with more freedom and stress on community development. The first Inuit community council was formed in 1958 at Baker Lake, and this form of local government began in all communities. The Northern Service Officers were re-named Area Administrators as more government staff moved north.

In 1958 a group of Inuit representing all regions except Labrador accompanied government officials on a visit to Greenland, the first of its kind. They were Elijah Menarik of Fort George, George Koneak of Fort Chimo, Davidee of Frobisher Bay, Kakasilk of Pangnirtung, Adamie Tootalik of Spence Bay, Kananginak of Cape Dorset, James Kavanak of Cambridge Bay, Idlaut of Resolute Bay, and Charlie Smith and Charlie Gordon of Aklavik.

In 1957 Abraham Okpik of Aklavik, George Koneak, and Ayaruak and Shingituk of Rankin Inlet made another historic first appearance at the Eskimo Affairs committee meeting in Ottawa. The days of conferences, committees, and councils had begun for the Inuit.

Changes in the provinces and territories   When *Newfoundland and Labrador* joined Canada the agreement signed on December 11, 1948, did not mention any definite federal responsibility for Indian and Eskimo people in the new province. The main reason given was that the people of Labrador had mixed to the point where it was difficult to say who was Indian, Inuit, or "white", economically or socially. In 1950, however, the federal government began to provide money to Newfoundland for health and welfare assistance to the native people of Labrador. In 1954 a new agreement was made, giving the federal government full responsibility for native health in Labrador for a ten-year period, and for assistance to the province in education and social welfare. Since then about 90 percent of all expenditures by the province on native peoples has been provided by the federal government.

The whole province of Newfoundland has been poor, and the people of remote Labrador have been neglected. Since 1970, however, people in Labrador and visitors from outside have demanded change and improvement. Gerry Sillit, a leader of the Inuit in Nain, has demanded protection of the local cod-fishing and sealing industries against foreign fleets. Indian and Inuit associations have been formed, and several federal government departments have given money and staff to develop communications, local industry, and organizations. In 1972 a royal commission set up by the province began to try to find ways to improve the life of the Labrador people, particularly the native residents.

In *Quebec* the provincial government increased its northern activities during the late 1950s. Survey crews began to explore the hydroelectric possibilities and prospectors discovered promising mining areas. Provincial pensions and allowances were made available to the Inuit, and in 1961 the provincial police replaced the RCMP in northern Quebec.

A new government had come to power in Quebec in 1960 and in April 1963 it created the General Branch of New Quebec, in the Department of Natural Resources, to assume all the provincial responsibilities in the non-organized parts of northern Quebec, with the exception of the services administered by the provincial departments of Justice, and Lands and Forests. Schools and administration offices were built in all communities, and at the request of several families the old campsite of Tasiuyaq was provided with a school, community store, and houses. The province assumed medical and health services for some northern Quebec settlements, and a new hospital with a resident doctor was opened at Fort Chimo. Like its James Bay counterpart, the provincial hospital is administered by a local elected board.

The whole question of government services to the Inuit of Quebec has been complicated by language, culture, and religion. The movement of the provincial government into Inuit affairs was made after a long association between Inuit and the English-speaking Hudson's Bay Company and the Anglican clergy who represent the majority religion of the Quebec Inuit. The RCMP during their years of duty in northern Quebec were mostly English-speaking, and between 1948 and 1963 a large federal English-speaking staff had gradually been established in administration, economic development, and education.

The Quebec entry into this federal-English-Anglican atmosphere was made quite quickly. Schools and administration offices were built side by side with the federal ones in all communities except at Tasiuyaq, where there is no federal office. The Quebec staff who first went north were naturally anxious to establish French as the second language of the Quebec Inuit.

All peoples of the world resist change, and the Inuit and the

English-federal group resented the changes brought by the first
Quebec appearance. To complicate matters more, a French-speaking fur company, Revillon Frères, had defrauded many Quebec
Inuit during the early 1900s and left a distrust for French-speaking people in general.

The Inuit were caught in between the two administrative power
groups, and each side tried to win the Inuit over. In turn the Inuit
sometimes played one side against the other for their own advantage. There were several years of such confusion, but gradually
things improved.

A compromise was made by placing the federal conduct of Quebec Inuit affairs under the Regional Director of Indian Affairs in
Quebec City. The majority of federal administrative staff in New
Quebec are now French-speaking, and there is close co-operation
between the federal and provincial administrations.

The provincial education program established in 1963 set out to
improve upon the federal one in its use of the Inuit language as
the sole teaching language in kindergarten and grades 1 and 2 and
its recognition of the Inuit culture. The use of the Inuit language
and the training of Inuit teachers were implemented, but there
were administrative problems which undermined the new system.

In July of 1968 the School Board of New Quebec was created,
under the provincial Department of Education, and charged with
the education of the territory of New Quebec, including Inuit education, but this Board started to operate only two years later.
The Quebec Union of Teachers submitted in January 1973 a brief
to the provincial government calling for changes in the Inuit
school system to suit Inuit cultural, linguistic, and economic needs.

The Inuit increased their consultations with the Indian Association of Quebec on their status and rights and realized that they
had some common interests in New Quebec, legally recognized in
the 1912 Extension Boundary Act by both the government of
Canada and the government of Quebec.

The federal-provincial and English-French questions are still not
resolved, but those concerned are working out solutions and time,
as always, helps to smooth things out. The years of struggle over
these problems, and over the James Bay development in association with the Quebec Indian organizations, have given the Que-

bec Cree and Inuit a new degree of political awareness and unity.
The Naskapi have not yet organized.

The Quebec Teachers Union and the New Quebec Co-operative
Federation have both sponsored the idea of a regional government
controlled by the native majority, but little progress has been
made so far. Two studies commissioned by the Quebec government may have important results for the Inuit. One is the Dorion
Commission Report of 1971, the other a report on the Administration of Justice beyond the 50th parallel, 1972. Among many
recommendations is one that the native people of New Quebec
should have their own members of parliament.

Ontario in 1968 formed a Ministry of Community and Social Services with an Indian Community Branch. This organization works
closely with federal Indian Affairs, but also deals with the many
Métis and non-status Indians who do not receive federal services.

In *Manitoba* a provincial Ministry of Northern Affairs has housing and other programs for residents of the northern part of the
province, most of whom are Indian or Métis. A Cree trapper and
author, Maxwell Paupanekis, was appointed in 1969 by the Manitoba government to be magistrate and family court judge for Norway House and its region. In 1973 he became a court communica-
tor, giving legal aid, and Chief Mrs. Jean Folster became magistrate. In 1970 a northern citizens' group presented a report, *Northern Task Force*, to the Manitoba legislature, recommending
important changes affecting native people.

Saskatchewan has its own Indian and Métis branch of government, and in *Alberta* the Human Resources Development Authori-
ty deals with native people as well as other groups in the province.

The province of *British Columbia* has a First Citizens' Fund
which pays for services to Indian residents, particularly those not
included in federal programs.

In each of the provinces one of the main problems is the gradual
loss of native hunting, fishing, and trapping lands due to mining,
hydro-dams, and water pollution. Mercury poisoning in Ontario,
the drying up of swamp land in northern Alberta, and the re-
settlement of Indian bands in several provinces are the result of
industrial action. In the case of the Fort Chipewyan delta, the
problem was caused by the Bennett Dam in the next province.

The situation of the native residents of the *Northwest Territories* is unique in that they total more than half of the population. The more independence is given to the territorial government, the more the native vote will influence what happens. Although the N.W.T. Council has existed since 1877, until quite recently it was controlled entirely by the federal government in Ottawa. In 1951 the Council was changed to include elected members and to meet in the north as well as in Ottawa.

In 1965 Abraham Okpik of Aklavik was appointed to be the first native member of the Council. In 1966 Simonie Michael was elected to the Council from southern Baffin Island, and in 1967 Chief John Tetlichi of Fort McPherson was appointed. A commission led by Dr. A. W. R. Carrothers brought out their report in 1966, recommending more independence for the Northwest Territories. Most of the ideas were accepted by the federal government.

The Council Headquarters were moved to Yellowknife, and at present (1973) five of the new elected members are of native origin — James Rabesca, Nick Sibbeston, Willy Adams, Lena Pedersen, and Paul Koolerk.

The Territorial Civil Service was enlarged to take over education, welfare, economic development and other services, and absorbed many of the former federal staff.

Under the Territorial Government the title of Area Administrator was changed to Settlement Manager, and an emphasis placed on the development of local government. Communities are classed as settlements, hamlets, towns, and cities. In general the bigger the community the more independent its council. Most of the settlements and hamlets have a majority of native people on their councils. There has been difficulty, however, in fitting the system of local government to the older system of elected Band Councils in communities of treaty Indians.

As described earlier, the education system of the N.W.T. has been changed to accommodate the needs of the native majority. A native federal M.P. and the native councillors are also assets to self-determination for the Inuit, Indian, and Métis people, but there are administrative problems.

Because the federal government retains overall control of the N.W.T. and particular control of major resources, the growth of the territorial government is limited and there is confusion among the many government agencies and programs. The native organizations sponsored by federal departments in the N.W.T. are seen by some N.W.T. councillors as undermining the value of a councillor as spokesman for the native voters.

One out of every six residents of the *Yukon* is either Indian or Métis; there are no Inuit residents. The federal Department of Indian Affairs and the Territorial Government share the programs affecting native people. So far no native has been elected to the seven-person Council, but a change of electoral boundaries in the future could result in a native representative on the council.

10 SNOWGEESE AMONG MOSQUITOES

In this rambling book we have traced the history of northern native peoples from their first arrival in an unpopulated land to the beginnings of their tribal groups, languages and customs. We have seen some of the changes resulting from foreign intrusion: fur trading, whaling, and new religions. From those times we have passed to the days of military, industrial, and government power.

Now it is time to sum up the long story, and to sketch in words the place of native people in their made-over homeland.

For the reasons we have considered in other chapters, northern native people have come to fit more and more into the southern Canadian pattern of life. Most people now live in houses with electricity, washing machines, and spring beds, close to stores, schools, and medical centres. Anywhere in the north the pilot of a plane, its mechanic or stewardess, the driver of a taxi, the clerk at the store check-out desk — even the anthropologist — may be Inuit, Indian, or Métis.

Little by little the native languages have given way to English and in areas such as the Mackenzie Delta, where very few young people speak the language of their grandparents, a special kind of English language has come into being. A father will ask his young son "Where you was?" and both will know exactly what is meant.

The sexual mingling of various peoples in the north has reduced the differences in appearance between native and non-native, tribe and tribe, Inuit, Indian, and Métis. Several of the most active native leaders are married to non-natives.

The word Métis usually means the people who emerged during the days of the Red River buffalo hunt. Some of them have suffered more than the "official" native people during the past century, as described by Maria Campbell in her book, *Halfbreed.* In the Mackenzie Delta, Labrador, and Yukon there are many of mixed blood for whom no general name exists, but who have lived, like the Red River Métis, close to the land and native ways.

In Inuit lands particularly there is a growing number of ethnically mixed marriages in which the parents are at the top of the salary and social scale. It will be interesting to see the part their children will play in the future of the north.

Two words are often used to describe the mixing of languages, cultures, and races. One is *integration*, which means fitting various parts together to make a complete way of life. The other is *assimilation*, which means that one way is absorbed by and disappears into the other. Both words could be used for what is happening in northern Canada. Integration and assimilation have always been a part of human history, and what is happening in the north is being repeated all over the world. What is probably most important is how much happiness or misery goes into the process, and this depends on the degree of true civilization in the stronger party.

One foot in each canoe

The past few years have been full of mixtures of the very old and the very new. A hunter going up the Eastmain River may use his skin drum in a ceremony to find caribou and his transistor radio to listen for news. A hostess at Eskimo Point will cut potatoes with her ulu, but slice the caribou roast with an electric carving knife.

At Pangnirtung, people move out of their houses each summer into tents, but wires run from house to tent so that electric guitars and tape recorders, both part of the modern Inuit culture, can be plugged in. Only one year-round group of hunters lives near Pang-nirtung. They come to visit the town on powerful snowmobiles, but heat their tents with kudliks of ancient form, burning a wick of moss. There is another twist even to this, for the kudliks are made from old oil barrel metal, and the seal-oil is carried in plastic jugs.

A young Indian delegate bound for his tenth conference that year may board a jet airplane and fasten the seat-belt around a moosehide jacket scraped, smoked, and beaded by his mother.

The changer changes

To complicate the picture of northern change still more are the changes going on in southern Canada and most of the industrial world. When the industrial nations first began to grow, very few people worried about the pollution of rivers, the loss of wildlife, or the ugliness of chimneys and mining-dumps. As the industrial countries have grown richer and machines do more of the work, people have begun to worry about balancing necessary industry with beauty, wildlife, and the thought of the future, all equally necessary. *Pollution, ecology,* and *environment* have all become powerful words.

At the same time in many parts of the world people have become concerned about the effect of strong human groups on smaller, weaker groups. Although many injustices are still happening, there is an important movement to protect *human rights,* including minority rights and native rights.

There is a third movement too, connected with the others — a feeling that rigid hours of work, assembly-line work, skyscrapers and huge cities, too much struggle for money and possessions, are producing unhappy, unhealthy people. Experiments are being made to change hours of work, to teach people to understand each other more, to change the design of schools, factories, and cities.

The northern native people are very much affected by these ways of thinking. In the debate and struggle, the many points of view between "back to nature" on one hand and "roll on industry" on the other, the Indian, Inuit, and Métis are at the centre. To some people they are a pushed-around minority who are in danger of losing the very natural qualities which industrial peoples are trying to win back. The northern land is seen as a last chance to develop a new, less destructive way of life. Many people in the south envy the clear identity and natural culture of the native people, particularly those of the north.

In a flood of conferences, a host of research programs, constant newspaper reports, radio and television shows, native people are involved. Women's Liberation, Northern University, Birth Control, Pipelines — for these and many other causes the northern native people are interviewed, invited, quoted, pushed, and pulled. At times — as we shall see — they are able to play the game to their own advantage. There are no clear-cut sides to take, for a trapper and hunter might support conservationists to stop oil exploration near his territory, but oppose their efforts to halt the trade in seal-skins and fox furs.

Petition power

One very good example of the kind of thing we have been talking about has taken place in Alaska. A growing movement by native people, supported by many other Americans, was brought to a head by the probability of an oil pipeline across Alaska. The result was the Alaska Native Claims Settlement Act of 1971. All Alaskan-born United States citizens of at least one-quarter Inuit, Aleut, or Indian blood and born on or before December 18, 1971, are entitled to share in the settlement, including some now living in Canada. So far some 77,000 applications have been received.

The native people of Alaska will receive recognition of full ownership on 40,000,000 acres of Alaskan land to be selected by them, and $962.5 million in cash and royalties as compensation for past losses. Most of the money will be placed in development funds to be controlled by regional native corporations. At the same time there is a growing unity of purpose among the native races to protect their hunting rights, to regain some of their losses in art, language, education, and self-government.

In 1967 the Nishga Tribal Council of northwestern British Columbia challenged the right of the government of British Columbia to control over 1,000 square miles of land. The Nishga people claimed ownership based on possession before Europeans came and confirmed by the Royal Proclamation of 1763.

Last year the Supreme Court turned down the Nishga case, but only just, with three judges for, three against, and one rejection on a technicality. Frank Calder, who presented the case for his people, has been a Minister in the provincial government of British Columbia.

In 1972 the Old Crow Indians of the Yukon Territory submitted a similar petition to the Canadian Parliament. They claim that since no treaties were ever made with them, about 60,000 square miles of territory belongs to them, not to Canada. Later the Yukon Native Brotherhood presented their brief demanding settlement of native land claims along similar lines to the Alaskan settlement.

The Old Crow petition was the result of oil and gas exploration work and the possibility of pipeline construction within their hunting and trapping grounds. Within the past three years several similar situations have occurred. The Indian people of the Mackenzie Valley are concerned over the effects of proposed oil or gas pipelines through their Treaty areas. The people of Tuktoyaktuk, Sachs Harbour, and Coral Harbour have been alarmed by the possible effects of drilling, explosions, and traffic on the wildlife of their areas. The James Bay hydro project is another current question of concern to Indian and Inuit — the biggest, but not the only hydro scheme in the north. As in Alaska, the land question is the main one, but along with it go language, education, and the whole feeling of native people to retain their identity, to have some say in their own future.

The government of Canada has been influenced by the social and environmental currents in north and south, and by the interest in minority rights. In March 1972 the Minister of Northern Affairs announced his government's proposals for northern matters. These include seven national objectives in the north, five priorities, and guidelines for social improvement. Despite the complicated wording it is clear that the government has taken public opinion into account; the proposals show an attempt to balance industry, nature, and the welfare of native people. A native land claims commission was set up by the federal government early in 1972, and in 1973 the Prime Minister said that he was ready to begin serious discussions about settlement.

Parka politicians

One of the reasons for the growth of the industrial way of life is organization. In the north, trading companies, churches, government departments, oil companies, and aircraft companies are all well organized, with headquarters, branch offices, and bank accounts.

Northern native people, divided into tribal and local groups, without a strong voice, have been over-run by organized southerners. The southern power groups did what was to their advantage and even did what they thought was best for the native people without discussing their plans or getting native approval. This combination of southern speed and paternalism, or "father knows best", was shown in most government programs.

The housing scheme of 1966 and the Baffin Island National Park of 1972 are both programs having tremendous effect on native people — the first all over the north, the second in two communities. In both cases the government planned and decided without first consulting the people most affected. Finding themselves without power to control what has been happening to them, the northern native people have begun to organize themselves in a political way.

In order to deal with modern or foreign problems, native people have had to model their organizations along southern standards. For years there have been small examples such as community councils, housing committees, and similar groups. The new political groups are more native-controlled, concerned with large-scale problems, and can speak at high levels on behalf of communities or people who might otherwise go unheard.

Because of the strong concern in southern Canada for environment, minority rights, and similar problems, the native organizations have been supported by citizens' groups of various kinds, and by both provincial and federal governments. Non-native experts are important at this stage, and it cannot be otherwise, for the new organizations are dealing with things outside the experience of their peoples.

Most of the financial support for the native groups is given by the federal government, and there are various ways of looking at this. It can be said that the money given is nothing compared to what native people have lost in the past. It can also be said that the government is "buying off" the native leaders in order to avoid future trouble. More favourably the support of native organizations can be seen as a real attempt to give power to the people and let them fight for their own rights in their own way.

This book has criticized federal and provincial governments for their dealings with native people, but there are changes for the better, and certainly the Canadian scene looks good when compared with some other countries, particularly those South American states in which Indian tribes are being slaughtered.

Each province and territory has its own association of registered Indians and its association of non-status Indians and Métis. The national headquarters for both parallel organizations are in Ottawa. The Inuit have a national organization based in Ottawa, and the COPE committee in the Mackenzie Delta includes all native people. There are regional cultural and educational groups like the Tree of Peace in Yellowknife, Skookum Jim Hall in Whitehorse and East Three, Inuvik.

The Inuit Cultural Association of Igloolik is an example of a local organization, concerned more with the survival of the native language and culture than with economic and political things.

Most of the organizations publish newspapers and newsletters. They conduct research and investigations into many things affecting native people such as game laws, treaties, education, and industrial projects. They hire lawyers and other specialists, and in general use the methods of modern business while keeping in touch with native ways locally.

The list of native organizations shown in Appendix A may not be complete, but it includes most of those in the north or dealing with the north. The "people power" of the northern native associations will be of increasing importance in the years ahead.

Surviving and succeeding

The title of this chapter is taken from a speech made by Victor Allen of Inuvik, who said that without their languages and cultures the native people who are special, like snow geese, will disappear into the Canadian mass, the mosquitoes. So far the mos-

quitoes are winning, and any history book that painted a very
happy picture of the northern situation would simply be untrue.

Because of the swamping of native life by foreign or southern
ways, the majority of northern Indian, Inuit, and Métis people feel
lost and helpless to some degree. For native men in particular the
change from proud independent hunter to "apprentice white man"
has been deep and bitter. The results show in chronic alcohol problems, battered women, and children without guidance. To make
matters worse the whole of western industrial society, including
Canada, is going through a social and economic crisis. Crime, violence, drugs, and other problems are part of this complex scene, so
that there is no firm, clear, workable system to which native people
can adapt.

If the situation of northern native people is to improve there are
two levels of action needed. First, Canadian society as a whole will
have to sort itself out, to come together and work toward a new
set of national goals. Although it may now be too late, one of these
goals could be a real effort to understand the needs, nature, and
situation of northern native people. What is needed also is the
courage to give way and in some cases "back-off".

At the second level, that of the native northerners themselves,
hope for the future seems to lie in learning to see history, present
and future, as systems. As men once calculated the conditions of
ice, wind, and wildlife in order to make decisions for the survival
of their people, they must now choose among other conditions.
Money, calculation, education, and organization can be used, just
as nature was used, to plan the best life possible for children and
the cultures they carry.

These two courses of action will require tremendous effort and
adaptability from Canadian society on one hand and from individual native people on the other. There are hopeful signs on both
sides, and it seems fitting to end with a few examples of a new
spirit of native pride and identity.

Apart from the many formal native groups there are events
such as the Arctic Games. In the Inuvik version, for instance, organized by people like Billy Day, Edward Lennie, and Nellie Cour-
noyea, native contestants from all over the Mackenzie Valley,
Yukon, eastern Arctic, and Alaska meet. For a few days the town

is dominated by people who can skin seal and muskrat, bake bannock, drum dance, do the Red River jig and the Eskimo high-kick.

Johnny Tetso, Thomas Boulanger, Nuligak, Ayaruak, and Markoosie are some of a growing list of native authors, and one of the most delightful films made recently by the National Film Board contains the art and music of the Tagoonaks, Germaine Arnaktauyak, and other Inuit.

The Inuvik ski team has become a symbol of what young northern people can do. Names like Kelly, Allen, Firth, and Bullock have become well known in world competition cross-country skiing. Vic Mercredi of Yellowknife signed with the Atlanta Flames N.H.L. hockey team for a $200,000 contract. Kayak of Pond Inlet, Nashook of Igloolik, and Charlie Crow of the Belcher Islands have each received the Order of Canada, Kayak for RCMP service, Nashook and Charlie for community work. Frank Hansen of Aklavik is a director of C.B.C. Other leaders and prominent people have been mentioned in previous chapters of this book.

All of these public figures and events, as anywhere in the world, are only the tip of the iceberg, the results of the quiet lives of those native people who are simply doing the best job they can of being themselves. From Labrador to the Yukon there are many men and women who like their parents have kept their pride and native sense of humour despite all upheavals. While coping with the demands of the industrial world they have kept and will pass on the visible skills, the ways of looking at life, and the feeling inside which add up to being native, to being one of those people whose roots go deep below Canada.

APPENDIX A

List, by Location, of Associations Serving Northern Native People

YUKON
Yukon Native Brotherhood, P.O. Box 2452, Whitehorse.

Yukon Association of Non-Status Indians, 22 Nisutlin Drive, Whitehorse.

United Native Youth Council of the Yukon, 3159 3rd and Alexander, Whitehorse.

NORTHWEST TERRITORIES
Indian Brotherhood of the N.W.T., P.O. Box 2338, Yellowknife (publishes *The Native Press*).

Métis and Non-Status Native Association of N.W.T., Box 295, Hay River.

Committee for Original People's Entitlement, Inuvik.

East Three, Inuvik.

Tree of Peace, Box 222, Yellowknife (publishes *Tsigoinda*).

Inummarit (Inuit Cultural Association), Igloolik (publishes *Inummarit Quarterly*).

BRITISH COLUMBIA
Union of British Columbia Chiefs, 2140 West 12th Ave., Vancouver.

B.C. Association of Non-Status Indians, 1027 West Broadway, Vancouver.

ALBERTA
Indian Association of Alberta, Room 203, Kingsway Court, 11710 Kingsway Avenue, Edmonton.

Métis Association of Alberta, Room 303, 10826-124 Street, Edmonton.

Alberta Native Communications Society, 114-27 Jasper Avenue, Edmonton (publishes *The Native People*).

SASKATCHEWAN
Federation of Saskatchewan Indians, Box 1644, Prince Albert (publishes *The Saskatchewan Indian*).

Saskatchewan Métis Society, 1935 Scarth Street, Regina.

MANITOBA
Manitoba Indian Brotherhood, 604-191 Lombard Avenue, Winnipeg (publishes *Manitoba Indian News*).

Manitoba Métis Federation, 374 Donald Street, Winnipeg.

ONTARIO
Union of Ontario Indians, Suite 804, 1300 Yonge Street, Toronto (publishes *Ontario Native Examiner*).

Ontario Métis and Non-Status Indian Association, 809 Victoria Street, Thunder Bay "F".

QUEBEC
Indians of Quebec Association, Huron Village, Loretteville (publishes *The Wolverine*).

Laurentian Alliance of Métis and Non-Status Indians, Room 308, 1280 St. Mark Street, Montreal.

Inut Movement of Quebec, Cité Roberval, Pointe Bleue.

Northern Quebec Inuit Association, Fort Chimo, New Quebec.

Fédération des Coopératives du Nouveau-Québec, 51 rue Bel-Air, Lévis (publishes *Kanguq*).

LABRADOR AND NEWFOUNDLAND
Labrador Inuit Association, Nain, Labrador.

Native Association of Newfoundland and Labrador, 393 Water Street, St. John's, Newfoundland.

ALL CANADA
National Indian Brotherhood, Suite 1610, 130 Albert Street, Ottawa (publishes monthly bulletin).

Native Council of Canada, Suite 1010, 77 Metcalfe Street, Ottawa (publishes *The Forgotten People*).

Inuit Tapirisat of Canada, Royal Trust Building, Suite 409, 116 Albert Street, Ottawa (publishes *Inuit Monthly*).

Native Youth Association of Canada, 327 Waverly Street, Ottawa.

APPENDIX B

LIST OF SUPPLEMENTARY READINGS

Research for a book of this type draws upon hundreds of written sources and the memories of many people. Time and other considerations do not permit the compiling of a complete bibliography of sources, but as second best here are a few suggested readings and bibliographies for further study.

PREHISTORY

Bandi, Hans-Georg. *Eskimo Prehistory.* Translated by Ann E. Keep. University of Washington Press, Seattle, 1972.

Beals, C. S., editor. *Science, History and Hudson Bay.* Vol. 1. Chapter 1 by W. E. Taylor, W. N. Irving, and J. V. Wright. Department of Energy, Mines and Resources, Ottawa, 1968.

Birket-Smith, Kaj. *The Paths of Culture.* Translated by Karin Fennow. University of Wisconsin Press, Madison, 1965.

Coon, Carleton S. *The Story of Man.* Alfred Knopf, New York, 1962.

Harington, C. R. "Ice Age Mammals in Canada." *Arctic Circular,* Vol. 22, No. 2 (1971), pp. 66-89.

Howell, F. Clark, editor. *Early Man.* Life Nature Library. Time-Life Books, New York, 1968.

Jennings, Jesse D. *Prehistory of North America.* McGraw-Hill, New York, 1968.

MacDonald, Robert. *The Romance of Canadian History.* Vol. 1, *Years and Years Ago, a Prehistory.* Ballantrae Foundation, Calgary, 1971.

McGhee, Robert. "The People of Arctic North America." Chapter 16 in *Arctic and Alpine Regions,* edited by J. Ives and R. Barry. Institute for Arctic and Alpine Research, University of Colorado, Boulder, 1972.

———*Summary of N.W.T. Prehistory.* Archaeology Division, National
Museum of Man, Ottawa, 1970.

Prest, V. K. *Retreat of Wisconsin and Recent Ice in North America.* A map.
Geological Survey of Canada No. 1257A, Ottawa, 1969.

Stalker, A. and Churcher, C. *Deposits near Medicine Hat, Alberta.* A chart.
Geological Survey of Canada, Ottawa, 1970.

Willey, Gordon R. *An Introduction to American Archaeology.* Vol. 1. Prentice-
Hall, Englewood Cliffs, New Jersey, 1966.

LEGENDS AND ORIGINAL CULTURES

Basile, M. J. and McNulty, G. E. *Atanuka, legendes Montagnaises.* Centre
d'Etudes Nordiques. Les Presses de l'université Laval, Québec,
1972.

Birket-Smith, Kaj. *The Eskimos.* Crown Publishers, New York, 1971.

Bleeker, Sonia. *The Eskimo.* William Morrow, New York, 1959.

Boas, Franz. *The Central Eskimo.* University of Nebraska Press, Lincoln,
1964.

Clark, Ella E. *Indian Legends of Canada.* McClelland and Stewart, Toronto,
1960.

Desbarats, Peter, editor. *What They Used to Tell About, Indian Legends
from Labrador.* McClelland and Stewart, Toronto, 1969.

Helm, June and Leacock, Eleanor B. "The Hunting Tribes of Sub-Arctic
Canada." Chapter 12 in *North American Indians in Historical
Perspective,* edited by Eleanor B. Leacock and Nancy O. Lurie.
Random House, New York, 1971.

Indians of North America. A map. Supplement to *National Geographic,* Vol.
142-6 (December 1971), page 739A.

Jenness, Diamond. *The Indians of Canada.* Queen's Printer, Ottawa, 1967.

Leechman, J. D. *Native Tribes of Canada.* Gage, Toronto, 1956.

McClellan, Catharine. *My Old People Say.* (Southern Yukon Indians.)
National Museums of Canada Bulletin, Publications in Ethnology No. 6. Ottawa, in press.

Morriseau, Norval. *Legends of My People, the Great Ojibway.* Ryerson Press,
Toronto, 1965.

Oswalt, Wendell, H. *This Land Was Theirs.* Second edition. John Wiley &
Sons, New York, 1973.

Royal Ontario Museum. *Naskapi, Wood Cree, Musical Instruments,* and
other R.O.M. wall charts. Texts by E. S. Rogers. In cooper-
ation with the Federal Department of Indian Affairs and
Northern Development, 1970.

Savoie, Donat, editor. *The Amerindians of the Canadian Northwest in the 19th Century, as seen by Emile Petitot.* Vol. 1, *The Tchiglit Eskimos,* MDRP 9; Vol. 2, *The Loucheux Indians,* MDRP 10. Northern Science Research Group, Department of Indian Affairs and Northern Development, Ottawa, 1973.

Weyer, E. M. *The Eskimos, Their Environment and Folkways.* Archon Books, London, 1969.

EARLY EUROPEAN SETTLEMENT IN THE EAST

Creighton, Donald. *Dominion of the North.* Revised edition. Macmillan, Toronto, 1957.

Giraud, Michel. *Histoire du Canada.* Les Presses universitaires de France, Paris, 1966.

Grenfell, Wilfred T. and others. *Labrador, the Country and the People.* Macmillan, New York, 1910.

Kenyon, W. A. and **Turnbull, J. R.** *The Battle for James Bay.* Macmillan, Toronto, 1971.

Soeur, Paul-Emile. *La Baie James, trois cent ans d'histoire.* Université d'Ottawa, 1952.

Trudel, Marcel. *L'Esclavage au Canada français.* Les Presses de l'université Laval, Québec, 1960.

THE FUR TRADE AMONG NORTHERN INDIAN PEOPLES

Boulanger, Thomas. *An Indian Remembers, My Life as a Trapper in Northern Manitoba.* Peguis Publishers, Winnipeg, 1971.

Dall, W. H. et al. *The Yukon Territory.* Downey and Co., London, 1898.

Franklin, Sir John. *Narrative of a Journey to the Shores of the Polar Sea, in the Years 1819, 1820, 1821 and 1822.* Reprint. M. G. Hurtig, Ltd., Edmonton, 1969.

Hearne, Samuel. *A Journey to the Northern Ocean, 1769-72.* Macmillan, Toronto, 1958.

Hudson's Bay Record Society Journals. London. Several volumes of historic documents such as the Northern Quebec and Labrador Journals, 1819-35. In most major libraries.

Innis, H. A. *The Fur Trade in Canada.* Revised edition. University of Toronto Press, Toronto, 1956.

Journals of the Champlain Society. Toronto. A variety of historic documents such as the journals of Samuel Hearne. In most major libraries.

Neatby, L. H. "History of Hudson Bay." Chapter 2 in *Science, History and Hudson Bay*, Vol. 1. Department of Energy, Mines and Resources, Ottawa, 1968.

Paupanekis, Maxwell. "The Trapper." In *People and Pelts*, edited by Malvina Bolus, pp. 137-43. Peguis Publishers, Winnipeg, 1972.

Rich, F. E. *The History of the Hudson's Bay Company 1670-1870.* 2 Vols. Hudson's Bay Record Society, London, 1958 and 1959.

——— "The Indian Traders." *The Beaver*, Winter 1970, pp. 5-20.

Tetso, John. *Trapping Is My Life.* Peter Martin Associates, Toronto, 1970.

Wilson, Clifford. "Milestones in the Progress of the Hudson's Bay Company." *The Beaver*, December 1941, pp. 27-41.

TRADING AND WHALING AMONG THE INUIT

Ayaruaq, John. *John Ayaruaup Unipkarnga, Inushimini.* (Autobiography in Eskimo only.) Department of Indian Affairs and Northern Development, Ottawa, 1968.

Bruemmer, Fred. "Whalers of the North." *The Beaver*, Winter 1971, pp. 44-55.

Hawkes, E. W. *The Labrador Eskimo.* Memo 91 of the Geological Survey of Canada, 1916.

Metayer, Maurice. *Arlok l'esquimau.* Nouvelles Editions Latines, Paris, 1965.

———, translator. *I, Nuligak, 1895-1966.* Peter Martin Associates, Toronto, 1966.

Millard, A. E. *Southern Baffin Island.* Department of the Interior, Ottawa, 1930.

Ross, W. Gillies. "American Whaling in Hudson Bay, The Voyage of the Black Eagle, 1866-1867." *Canadian Geographical Journal*, Vol. 75, No. 6 (December 1967), pp. 198-205.

Usher, Peter. *The Bankslanders, Economy and Ecology of a Frontier Trapping Community.* Vol. 1, *History;* Vol. 2, *Economy and Ecology;* Vol. 3, *The Community.* NSRG 71-1, 2, and 3. Northern Science Research Group, Department of Indian Affairs and Northern Development, Ottawa, 1971.

——— *Fur Trade Posts of the Northwest Territories.* NSRG 71-4. 1971.

Washburne, H. C. and **Anauta.** *Land of the Good Shadows, the Life Story of Anauta, an Eskimo Woman.* John Day Co., New York, 1940.

THE GOLD RUSH, EXPLORATION, MISSIONS, AND EPIDEMICS

Baird, P. D. "Expeditions to the Canadian Arctic." *The Beaver,* March, June, and September 1949.

Berton, Pierre. *Klondike.* McClelland and Stewart, Toronto, 1958.

Carne, J. *A History of the Missions in Greenland and Labrador, 1789-1844.* Land and Tippett, New York, 1848.

Carrière, Gaston. *Histoire documentaire de la Congregation des Missionaires Oblats... dans l'est du Canada.* Université d'Ottawa, 1957-70.

Carrington, Philip. *The Anglican Church in Canada, a History.* Collins, Toronto, 1963.

Cooke, A. and **Holland, C.** *A Chronological List of Arctic and Sub-Arctic Expeditions and Historical Events.* Scott Polar Research Institute, Cambridge, England, 1969-73.

Duchaussois, R. P. *Aux Glaces polaires.* Oeuvre des Missions, OMI, Editions SPES, Paris, 1935.

Miller, James. *The Moravians in Labrador, 1764-1805.*

Morgan, Murray. *One Man's Gold Rush.* University of Washington Press, Seattle, 1967.

GENERAL READINGS

The Beaver. Quarterly from Hudson's Bay House, Winnipeg, Manitoba. Contains many articles on Indian and Inuit history.

Campbell, Maria. *Halfbreed.* McClelland and Stewart, Toronto, 1973.

Cumming, Peter A. and **Mickenberg, Neil H.,** editors. *Native Rights in Canada.* Second edition. The Indian-Eskimo Association of Canada in association with General Publishing Co., Toronto, 1972.

Gooderham, Kent, editor. *I Am an Indian.* J. M. Dent and Sons, Toronto, 1969.

Handbook of North American Indians. Smithsonian Institute, Washington, D.C. This 20-volume encyclopedia will be published in 1976, but extracts may be available before then from the general editor, W. C. Sturtevant.

Helm, June et al. "Synoptic Chart of North-Western Indian History 1690-1970." In *Athapaskan Conference Volume,* Ethnology Mercury Series. National Museum of Man. Ottawa, in press.

Jenness, Diamond. *Eskimo Administration.* Vol. 2, *Canada;* Vol. 3, *Labrador;* and Vol. 5, *Analysis and Reflections.* Arctic Institute of North America Technical Papers Nos. 14, 16, and 21. Montreal, 1964, 1965, and 1968.

Ornstein, Toby E. *The First Peoples in Quebec.* 3 Vols. Prepared at the Native North American Studies Institute for the Indians of Quebec Association. Thunderbird Press, La Macaza, Quebec, 1973.

Renaud, André. *One Hundred Books for Indian School Teachers.* Indianesco Inc., Ottawa, 1963.

Richardson, Boyce. *James Bay, the Plot to Drown the North Woods.* Sierra Club, San Francisco, with Clarke, Irwin, Toronto, 1972.

Senungetuk, Joseph. *Give or Take a Century.* Indian Historian Press, San Francisco, 1971.

Symington, Fraser. *The Canadian Indian.* McClelland and Stewart, Toronto, 1969.

Textbooks and the American Indian. Indian Historian Press, San Francisco, 1970.

Willis, Jane. *Geniesh, an Indian Girlhood.* New Press, Toronto, 1973.

BIBLIOGRAPHIES

Arctic Bibliography. 15 Vols. Arctic Institute of North America, Montreal, 1953 —. In all major libraries.

Bibliography of the Quebec-Labrador Peninsula. 2 Vols. G. K. Hall and Co., Boston, 1968.

Carney, R. J. and **Ferguson, W. O.** *A Selected and Annotated Bibliography on the Sociology of Eskimo Education.* Occasional Publication No. 2. Boreal Institute, University of Alberta, Edmonton, 1965.

The First Americans. Indian-Eskimo Association of Canada DLS 4, Toronto.

Fortuine, Robert, M.D. *The Health of the Eskimos, A Bibliography, 1857-1967.* Dartmouth College Library Press, Hanover, New Hampshire, 1968.

Hemstock, C. A. and **Cooke, G. A.** *Yukon Bibliography Update 1963-1970.* Occasional Publication No. 8-1. Boreal Institute, University of Alberta, Edmonton, 1972.

Jones, Mary Jane, editor. *Mackenzie Delta Bibliography.* MDRP No. 6. Northern Science Research Group, Department of Indian Affairs and Northern Development, Ottawa, 1969.

Lotz, J. R. *Yukon Bibliography.* YRP No. 1. Northern Coordination and Research Centre, Department of Northern Affairs and National Resources, Ottawa, 1964.

McCormack, Pat A. "Athabascan Bibliography." Unpublished. Department of Anthropology, University of Alberta, Edmonton.

Poppe, Roger. *Bibliography of the Kutchin Indians.* Canadian Wildlife Service, Edmonton, 1971.

Available from the Cultural Development Division, Education Branch, Indian and Eskimo Affairs Program, Department of Indian and Northern Affairs:

Arts and Crafts (1) General, 1969 and 1972 lists; (2) Ojibway only
Audio-visual materials
Indian Artists of Canada
Indian and Eskimo Authors
Indians of Canada
Indians of the Fraser District, B.C.
Languages
Legends
Religions and Ceremonials